TWELVE WAYS OF SEEING THE WORLD

PHILOSOPHIES AND ARCHETYPAL WORLDVIEWS FOR UNDERSTANDING HUMAN CONSCIOUSNESS

Mario Betti

Hawthorn Press

Translated by Matthew Barton

Twelve Ways of Seeing the World was first published as *Zwolf Wege, die Welt zu Verstehen,* in 2001© Verlag Freies Geistesleben, Stuttgart, Germany.

Twelve Ways of Seeing the World © 2019 Hawthorn Press.
Published as an English edition by Hawthorn Press, Hawthorn House, 1 Lansdown Lane, Stroud, Gloucestershire, GL5 1BJ, UK
info@hawthornpress.com www.hawthornpress.com

Cover design by Lucy Guenot
Typesetting in Minion Pro by Mach 3 Solutions Ltd (www.mach3solutions.co.uk)

Printed by Severn, Gloucester

Acknowledgement: Hawthorn Press acknowledges the generous support of The Cloverleaf Foundation, www.cloverleaffoundation.com, which made the translation of *Twelve Ways of Seeing the World* possible.

Translation by Matthew Barton

Printed on environmentally friendly chlorine-free paper sourced from renewable forest stock.

British Library Cataloguing in Publication Data applied for

ISBN 978-1-912480-12-8

Twelve Ways of Seeing the World

In today's multicultural society, religious and philosophical outlooks of all kinds often seem to clash irreconcilably. Mario Betti is concerned to see the validity in each worldview, and to seek truth not in one narrow perspective but in the overall context of all the possible different outlooks. In clear, accessible language, he helps readers engage with twelve perspectives on the world, at the same time offering insight into anthroposophy, and new understandings of it.

Mario Betti was born in Lucca, Italy, in 1942. Following studies and work in Italy, Germany, Spain, Switzerland and England, he settled in Germany. He studied Waldorf pedagogy and subsequently worked for many years as a teacher of English, history, history of art and religion. From 1985 to 2001 he was a lecturer in pedagogical anthropology, history of art and anthroposophy at Alanus University, Alfter, near Bonn, and was an art teaching advisor to Waldorf schools. From 2001 to 2006 he was a lecturer at the Waldorf teacher training course in Stuttgart. Mario has published various books on literature and spiritual science.

Four blind men are trying to decide what an elephant is.

They each feel and touch the elephant, clearly a patient creature, and thereupon each gives his view:

'A pipe', says the first, touching the trunk.

'A wall', says the second, feeling its side.

'A whip', says the third, feeling its tail.

'A tree', says the fourth, who has got hold of a leg.

Old legend

Twelve Ways of Seeing the World

Contents

Contents

Foreword

Robert McDermott and Matthew T. Segall

Rudolf Steiner was one of the twentieth century's few true Renaissance men. While modern science, art, religion, politics and philosophy continued to fall into increasing specialisation, fragmentation, deconstruction and narrow-minded conflict, Steiner laboured tirelessly to create new integral approaches to education, agriculture, medicine, architecture, social reform, banking, visual and performance art, esotericism and more – all inspired by a deep commitment to humanity's spiritual potential. Mario Betti, a lifelong practitioner of Steiner's anthroposophical method, has written a book that succeeds not only in its clear interpretation of a sometimes enigmatic thinker's ideas, but in its brilliant amplifications and applications of these ideas to our present-day circumstances.

Betti offers his book as a stimulus or seed to support the growth of a still-fledgling pluralistic society. Achieving a planetary humanity guided by freedom and love out of the ashes of the modern pathologies of fascism, totalitarianism, nationalism, oligarchism and terrorism (the list goes on...) will require more than a shallow, relativistic multiculturalism that settles for mere tolerance. Betti draws on Goethe to remind us that *tolerance can only be a temporary position*. Genuine pluralism, Betti demonstrates, requires more than toleration: it requires a willingness to engage the whole of our being in deep communication with, and mutual affirmation of, other worldviews. We must strive to reach across our differences through an inner development that is capable of seeing their holistic interdependence. Betti's amplification of Steiner's twelve worldviews is a profound aid in this effort of inner development. Significantly, it shows the dignity and merit of each way of seeing the world at the same time as revealing the danger of exclusivism. *Every worldview becomes false, the moment it claims to be the whole of the world.*

Albert William Levy's *Philosophy and the Modern World*, a particularly expert and readable account of twentieth-century philosophies, summarises our present situation well:

> ... philosophical movements of the recent past are to be viewed as waves of successive reform beating upon an infinite shore, with each group of partisans committed to a conception of philosophy which assures them a virtual monopoly of its legitimate practice.... And to pragmatists, logical empiricists, and linguistic analysts alike, any alternative conception of what philosophy is rests upon a tragic mistake.

Who would dare an attempt to overcome such differences of opinion, each supported by knowledge and powerful arguments? An ideal candidate would be a teacher whose thinking is lifted by creative pedagogy and artistic imagination. Mario Betti would appear to be such a teacher. Every page of this book reveals an author who teaches thinking as a contribution to individual lives, to relationships and to a sane society. He is invested not in scoring philosophical points but rather in helping his readers cope with intellectual confusion and conflict.

Betti succeeds in his purpose by giving a positive account of twelve worldviews. He takes as his model Goethe, who held in one view both universal harmony and plurality (p. 3). We are led to appreciate that each worldview is convincing up to a point. His treatment of Idealism, for example, invites the reader to see that all reality is, or at least emerges from, ideas – from a realm that Plato described so convincingly. But then Betti draws on Aristotle, an equally brilliant and equally influential philosopher, to show the need for a more positive account of particulars, whether moments, thoughts or objects. Betti refers to this combination of Plato's and Aristotle's philosophy as Realism, the philosophy that occupies the top-most spot on the philosophical compass (more on this below).

In a similar way – the way of showing polarities – Betti makes a case for Rationalism, the philosophy of ethical order and proportion, and then shows how it virtually solicits its polar complement, the philosophy of Dynamism: structure needs process to be effective; and process, in order to avoid chaos, needs structure. As an introvert needs at least a little extroversion to get through the day, and as melancholic and phlegmatic temperaments need at least a touch of choleric and sanguine temperaments, so does Psychism, a philosophy ready-made for psychology, need a little Phenomenalism, a philosophy that emphasizes the reality of external objects and events but is not sufficiently affirmative of the interior depths of the soul. 'Psychism is the inner version of phenomenalism' (p. 95). These pairs, furthermore, are not only complementary, as in two static halves that make a whole; rather, they need and benefit each other but also oppose each other – like individual and community, inner and outer, and of course, like gender. The twelve views are also like gender in that they exist not only as pairs of clearly demarcated opposites but as a spectrum with fluid boundaries, a perspective that contemporary social justice movements have made increasingly clear (p. 115).

In addition to an emphasis on the conflict of worldviews, Betti emphasizes the importance of mutually enhancing polarities: 'Each worldview is both a genuine opposite and an enhancement of its opposite' (p. 95). By plunging downward into the domain of gravity, the Materialist worldview has produced marvels of human understanding like the periodic table of elements, just as the 'Spiritualist' worldview has revealed its own '"levitating" periodic table of spiritual elements': the angelic hierarchies (p. 130). While Materialism risks digging itself ever deeper into the sand like a crab, 'Spiritualism' (see note, in p. 15) risks fleeing the Earth entirely. Such polar tensions are the engine of the evolutionary adventure that has produced all that we see around us and feel within us.

As was mentioned above, despite insisting on the equal value of each of the twelve views, Betti follows Steiner in giving pride of place to Realism. 'All worldviews rest like a bud within [it]', as it is '*the* fundamental human outlook *par excellence*' (p. 173). 'Cognition', Steiner tells us in his autobiography, 'is not the depiction of intrinsic being but rather the soul living its way into this intrinsic being' (quoted by Betti on p. 180). In other words, an act of knowing is not an internal mental representation of an external physical world; rather, knowing is a participatory event that is immanent to the world-process itself. 'If knowledge did not exist', Steiner continues, 'the world would remain incomplete' (quoted by Betti on p. 181). This is obviously not a *naïve* realism: it is a higher realisation rooted in Steiner's participatory approach to knowledge and reality.

This higher or participatory Realism is a developmental culmination of the other eleven worldviews, whereby through a sort of alchemical transfiguration, the distinct capacities of thinking, feeling, sensing and willing (each emphasised by their respective worldviews) are etherialized into what Betti calls 'a new earth substance' (p. 183). In this primordial etheric life substance, Betti tells us, the opposition between spirit and matter is overcome so that human consciousness can be raised and transubstantiated by the power of the Logos-Christ.

Some readers may have trouble following Betti and Steiner at this point, as these are rather mysterious matters, to say the least. But Betti's book succeeds at least in leading all spiritually striving individuals to the point where they are able to perceive the intrinsic value of all worldviews. At that point, it is up to each of us to discover the true integral potential of our human existence. 'The whole world, apart from the human being, is an enigma,' Steiner tells us. *'And the human being is its solution'*.

Professor Robert McDermott, PhD
Philosophy, Cosmology, & Consciousness Program
California Institute of Integral Studies, San Francisco, USA

Matthew T. Segall, PhD
Assistant Professor
Philosophy, Cosmology, & Consciousness Program
California Institute of Integral Studies, San Francisco, USA

4 February 2019

Introduction

Kathelijne Drenth

You are about to embark on a journey with Mario Betti's *Twelve Ways of Seeing the World* which may well change your life as much as it did mine.

My journey started when Herbert Wolpert, an organisational development consultant colleague, heard that I was involved in the development of a holistic framework for organisations based on twelve different perspectives. These were inspired by Rudolf Steiner's descriptions of twelve archetypal worldview philosophies in his book *Human and Cosmic Thought.* Herbert suggested that I should contact his business partner Albrecht Hemming, who had recently made a presentation titled 'Zwölf Wege Mensch und Welt zu Verstehen', or 'Twelve Ways of Understanding People and the World'. Albrecht sent me his script, and in it I came across a reference to Betti's book. I bought it, at the time available only in German, and devoured it.

Betti describes twelve different worldviews, from idealism to realism, and from spiritual will to material embodiment. He explains and anchors each worldview within a twelvefold constellation of the different perspectives of a comprehensive range of philosophers.

What becomes very clear is that throughout history no one philosopher can claim to have identified the 'absolute' truth. Rather, it is evident that advocating only one philosophy to the exclusion all others will give one a severely limited and very partial view of the world. No one perspective is more important or more crucial than any of the others; and not only are they equally important, they also complement each other seamlessly, all mutually reinforcing one another. Philosophy is usually presented as a battlefield of ideas, with each school struggling to claim the one true crown. Betti's suggestion is that all schools contribute, each offering within the whole one particular genius that illuminates that philosophical perspective, but together all twelve perspectives cohere to present one all-embracing and inclusive big picture of the whole.

Betti suggests that those twelve perspectives collectively embrace every possible worldview of which the human mind is capable, each one of which comprises one crucial dimension of our whole cognition. We all 'sit' within the constellation of those twelve perspectives. And even though we may be committed to one particular philosophical perspective and contest all others, our capability nevertheless spans all twelve, whether we are conscious of that or not. To optimally exploit our full systemic potential we need to recognise and engage not only with every single one of those perspectives but also with their collective totality.

Betti introduces the reader to revelatory insights, paths and developmental understandings that explain, embrace and explore that bigger whole constellation. His book invites us to engage and connect with all twelve worldview perspectives, and asks us to make the effort to understand them both individually and as a whole. The fact is that if we want to really master what it is that brings coherence to us as a whole, whether as individuals, groups, organisations or even nations, we need not only to master all twelve worldviews but also to grasp their *collective* integration within one overall picture. They enable us not only to see the whole expanse and potential of our capability, but also to *experience and act* that wholeness, knowing ourselves as *one* in our unique striving to bring value into the world and to give meaning to our life.

Had it not been for this profoundly transformative book, I would not have recognised, properly begun to understand and increasingly to trust the cohesive power of the framework of twelve leadership domains that my colleagues and I introduce in our work in organisations. I was working with the board of a multinational company back in 2008 in one of our first client cases using this framework for the purpose of defining an organisation's uniqueness. Then, at a certain moment, something magical happened, as if they had collectively found the 'holy grail' of their organisation. All of their differences, whether in their perspectives, professional background, individual capability or personality, suddenly appeared to be essential to guiding the successful striving of the bigger whole. The board was experienced by its members as one team, with a shared overarching intent and commitment to the core – the who, what, why and how of their whole organisation. This same phenomenon has emerged within all of the client boards with whom we have worked since then.

What is very clearly demonstrated by our experience with working in all kinds of organisations facing a variety of developmental questions is that the twelve worldviews work as *ordering principles*, creatively applicable within any and every situation. Engaging with this twelve-fold framework enables groups both to clarify what brings them together and to move forward as one integrated whole. Acting within their shared twelve worldviews, they can connect with the collective meaning of the whole organisation, which they experience as one uniquely differentiated whole. And the worldviews work equally with individuals; enabling the comprehension of the whole of our own unique capability, each of us can likewise begin to experience ourselves as complete, powerful and fully integrated in the world.

All of the twelve worldviews lie within each and every one of us, by virtue of our common human condition. Some are more dominant than others, but all have a key role to play. Engaging seriously with the awareness-raising process that Betti invites in this book empowers all of us to deal more confidently and constructively with the world we live in today.

Framing one's understanding of the world within the twelve perspectives is extraordinarily powerful, inspiring and transformative. It is that experience that has encouraged the Cloverleaf Foundation to bring Mario Betti's beautiful and masterful book to an English-speaking readership.

The Foundation has funded the translation from the original German. We are delighted with the outcome, with many thanks to the outstanding translator Matthew Barton. We are also very happy to be collaborating with Martin Large, publisher of Hawthorn Press. And Mario Betti has been a pillar of strength and encouragement throughout what has been a long and often challenging process. From our very first contact almost ten years ago our relationship has been nothing but inspiring and dear, and I thank him deeply for the meaning his work has had for my own life and work.

I wish you a wonderful journey in reading this inspiring book. Enjoy!

Kathelijne Drenth, Chair, Cloverleaf Foundation,
Netherlands. www.cloverleaffoundation.com

Note: Study Guide for Individuals and Groups

At the end of this book you will find a Study Guide that Mario and I have compiled for the English edition. The purpose of this guide is to facilitate individual study and also group study. A version is also available in German, which can be downloaded from www.cloverleaffoundation.com.

Foreword to the 2001 German Edition

Mario Betti

This book is an attempt to present twelve worldviews that offer twelve different ways of understanding ourselves and the world we live in. Each can gradually help us to penetrate secrets of the human being and the cosmos, since, in the words of Goethe's Faust, they together embody 'what makes the world most inwardly cohere'.

First and foremost, especially in regard to our currently developing multicultural society, the book aims to stimulate new ways of thinking, rather than just being a compendium of worldviews or an historical outline of philosophical ideas. Where the context requires it, the book draws equally on science, art and religion, and in the process it will become apparent that Goethe's whole oeuvre was ultimately a striking realisation of the 'huge undertaking' to which he referred when looking back at his unfinished poem, 'The Mysteries', in which he had wanted to give artistic expression to twelve outlooks on the world.

Moreover, the universalist approach of Rudolf Steiner's anthroposophy also develops naturally and fittingly into a study of twelve worldviews.

This book is the result of over 20 years of study and research, and owes much to the many generations of students at Alanus University, near Bonn, Germany, who repeatedly urged me to write it. At the start of every year, I spend several days speaking about the twelve worldviews to each new group of students. I offer my warmest thanks to them, and to the colleagues who have worked alongside me.

My special thanks go to the Hausser and Mahle Foundations, without whose kind support this book would not have seen the light of day so quickly.

Mario Betti

21 March 2001

1

Goethe's 'The Mysteries', and Today's Multicultural Society

And so without delay take hold
Of sacred, open secret, and behold.
From Goethe's poem 'Epirrhema'

> If this poem had been published in full 30 years ago, when it was conceived and begun, it would have come somewhat ahead of its times. And today, although ideas have developed since then, feelings have purified and views have grown more enlightened, the reader may perhaps be glad to see in poetic garb what has, in the mean time, come to general acknowledgement, and thereby find an affirmation of views which alone can bring contentment and peace to each person upon his personal Mont-Serrat.[1]

Goethe was already 67 when he published these words in 1816, in the *Morgenblatt* (*Morning News*). Addressed to 'a society of young students', his aim was to affirm the plan and purpose of 'The Mysteries', a poem that he had never completed. He had started it in 1784, very shortly before his 35th birthday, and written the poem 'as it stands… quickly, and all at once'. For nine months Goethe kept trying to return to it, but on 28 March 1785 he wrote to Knebel to say that 'the undertaking is too huge for my capacities'.[2] The work had faltered, and was never picked up again.

What is this 'affirmation' about? Mont-Serrat, a rocky, almost isolated mountain range in Catalonia, today much frequented by pilgrims and tourists, has been linked in diverse ways with the Grail tradition.[3] In 1800,

Goethe himself had received an account from Wilhelm von Humboldt of hermitages in the mountains of northern Spain, later to be his inspiration for the figures of the holy Fathers in the last scene of *Faust*. In retrospect he connects this mountain with the one in 'The Mysteries': it becomes for him a symbol of an 'ideal Montserrat' where each person can affirm the views and outlooks that can give him or her 'happiness and tranquillity'.

What kind of happiness? What kind of tranquillity?

The poem describes how a young priest, Brother Marcus, one evening comes in his travels to a quiet valley, to a monastery where he is invited to enter. Over the gateway of the monastery is a 'cross thick-woven with roses'. Goethe describes the situation as follows: Brother Marcus 'finds there twelve knights who, after the tumult and travails of lives full of exertion, suffering and danger, have taken a vow to live here and quietly serve God. A thirteenth, whom they acknowledge as their superior, is on the point of departing from them.' Brother Marcus is now welcomed most warmly, and led into a hall.

> Here was no ornament to distract the eyes,
> A daring cross-vault rose aloft
> And by the walls stood thirteen chairs
> Arranged in a ring, as for a pious choir,
> Each gracefully carved by able hands;
> Before each chair there stood a little desk.
> You had a sense of reverence everywhere,
> And peace, and sociability together.

This mysterious brotherhood is gathered around a figure named Humanus, described as the archetype of true humanity, and someone who has the ability to act as a mediator between them. Goethe described the twelve as representatives of the 'most diverse modes of thought and feeling', or in other words as belonging to very different worldviews or religions. They are people who, while strictly maintaining each one's inner freedom, seek harmony between their different perspectives. Thus, Humanus is at the centre of a world of thought and feeling conceived in universal terms. From their master, the twelve have learned the kind of tolerance in which, despite differing professions of faith, they can live harmoniously together, complementing and enhancing each other. They had all felt 'a resemblance with and sympathy for him', and now, 'after long living together, Humanus could depart from them since his spirit was embodied in them all, belonged to all, and no longer needed earthly raiment'. The young pilgrim, who has been sent to them by divine direction, is now to become the master of this brotherhood as the earthly representative of Humanus.

The core message of this poem, in Goethe's own words, is this:

> If, after this outline, the listener, the participant, is then led in spirit through all lands and times, everywhere experiencing the most joyous things that the love of God and man brings forth in so many different forms, this should give rise to the most pleasant sense in which the aberrations, malpractices or distortions of which every religion is sometimes accused in certain epochs nowhere become manifest. If this whole enactment takes place in the week of Easter, and the chief symbol of this community is a cross inwoven with roses, it is easy to envisage that the eternal preservation of higher human conditions will have also been revealed here, in consoling fashion, at the point when Humanus departs.

'And so without delay take hold / of sacred, open mystery, and behold' are words we might, in view of the above, gladly call out to our contemporaries. For it is true to say that the human qualities in human beings – which Goethe symbolised so profoundly in the figure of Humanus – struggle to see the light of day in our era. And it is indeed difficult, given the wealth of outlooks and perspectives on God, nature, history, etc. which live in our developing multicultural society, to imagine the possibility of true connection with each other, let alone to grasp the idea that they – in their archetypal qualities – are part of one all-embracing whole. Goethe, with his universalising outlook, *was* able to conceive of a cosmos of twelve different 'modes of thinking and feeling', not only in terms of religion. And he also recognised why, unlike Eckermann for instance, he never demanded that human beings should 'harmonise' into one and the same outlook. On 2 May 1824 he said to Eckermann:

> I have always regarded a person only as a self-contained individual whom I sought to understand, and with whose particularity I endeavoured to acquaint myself, without demanding from him any further sympathy. By this means I have now become able to relate to every human being, and through this alone arises a knowledge of manifold characters as well as a necessary adroitness in life. You see, especially when one encounters obstinate natures, one must get a grip upon oneself to get through to them, and by this means all the different aspects in us are enlivened and developed, so that one soon feels equal to every

> encounter.... You must venture forth into the greater world, whatever position you wish to adopt.[4]

About six years previously, in 1816, Goethe had written down the passage about 'The Mysteries' that we quoted above. The two statements should be seen in the same context. In his monograph on Goethe,[5] Rudolf Meyer is right to remark that this outlook is entirely in accord with the idea of tolerance that was at last making headway in the eighteenth century after fanatical denominational disputes had convulsed European culture for centuries. He goes on to write:

> But tolerance can also culminate in an unfruitful neutrality of view, one that makes no effort to engage with the specific and particular nature of a different stance. For this reason Goethe says: 'Tolerance should actually only be a temporary position: it must lead to recognition and acknowledgement. Sufferance signifies insult.' It is clear that this high ideal at the same time points to a developmental goal embracing all human society and the community of nations.

In this sense this core concern of Goethe's, seen now in sociological terms, offers a deeper view of what is nowadays called 'the multicultural society', in so far as its goal – with all diversity of languages, traditions, religious confessions, values and lifestyles – is a community of human beings founded on tolerance and acknowledgement. The two cornerstones of such a society are no doubt a culture of dialogue – including dispute – and a new kind of introspection. Whereas the latter can first provide us with insight into our bodily, psychological and cultural or spiritual identity, the former gives us deeper acquaintance with the other.

But Goethe goes still further than this – and here we can see how far ahead of his time he was, his very specific vision becoming apparent from his unusual view of 'Easter Sunday', which displays a truly cosmopolitan outlook. In relation to 'The Mysteries', Rudolf Meyer writes of this:

> The figure of Humanus who, under the sign of the Rose Cross, gathers round him the representatives of all religious and cultural streams and can unite them in true fraternity, seeks to offer this outlook of a future, inter- and supra-denominational Christianity.[6]

It could of course be objected that Goethe was simply Goethe, and nowadays is nowadays; that everywhere we witness war and conflict between people, worldviews, racisms, nationalisms and fundamentalisms. At the same time, society has fallen under the sway of increasing connectivity and globalisation – or in other words a levelling of all conditions, which is really only a variation on the rule of power prevalent from ancient times. And then too, ultimately, it might be said, world society is slowly but surely heading towards its dissolution: a clash of cultures is imminent, rather than a global 'round table'. These widespread views about our contemporary world have partial justification. And yet more and more round tables *are* coming into being, corrupt, inhumane political systems, and power blocks are crumbling and humanity is increasingly struggling through to greater unity. Reality is of course not a gigantic woodcut with fixed areas of light and dark, but rather a developing landscape that each and everyone can help to shape, the smallholder as much as powerful politicians.

We are concerned here also with an awareness of our potential freedom, and spiritual and social capacities. This is a creative process. We need to dig in with the will. Hegel says this:

> Development is... tough, reluctant work against oneself; and moreover it is not merely the formal nature of development in a general sense but the bringing forth of a purpose with specific content. This purpose is one we determined upon from the beginning: it is the mind and spirit, and accords with their true nature, the idea of freedom. This is the founding and thus also the governing principle of development, through which it gains sense and meaning.[7]

And 'World history, as has been previously determined, embodies the development of the spirit's consciousness of freedom, and the realisation or implementation produced by such consciousness.'[8]

Here, where the individual as such is involved, we can of course offer no fixed prognoses. But it is enough to recognise that human beings can shape world history in a humane way if they are moved to act. Related to our theme, the realisation of the mind or spirit, which Hegel postulates so urgently, can also consist of enlarging our own view of things in scientific, artistic, social and religious dimensions, so that the full reality of life increasingly becomes the reality we experience. The world reveals its riches to us to the degree that we possess organs to perceive it. Thus we need not only to revise our views but to furnish our mind in a more comprehensive way. It is a matter not simply of replacing one theory with a 'better' one, but of justified diversity when considering any set of circumstances.

In this context, Thomas Kuhn's essay on the structure of scientific revolutions is extremely apposite. Without discussing the ultimate unity of diverse worldviews, he shows how absolutist claims to truth are untenable. He applies the familiar definition of 'paradigm' – as a model and standard according to which experience can be compared and evaluated – in particular to the basic views that hold sway in an academic or scientific discipline at any one time, testing them chiefly in respect of subject and methodology. The paradigm establishes what can be regarded as a scientifically satisfactory solution, and what questions can be seen as allowable. Kuhn's thesis is that 'revolutions' – in the sense of changes of paradigm – continually arise in the history of science, and that scientific theories relating to particular fields cannot be compared with one another because of the paradigms upon which they are founded; thus they are 'incommensurable'. And, since the concepts used, such as space, time and mass, have different significance in, say, Newton's or Einstein's view of mechanics, they are also irreconcilable. Here is a passage from his book that brings the debate in this realm right up to date:

> We will therefore take as proven that the contradictions between successive paradigms are as necessary as they are irreconcilable. And can we then say more clearly what kinds of opposition these are? The most noticeable kind has already been cited several times. Successive paradigms tell us various things about what exists in the universe and how it behaves. That is, they deviate from each other in questions such as the existence of subatomic particles, the materiality of light and the conservation of heat or energy. These are the essential differences between successive paradigms, and they require no further explanation. Paradigms, however, differ in more than substance, for they relate not only to nature but also reflect back on the science that produced them. They are the source of all methods, problem areas and solution norms as these are acknowledged at any time by a mature scientific community. In turn this means that adoption of a new paradigm often requires a new definition of the science in question. Various old problems can be diverted to a different field or be declared completely 'unscientific'. Others in turn, which did not previously exist, or were entirely insignificant, can, with the arrival of a new paradigm, become a primary type of important scientific achievement. And in the same way that the problems change, so also the norm which distinguishes a truly scientific solution from mere metaphysical speculation, wordplay or mathematical gimmickry. The normative scientific tradition that arises from

> a scientific revolution is not only irreconcilable with the past but often, indeed, incommensurable.[9]

The paradigms themselves are thus not worldviews as such but, as already suggested, more like ordering principles, models of explanation in the context of an already fairly well-developed worldview such as materialism or mathematism.

An outlook close to our own position here is that of Neil Postman, who has come to prominence in recent years with his works of cultural critique. In his book *The End of Education*, which was published in 1995, he writes as follows:

> Educators may bring upon themselves unnecessary travail by taking a tactless and unjustifiable position about the relation between scientific and religious narratives.
>
> We see this, of course, in the conflict concerning creation science. Some educators representing, as they think, the conscience of science act much like those legislators who in 1925 prohibited by law the teaching of evolution in Tennessee. In that case, anti-evolutionists were fearful that a scientific idea would undermine religious belief. Today, proevolutionists are fearful that a religious idea will undermine scientific belief. The former had insufficient confidence in religion; the latter insufficient confidence in science. The point is that profound but contradictory ideas may exist side by side, if they are constructed from different materials and methods and have different purposes. Each tells us something important about where we stand in the universe, and it is foolish to insist that they must despise each other.[10]

Cultural commentator Hartmut Böhme highlights a different aspect of the whole issue. In an article in the periodical *Die Zeit*,[11] on the theme of bio-sciences and the tasks of cultural studies, he expresses ideas that once again underline the topicality of the attempt, undertaken here, to survey a range of different worldviews and their interrelationship. This also offers further proof of the modernity of Goethe's vision.

> Since modern science and technology existed, nature and humankind have been overrun by ever-new models of monopolistic explanation. At a time when the cosmos seemed to be created in the image of a clock, everything from the smallest living entity, through humankind, to the heavens was explained in terms of mechanics and machines. Whereas

> at one time circulation was seen as the principle governing both the blood and the motions of the planets, at another an infinitesimal mathematics made it possible to enumerate the world from its smallest creature to the infinite universe. With the discovery of electromagnetism it seemed we had found the energy responsible for the life of animal and human organisms as well as the order of the universe. Darwinism enchanted thinkers with its thesis of the genetic mechanisms of selection regulating all life. The theory of relativity, and quantum theory, explained physical structures from elementary particles through to the macrocosm, but was at the same time also adapted as a model of society and history.
>
> Today the 'life sciences' have taken on the mantle of such universal generalisations and euphoric promises of salvation. History teaches that these great claims are always followed by repudiations. It is therefore to be suspected that even scientists who at present flock to the banner of what is rather immodestly called 'life science' will eventually realise that they have not actually understood 'life' at all, and will be succeeded by other claimants to the forefront of knowledge. But let us not wait until this happens, for the assertion that the bio-sciences are 'sciences of life' demands scientific, political and cultural responses right now.

These examples, only a few of the many that could be cited, testify to the willingness of alert contemporaries to depart from the narrow and linear paths of reductionism and come to a universally human, multi-layered worldview. Or to put it another way: more or less consciously there is a growing willingness for creative self-realisation as Hegel understood it, and an all-embracing humanity as Goethe described.

2

The Twelve Worldviews: What Is Meant by Them

Since Kant introduced the word 'worldview' into philosophical discussion, it has assumed many different shades of meaning. In his *Critique of Judgement*, Kant uses it to refer to a subjective summary of the world multiply grasped by the senses. Max Scheler, on the other hand, characterises 'worldview' as

> A mode of selection and categorisation that holds sway over a whole cultural milieu or a person, assimilating *de facto* the pure truths of physical, psychological and ideal things irrespective of whether and how it either does or does not reflexively know this.[12]

Scheler died in 1928. A contemporary of his, Rudolf Steiner, goes a step further in seeing 'worldview' as real ontology by connecting it more strongly both to the human being and the cosmos. In his lecture of 21 January 1914,[13] Steiner initially tackles questions of the universality of thinking, and the dangers of one-sided perceptions. 'If one seeks to form any idea of thinking at all,' he says, one must be clear 'that the truth of a thought in its particular field does not yet tell us anything about its *general* validity. A thought can certainly be correct in its field but this has no bearing on its general validity.' He continues by emphasising 'that one-sidedness is the greatest enemy of all worldviews and should be avoided at all costs'. People such as Kuhn, Postman and Böhme would very likely agree with him here.

In the lecture, Steiner then goes on to outline twelve justified worldviews, in a sense as universal categories of outlook, though of course without entertaining a shallow pluralism. He is describing an organism of worldviews – that is, of perceptions of the principles that constitute the world and the human being. In the words of Faust, once again, he is examining 'what makes the world most inwardly cohere'. Steiner, though, summarises as follows:

> Between these worldviews we can conceive of others too, but they are only subtly different from the ones I have described, and can be assigned to the chief types. If we seek to acquaint ourselves with the fabric of the world, we have to recognise that we come to know it through these twelve gateways.

The *Brockhaus Encyclopaedia* identifies around 90 worldviews current today. Based on the relevant literature – including Dilthey, Jaspers and Spranger – it states: 'Insofar as worldviews seek completeness, they must include characterisations of the human being and the world, and views about value, life and morality.'[14] This statement relativises the scientific validity of worldviews in that they are 'interpretative outlooks in the form of personal convictions about the fundamental structure, modality and function of the whole world'. But then it states, somewhat more authoritatively, that,

> Today, distinctions made according to the six most important governing principles take precedence over any worldview. These are: the individual (for instance, humanism), the community (for instance, socialism), the future (life of future generations, utopian ideals), omnipotence (for instance, religions), action (for instance, materialism, anarchism), reality (for instance, pragmatism, monism). Many worldviews are currently in a crisis of coherence and relevance, which has led to the tendency to form 'private worldviews' composed of fragments of the most diverse outlooks. Orders of value founded on individual motivations and orientations become personally meaningful views of life. The need for 'cultural belonging' remains, however, in the form of universal explanations, as support and assistance in dealing with life, especially in 'borderline situations'.

Now Steiner's position – like that of the present author – is not a relativistic one. The twelvefold character, taken as a whole, supplies not merely some 'personal conviction', but rather a harmony of comprehensible worldviews, which separately and together give us what we could call a manifestation of the truth about the world and the human being. Just as we can see a house, a mountain and – of course – an elephant (see the Indian fable on p. iii) very differently, depending on our particular perspective, so also, in the sense of Steiner, we can see the 'fabric of the world'. The number twelve is no more 'mystical' than the six governing principles to which the *Brockhaus Encyclopaedia* refers, or the numbers three, four, five and seven which we encounter repeatedly in phenomena of nature, astronomy or cultural history.[15] From an epistemological perspective, and given the fact that the mesh size of a net is what determines the size of fish that will be caught, we have to resort to the full scope of our cognitive capacities if we are gradually to delve into the domain of truth. The 'whole truth' is comparable to an ocean. We swim close to the beach and cannot therefore encompass the ocean's whole scope, but we *are* already in the water and can swim out ever further. It is only important to know that there are other 'shores' from which to embark for the open sea. The problem of worldviews does not primarily lie in their irreconcilability but in the one-sidedness and exclusivity they can manifest.

More than almost any other of his contemporaries, Rudolf Steiner sought strenuously for a multiplicity of outlooks. Born in Kraljevec (modern Croatia) in 1861, he studied sciences in Vienna and was awarded a doctorate in philosophy in Rostock. After he had embarked on editing Goethe's scientific writings as part of Kürschner's 'German Literature' editions, he was employed at the Goethe and Schiller Archive in Weimar. In both Vienna and Weimar, and later, around the turn of the century in Berlin, he moved in the most varied circles. His research increasingly enabled him to comprehend both the material and the spiritual aspect of the world in a *single* process of cognition, and this was to form the basis of the anthroposophy that he later founded. In relation to this, looking back a few months before his death, he said of his book *Philosophy of Freedom*, published in 1894:

> In my book I sought to show that nothing unknown *lies behind* the sense world, but that the world of spirit is *within* it. And I tried to demonstrate that the human world of ideas exists in this spiritual world. Thus the reality of the sensory world is hidden from the human mind only for as long as the soul perceives *only* through the senses. When we experience the ideas that complement sense perceptions, our consciousness experiences the sense world in its objective reality. Cognition is not a reflection of reality but a process in which the soul finds its way into it. Within consciousness occurs an advance from an as yet inessential

> sense world to its essence. Thus the sense world only remains 'phenomenon' or appearance while the mind has not yet fathomed it fully. In truth the sense world is therefore spiritual world too; and the soul lives at one with this perceived world of spirit by extending consciousness to encompass it. The goal of the process of cognition is conscious experience of the spiritual world, in the sight of which everything resolves into spirit.[16]

This experience is one that draws on and existentially requires the whole human being's thinking, feeling and intent. And thus Steiner says:

> The world is full of enigmas. Cognition seeks to understand it. But mostly it tries to offer a thought content as solution to any riddle. But riddles – as I said to myself – are *not solved by thoughts.* These direct the soul towards solutions but do not themselves contain them. An enigma arises in the actual world, and exists there as a phenomenon; and so its solution must also arise *in reality.* Some essence or occurrence appears which embodies the solution to another. And so I said to myself: the whole world, apart from the human being, is an enigma, the world riddle if you like; and the *human being is its solution.* ... Human beings do not *create* the content of knowledge *for themselves,* but, with their soul, they offer the stage or setting where the world first comes to a partial experience of its existence and development. Without human knowledge, the world would remain incomplete.[17]

This is an extraordinarily keen conclusion which can lead us, already in close study of *The Philosophy of Freedom*, to a personal–transpersonal experience. For Steiner himself this increasingly intensified process of cognition went hand in hand with a social and existential embrace of different worldviews, as he experienced these in diverse friends and interlocutors.

It is important to become aware of this aspect of his endeavour and research. It is central to this book, which is founded on similar experience. While the chief focus here is on finding paths of deeper communication and mutual affirmation between people, at the same time there are pointers here – for each person can only experience this for themselves – that I and world, human being and cosmos, can grow together. Intensive engagement with the founding motifs of the twelve worldviews can in fact become a grand boulevard towards this goal.

In his unfinished *Autobiography*, from which the passages above are taken, Steiner writes sentences that must certainly be regarded in this light. They relate to his time in Weimar, during which he was 'in the liveliest discourse' with many different people:

> I liked visiting Suphan, and I liked visiting Hartleben. Suphan never went to see Hartleben, nor Hartleben Suphan. Neither could engage with the other's way of thinking and feeling. But I felt immediately at home with both of them. Yet neither Suphan nor Hartleben ever came to visit me properly. When they did visit, they stayed as it were at home. In spirit I did not experience them as visiting me. I saw the most diverse worldviews inwardly before me: the scientific, the idealistic, and many shades between. I felt the urge to engage with them, to move within them.[18]

Then:

> In this way I did not live without spiritual dangers and difficulties. Those who reject anything that does not conform with their way of thinking are not under pressure from the relative justifications of different outlooks. They can feel unreservedly the fascinating aspect of what has been thought in a particular 'school of thought'. This intellectual fascination lives in many people. They can easily deal with a thinking different from their own. But if you have a world of *visions, views, of tangible perceptions,* as the spiritual mode of enquiry *inevitably* does, you *see* the justification of different 'standpoints'; and you have to continually defend yourself inwardly against being too strongly drawn to the one or the other.[19]

And:

> This was an apt soul exercise, which life itself presented me with in order to get beyond the abstract either–or of rational judgement. *This* kind of judgement erects inward barriers to the supersensible world, which is not one whose realities and occurrences allow such binary alternatives. One has to become manifold and versatile in relation to supersensible reality. Theoretical learning is not enough; one must make it a habitual practice, right into the soul's inmost responses, to regard everything from the most diverse perspectives. 'Standpoints' such as materialism, realism, idealism, spirituality – which people with an abstract focus

> develop in the physical world into extensive theories in order to add significance to things themselves – lose all interest for the supersensible seer. The latter knows, for instance, that materialism can only be a view of the world from the perspective in which it appears in material garb.... No doubt it was the spirit of Goethe, so prevalent everywhere in Weimar, that made a certain aspect of my experience of what happened there into a practical soul exercise in adequate description of supersensible worlds.[20]

In 1897, Steiner moved from Weimar to Berlin. Developing anthroposophy there as a 'path of knowledge that seeks to lead the spirit in the human being to the spirit in the cosmos',[21] he may well have expected that the spark of keen engagement with different worldviews would kindle in a great many hearts. He gave the lectures on the twelve worldviews, referred to earlier, in 1914 in Berlin, for the Anthroposophical Society founded in 1912–13. There he explained:

> There is not only *one* worldview that can be defended, that is legitimate, but twelve. And it has to be admitted that there are just as many good reasons for one worldview as for every other of the twelve. The world cannot be regarded from the one-sided outlook of *one* worldview, one thought, but reveals itself only to those who know that one must circumnavigate it. Just as, in the Copernican worldview, the sun passes through the signs of the zodiac, shining upon the earth from twelve different regions, so likewise we should not position ourselves upon a single standpoint – that, say, of idealism, sensualism, phenomenalism or any other outlook that can be named – but instead, we should be able to encircle the world and live our way into the twelve different perspectives from which the world can be regarded.[22]

As far as I can tell, this seed did not produce copious fruits, either in the public domain or within the anthroposophic movement. I am referring here not just to the immediate practical and social consequences of such an outlook, but also the further dissemination and development of the twelve worldviews to which Steiner makes only passing reference. These are:

Phenomenalism
Sensualism
Materialism

Mathematism
Rationalism
Idealism
Psychism
Pneumatism
'Spiritualism'*
Monadism
Dynamism
Realism

[*Translator's note*: The terms 'spiritualism' and 'spiritualist' could easily be confused with the 'spiritualist' movement, with which it has next to nothing in common. It refers, rather, to a 'spiritual' mode of apprehending reality. When the term is used in the text, it is placed in quotation marks to indicate this crucial difference.]

An exception here is the philosopher and historian Sigismund von Gleich, who in the 1940s wrote a work entitled *The Truth as Full Compass of All Worldviews.*[23] This is the wonderful outline of a history of philosophy and culture from ancient times to the twentieth century, from the perspective of the twelve worldviews. It is a work of grandeur, and the present book could not have been written without thorough study of it. I whole-heartedly recommend it for readers who would like to explore these themes further.

Given the multi-layered complexity of the theme, this book will aim to bring the core of each worldview into clear focus and see it in relation to the others. Each worldview is in a sense an 'archetypal phenomenon', an originating picture that can appear in many shades, as it were prismatically fragmented – fragmented as many times, in fact, as there are human beings. Each person is unique, their depths and heights beyond grasp. Nevertheless there are strong proponents of very specific worldviews, even if, of course, they are not entirely subsumed by their outlook.

It must therefore be a matter not of pigeonholing people in a cultural or spiritual context but of *understanding* them, and doing so *also* within the specific values and characteristics they lend to a certain worldview. Ultimately we can recall here the phrase of Empedocles, that only 'like perceives like'; or the telling phrase of J.G. Fichte: 'The philosophy one has shows what kind of person one is.'[24] If we now start from the assumption that this twelvefold source springs within human beings themselves, then every encounter with another, but also with nature around and above us, will become an act of self-knowledge in a deeper sense. And the world will then always increasingly turn out to be constituted of, and pervaded by, the creative principles that manifest as a 'worldview' in any individual. In this case I as human being am the answer to the world's enigma.

The path highlighted here can therefore become a tangible stimulus for every open-minded contemporary individual, and a means increasingly to embrace a developing multicultural society, and to grow to be at one with the cosmos. Recalling Goethe's 'The Mysteries' we must say that Humanus in each of us is waiting to be born in our own, ideal Mont-Serrat, to work in socially practical ways for the humane progress of our culture.

3

Look at, and Listen to, the World – Phenomenalism

A deep red sun slowly sets on the horizon. As the sky grows ever darker behind you, in the West a glorious flare of colours is blazing: yellow, red, gold, and high above a bright mother-of-pearl shimmer accompanies the sun as it sinks slowly into the depths. Veils of cloud gleam in ever-changing shades of colour, and, as a gentle breeze seems to usher you towards the far breadths, you feel something like an inkling that you cannot put into words. Everything has fallen silent in you, in your surrender to the colours, light, air and wind. You feel a sense of wonder at intimations you cannot yet fathom, and a deep, joyful religious mood joins your reflections, like a musical undertone. Perhaps you think of a poem you learned long ago at school, such as this one by Eichendorff:

> A song sleeps within everything,
> In lasting dream that never will
> Awaken till you find the magic spell –
> And then the world at last begins to sing.

Over the millennia people have so often had similar experiences – in the mountains, by lakes, in forests and in their encounter with animals. The legend of St Hubertus, of which many variations exist, may have a similar experience at its heart. It relates how a deer fleeing from a hunter suddenly stops, turns and simply gazes with gentle majesty at the man who has already strung an arrow to his bow. The legend tells us that Hubertus saw a cross of light between the deer's antlers and heard a voice that called upon him to dedicate his life to God and the creature he was chasing. It may have been the regal, tranquil stance of the deer that called up this vision in Hubertus, but he changed his whole life. Later he became the Bishop of Lüttich, and today, somewhat cynically, is regarded as the patron saint of hunters.

Although this legend has a 'pneumatical' aspect – and we will return to what this means later – the first part of it is marked by alert attention and a perception permeated by a deeper reality. This is brought about by the majestic *phenomenon* or appearance of the deer itself, in the same way that the whole phenomenal world can become the 'song' of creation, or, in Shakespeare's words in his play *As You Like It*, the book in which we read:

> And this our life, exempt from public haunt,
> Finds tongues in trees, books in the running brooks,
> Sermons in stones, and good in everything.

In this kind of experience, as Nietzsche says, the world reveals 'depths deeper than the day'.

When this selfless perception arises, which can naturally assume different degrees of intensity, then we have a means for developing the worldview of phenomenalism. This is a mode of observation of varying kinds. It can have a spiritual dimension, or also not. Phenomenalism is rooted in the fact that we are perceiving beings, and in the more or less justified conviction that the sense world conveys truth and reality to us. The true phenomenalist is not misled by metaphysics, by ideas of a different, 'real' world hidden behind the visible one. This phenomenalist potential lives in all of us – since we all see, hear, etc. – but not everyone makes it into their philosophy or formulates an artistic aesthetic from it. Given all the subjective sensualism that can manifest here, as we will see, it is important that we follow Goethe in recognising that the senses do not 'dissemble'. The fact that we only become aware of sense perceptions through extraordinarily complex physical and physiological processes does not necessarily mean that they are 'untrue' or merely subjective. Just as we human beings are an integral part of the whole cosmos, already by virtue of our corporeality, so we have, as previously suggested, adequate means to recognise 'what makes the world most inwardly cohere' (*Faust*).

We find within us the same mineral world as in our surroundings, the same hydrosphere (over two-thirds of the body is composed of water). Likewise, we are part of the atmosphere through our 'air organism', while our warmth relates to and is connected with the warmth and heat in the world.

And yet, should our perception of the world and conscious life be seen only as the outcome of what unfolds in our subjective skull, and not also as part of a universal consciousness? It is much more realistic to assume that the whole human being is an answer to the 'world enigma', and that the world would remain incomplete without our perception of and thought about it. Justified as it is to question the objectivity of our sense impressions, there is nevertheless no evidence to suggest they are exclusively subjective.

The physiologist and philosopher Hermann Lotze once made some very interesting comments on the phenomenality of the world:

> Things are not intrinsically coloured but it is their living, active shining that looks out at us in colours. Their taste, their smell, are actions that approach us, in which their inmost essence comes towards ours, revealing to us what fills their forms within external, spatial confines, and is the true *reality* of their existence. Reflective listening perceives in the different voices of nature communications through which an enigmatic interiority of things speaks to us vividly, though one untranslatable into any other language. Thus we recognise how our sensory nature seeks to give us insight into the inmost living being of authentic, alien interiority.[25]

Goethe as scientist propounded this almost classical phenomenalism in outstanding fashion. It constitutes his working method. We can think here of his studies of bones, his metamorphosis of plants or the theory of colours which was so important to him; and although some aspects of his findings have been superseded today, his fundamental method and aims have not. These enquiries of his are treasures of scientific research. In his *Proverbs in Prose* he succinctly summarises the goal of his quest: 'The highest achievement would be to understand that all actuality is already theory. There is no need to search behind the phenomena; they themselves are the tenets.'[26] And: 'Truth resembles God; it does not directly appear to us, but we must grasp it from its manifestations.'[27] We can also return here to the short poem 'Epirrhema', which could stand as a kind of leitmotif for all phenomenological observation of nature:

> Observing nature, we must ever
> Attend both to single things and all;
> Nothing is inner, nothing outer:
> For inward is also outward, so

Without delay take hold
Of sacred, open secret, and behold.

Take delight in true appearance,
And in serious play:
Nothing alive is one thing alone
But always manifold diversity.

We can see, both from the passage by Lötze and the words of Goethe, that something like a selfless poetic sensibility accompanies rigorous scientific enquiry and can then culminate in a religious experience:

Nature conceals God!
But not from everyone.[28]

Phenomenalism requires a kind of chasteness of the senses, a very specific artistic-objective observation of the world, if it is to appear in a pure form. Only then is nature willing to divulge her secrets. In the pictorial arts we find this element, for instance, in the nature sensibility of the Impressionists, and in the way in which, through gradations of colour and their special technique of applying it, they try to record how things respond to the interplay of sunlight and shadow. This is a special form of naturalism, but one that captures the object at the moment of painting in an almost physiological way. What comes about in consequence is not just an expression of the painter but belongs to the things themselves. We might also cite Paul Klee's 'creative confession' here: 'Art does not depict the visible but *makes* visible.' This primary law of artistic work – the invisible becomes visible, or, in philosophical terms, hidden essence becomes phenomenon – by virtue of which we can directly 'read' the message of the artist, is also what Goethe means when he writes: 'Beauty is a revelation of secret natural laws which would have remained eternally concealed from us without its manifestation.'[29] And we can likewise quote Novalis here: 'Outward appearance is an inner quality raised into a secret condition.'[30]

An aesthetic rooted in phenomenalism does not regard intellectual patterns of meaning or abstract symbolisms very highly. This naturally represents only one aspect from the whole scope of artistic approaches and beliefs. But it is interesting that phenomenalism investigates the world exclusively in its mode of appearance: as it simply 'shines forth'. This manifesting and appearing is a fundamental quality of the world, and in itself is no reason to declare the world to be only materially constituted. If I look and listen properly, it is as if the world reveals itself: its being manifests within the phenomena. It becomes an 'open secret'. Even in Expressionism we find this law applied, except that here the source of coloration and line are largely not found outside in nature, but within the soul of the artist.

In former times, people's view of the world was very strongly marked by phenomenalistic traits. We find this, for instance, in the basic outlook of religions that regard nature and the whole cosmos as divine. The three examples below are not meant to substantiate this, but simply offer a further aspect of this worldview.

There is the old religion of Zarathustra, as it originally spread through the language and culture of Persia, modern Iran. Zoroastrianism was marked through the centuries by a fundamental polarity in the form of the battle of light – Ahura Mazda – against the 'bad' spirit Angra Mainju. In this context it is characteristic that Ahura Mazda is perceived to be living everywhere within Creation, 'for the heavens are his star-sown garment' and 'aspects of his being (Amesha Spentas) are embodied in the elements of this world'.[31] While he has his dwelling in the 'lights without beginning', he appears and is present in many good elements of the earth, whereas the 'darkness' is a direct expression of the evil principle. In the dark, demons have their existence. This also comes to expression in the bright figure of the God Mithra, who can be traced back most likely to non-Zoroastrian but still ancient Persian religious ideas. He is portrayed as the 'God of daylight'. He vanishes in the evening, and in the darkness returns 'from the West (over the earth) to the East, battling with the demons as he does so'.[32]

In dark Seth or Typhon in ancient Egypt, and in bright Horus, we find a certain correspondence to these beliefs. Characteristic here is the significance accorded to the world of sense phenomena, as an objective element. It is hardly surprising that people's experience back then was so primally vivid and human, since as yet no one-sided intellectualism in thinking had infected their trust in the natural capacity of the senses.

In Pharaoh Ekhnaton's reverence for the visible sun, which he called 'Aton', we also find the living experience of such things. In the new city that he constructed, he ordained that the disc of the sun and its proximity to human beings should be depicted everywhere, as light and warmth. It is worth noting the subtle phenomenalism in the beginning words of his famous hymn to the sun:

> Your rising is beautiful at the borders of heaven,
> Aton, who was before all else became.

> In your rising you fill the lands with brilliance.
> Your rays encompass what you have created,
> binding them with love.
> Infinitely distant, you are close, the day is the footprint of your presence.
> When you set, the earth is as if dead.[33]

Here, sunlight becomes tangible physiognomy: the phenomenon *is* already utterance, shedding light on the revolution in art that came with Ekhnaton, which of course has been seen and interpreted in a great many ways. (In purely phenomenalistic terms, there is, however, nothing to 'interpret' in art; it should simply be regarded or heard.) In sculpture, primarily, instead of the symbols that were widespread in ancient Egyptian art, forms suddenly directly manifest their content. For instance, the painted limestone busts of beautiful Nefertiti are devoid of the traditional stylisation, as are also the plaster masks from the workshop of the court sculptor Thutmosis, which are 'clearly portraits taken from life'.[34]

The Old Testament, too, knows the divine in sensory appearance – for instance, the physical, not symbolic, rainbow as sign of God's pledge after the Flood.

> And God said, This is the token of the covenant which I make between Me and you and every living creature that is with you, for perpetual generations: I do set My rainbow in the cloud, and it shall be for a token of a covenant between Me and the earth. And it shall come to pass, when I bring a cloud over the earth, that the rainbow shall be seen in the cloud.[35]

Of course, this picture isn't purely phenomenalistic. It has a clear symbolic content that displays an element of thought, as humankind would gradually come to embrace it. But the rainbow as such, in its transparency and ethereal brightness, its inner luminosity, is surely already something intrinsically special. A phenomenalist will not be surprised that the rainbow was chosen as a sign given by God!

That ancient, pure receptivity then increasingly gave way to a different mode – one that, for example, would acquire universal historical importance in Aristotle. In pre-Socratic natural philosophy, which was not science as we understand it today, there is still a good deal of phenomenalism. Aristotle founded instead a speculative science of sensory things which, while passing through multiple transformations, remains influential to this day. But Goethe's phenomenalism also bore much fruit in our own times – not only in his own day and directly afterwards – as is clear from the great number of conferences on Goethe held in 1999.[36] Even modern researchers of different schools, such as the physicist Werner Heisenberg, value the truth of Goethe's findings. Goethe's dispute with Newton, especially in the field of colour theory, is well known. In the general view, he was defeated in this altercation. But Heisenberg once wrote that

> Goethe's science, an anti-Newtonian science, oriented to perception of qualities in nature – Goethe called them '*ur*-phenomena' – did not lose in the dispute with Newton because it was not true. It is in fact just as true, perhaps even 'truer', but was held to have no application. People thought that nothing could be 'done' with it. By contrast, modern technology was developed from Newton's scientific doctrine, which could be 'applied'. This criterion of feasibility has been part and parcel of enquiry since the time of Bacon, since when all that can be reproduced experimentally, and is therefore 'feasible', is regarded as correct in principle.[37]

Heisenberg's comment is very significant!

Another important variant of phenomenalism is behavioural science, which has come to great prominence in recent decades in the fields of psychology and biology. We can think here, for example, of the wonderful observations of animals which Konrad Lorenz conducted and described in his books.[38] In one foreword he gives very fine expression to the phenomenalistic aspect of his research, though of course there were other aspects to it:

> The truths of organic nature are of endearing and awesome beauty and they become ever more beautiful the deeper one delves into their details and distinctive peculiarities. It is nonsense to think that the objectivity of research, knowledge, understanding of natural contexts would diminish our joy at the wonders of nature. On the contrary: we will be all the more deeply and lastingly moved by living reality, the more we know about it.[39]

This great researcher points to a very important aspect of phenomenalism. He has a deep affinity with the idea of 'beauty'. (The Latinate word 'beauty' in English replaced the Middle English 'sheen', which is cognate with the German 'schön'. The latter words signify that something *shines through*, or manifests in, the phenomenon.) Here we immediately recall the quotation from Goethe cited earlier: 'Beauty is a revelation of secret natural laws which would have remained eternally concealed from us without its manifestation.' This is phenomenalism!

Behaviourism, a psychological branch of behavioural science, is a school especially represented in the United States. It seeks to depart entirely from all self-observation and its evaluation, and merely describes behaviour externally. The twin concepts stimulus/response play a key role in this method of enquiry – which sees human behaviour in terms of a kind of automatic or mechanistic compulsion, according no value to inner participation. It is thought that this coupling of stimulus and response will allow human behaviour to be predicted in certain situations, and that rules can be derived from this for education and human society.

The ideas of B.F. Skinner, who died in 1990, were very influential in this field. He conducted animal experiments to research learning processes, and founded his systematic behavioural theory of learning on the outcomes. This also formed the basis for application in education, for example in what is known as 'programmed learning'. To put it simply, this involves the pupil engaging in a cycle of input/output of data. The teaching 'objectified' in this way is founded on a fixed, printed learning programme that the pupil must complete in stages. We get a tangible sense here of the impoverishment of education by detaching it from human qualities. The emotional aspect of a learning process, the enthusiasm, say, which can be felt as one learns, plays no role at all, and nor does the role of teacher as exemplar.

Every rigorous analysis of animal or human behaviour has a marked phenomenalistic aspect. Drawing conclusions from animal behaviour about human behaviour, however – and scarcely any behavioural researchers are free of this temptation – is a common *liaison dangereuse*, one that manoeuvres us almost unwittingly into the realm of a Darwinian materialism, and a reductionism applied to *all* human behaviour.

During studies in England in the 1970s I had a very important, albeit indirect, encounter with B.F. Skinner, which had significant consequences for my later outlook as a teacher. A psychology lecturer, who was also a scientific journalist for a major English newspaper, told us about meeting Skinner to interview him for the newspaper. They spoke together for a long time, and at the end of the discussion, as my lecturer was leaving, Skinner said to him: 'But don't imagine we have been conversing; we've just been behaving!' This gave me the sense of an outlook that regards the human being as a fixed, programmed machine – one in this case being a journalist, the other a scientist – that can do nothing other than act in accordance with the software implanted in it sociologically. It seems to me that this has, since then, become the more or less conscious view of countless people, with all the consequences it entails at a political and microsocial level of endless conflicts, disputes and divisions.

At the same time, inwardly developing a kind of unsullied phenomenalism can be of key importance in every situation that involves others, whether they be teacher, friend, partner or parent. As Lotze says, our perception of the world – and also of human beings – grants us 'insight into the inmost living being of an authentic alien interiority'.

Teachers can learn so much from the children entrusted to their care, by observing how they walk, the colour of their complexion or the way they speak. So likewise can a friend, partner, mother or father, if they really open their eyes to the *other* rather than being primarily concerned with themselves. Admittedly, not everyone has an innate talent for observing or listening, but practice can help us acquire it.

If only like understands like – and thus like affects like, as in homeopathy – learning to see and hear better is vital. Keen observation of nature, interest in people in all their diversity, can open us up to hitherto unknown depths of the world, as well as an artistic aesthetic. In *Knowledge of the Higher Worlds,* one of Steiner's ground-breaking books on spiritual development, he gives effective exercises to, among other things, keep developing our phenomenalistic potential. Here is one example that relates to the experience of tone quality:

> We should distinguish here between a tone that is produced by what we call lifeless things (a falling object, a bell or a musical instrument) from one that originates in a living creature (an animal or human being). Hearing a bell, we perceive its tone and connect a pleasant feeling with it; hearing the cry of an animal we will, beside this feeling, sense also the manifestation of inner experience.... We should direct our whole attention to what announces itself to us in the tone that is beyond or outside our own soul. And then we should immerse ourselves in this otherness. We should connect our feelings intimately with the pain or pleasure that reach us through the tone. We should move beyond what the tone is for *ourselves*, whether pleasant or unpleasant, enticing or displeasing, and fill ourselves only with what is occurring in this other creature from whom the tone comes. By doing such exercises regularly and intentionally, we can acquire the ability to, as it were, merge with the experience of another creature or person. A person with musical sensibility will find it easier to cultivate their inner life in this way than someone

> without it, but no one should think that musicality itself is a substitute for this practice. In this way we must… learn to respond to *everything* in nature…. All nature starts to offer up its secrets through tones and resonance. What was previously incomprehensible noise to us thus becomes meaningful as *nature's language*. And whereas we previously only heard tone when something 'lifeless' resounded, we now hear a new language of the soul. If we progress in this way in the cultivation of our feelings and sensibility, we will soon become aware that we can now hear things previously unsuspected. We begin to hear *with the soul*.[40]

We will end this chapter at this point, and pass on to consideration of another worldview that has a close affinity with phenomenalism, which we will also briefly outline.

To sum up phenomenalism as a worldview, we can say that the universe, as a whole and in its details, is an objective reality that reveals truth in its palpable appearance. This authentic quality of being is available to us if we are able to encompass it deeply and broadly enough with our – reliable and not deceiving – senses.

We find this idea formulated very strikingly in Schiller's poem 'The Artists':

> Only through beauty's morning gate
> Could you pass through into the land
> Of knowledge: reason first practises with states
> Of loveliness to learn radiance of a higher kind.
> The sweet tremor that through you passed,
> Summoned by the muses' lyre strings,
> Taught you to find a power in your breast
> That lifted you at last on wings
> Towards the spirit of the universe.
> …
> What we here feel as beauty, will one day
> Meet us again as truth upon our way.

4

Human Carnality – Sensualism

The worldview of sensualism takes seriously our purely sensory nature. Sensualists experience *their* own senses, and through them the sensory nature of the world so strongly that they may not even contemplate the idea, upon which phenomenalism is founded, that the senses could reveal something 'objective'. The senses give them meaning and fulfilment, and thus become the primary foundation of their self-awareness. Naturally we all have a sensory organisation, but not all of us make this into a philosophy, a worldview whose many aspects – as in all the twelve – are extraordinarily complex, but whose basic pattern is relatively clear: I and the world are merely the outcome of our sensory experience. Here we immediately sense the inherent problem in all worldviews: if they regard themselves not as aspects of an integral whole but each as *the* central source of truth, they easily succumb to misapprehension – even if, here and there, they connect symbiotically with each other.

Immediate sense experience is the first cornerstone of a sensualist outlook, while the second is established by commonly accepted sense physiology. The physicist and philosopher Ernst Mach gives fine expression to the first when looking back to an experience he had at the age of 17. If we compare the passage below with the words by Lotze from the previous chapter, we can sense the chasm that can divide a sensualist from a phenomenalist:

> I suddenly felt it idle to think in terms of 'things in themselves'. On a bright summer day in the open air, the world, together with my 'I', suddenly seemed like a connected mass of feelings and sensations, merely more connected within the 'I'. Although I didn't actually formulate this reflectively until later, this moment was decisive for my whole

> outlook.... Nature is composed of the *elements* given through the senses. Not things and bodies, but colours, tones, pressures, spaces, periods (which we usually call sensations) are the real elements of the world. It is not that bodies call forth feelings in us but rather, the bodies to which we refer in general terms are in reality complexes of feeling and sensation... and of these elements the *I* is constituted.[41]

The second cornerstone, sense physiology, also affirms this 'subjectivity'. In our day, a consistent general physiology of the senses has been established, based on increasingly detailed enquiries into the nervous systems of animals and humans, and the neurophysiological findings thus obtained, primarily as regards reception and processing of stimuli. This physiology is as interesting as it is complex, and both psychology and philosophy are often founded on these cornerstones. But the whole of empiricism and the positivism and pragmatism derived from them are in principle only a solid overarching structure if they are not separated from phenomenalism and other worldviews. Empiricism means more or less the same as sense experience and as such, in itself – and related to the totality of the world – does not provide the least cause to doubt its 'truth'. Josef Dudel writes interestingly about this:

> Sense physiology is thus divided into an account of the nervous system's reactions to stimulus – objective sense physiology – and a description of statements that the subject makes about their sensations and perceptions – subjective sense physiology. But the terms objective and subjective should not in this context be seen *in any way as value judgements* about the correctness of a statement. The sentence 'red is a warm colour' can be just as 'right' as the sentence 'the greater the intensity of a sensory stimulus, the greater the frequency of arousal in sensory nerve fibres'. As biologists, and especially as scientists investigating human experience, we must approach subjective statements about sensations and perceptions with as little preconception as we would deductions about cell potentials.[42]

And yet the same author reasonably regards this problem, referred to in the relevant literature as the 'psychophysical problem', as something that science cannot bridge:

> We feel sense experiences to be very personal ones, and our moods depend on them. In surroundings that exclude sensory stimuli, we

> become mentally unstable and ill (sensory deprivation). Thus a person 'is nothing other than the sum of his sense experiences' (D. Hume). On the other hand, schools of philosophy, struck by the strongly subjective components of all sense experiences, have asserted that only the subject exists, and our 'environment' is a product of our mind. The psychophysical problem which we have encountered so radically in sense physiology, is, for the time being at least, not soluble by the scientist.[43]

In the context of this study, we would have to add here: not soluble as long as the outlook remains a one-sided sensualist one, or succumbs to a reductionist model of explanation. In fact, this outlook logically cancels itself out: for if the sense world as I experience it is objectively a kind of illusion, then I myself would likewise be an illusion to an observer and to myself as a person grasped through the senses. It is worth pursuing this to its conclusion. What remains of us then? If our environment is a 'product' of our mind – a view common enough in the history of philosophy – then I, strictly speaking, am the product of my neighbour! In the course of this book we will keep coming up against the alarming fact that each outlook, narrowly conceived and applied, not only sunders us from the fullness of existence but ultimately leads to absurdity. None of the twelve worldviews is free of this danger.

Things look different when the findings ascertained by honest research are augmented by others – a demand that many now experience as pressing. A few years ago, Franz Mechsner wrote the following in an article on 'The problem with the soul':

> Those who seek to explain inner experience as part of the material world contradict our dualistic intuition, for the sensation 'red' is in fact something entirely different from the brain processes that accompany it. And those who see the world of inner experience as autonomous reality encounter problems, at the very least, when they try to explain the interplay between mind and matter. Or do we simply see things askew, and is our thinking wrong? Is it possible that more precise observation would resolve the paradox as one that does not exist in reality? Is there perhaps a way out of the cul-de-sac of the body–soul problem? A different theory that we have not yet considered?... All attempts to solve the body–soul problem thus lead, astonishingly, to a recognition of the untenable nature of the idea that science can 'in principle' explain everything we know about the world.[44]

At the end of his essay, Mechsner then mentions the neurologist Hans Flohr, 'who is seeking the collaboration of biologists, psychologists and philosophers to work on this problem'.

These comments are remarkable, and may come as a relief to people today. The problem of a materialistic or merely 'dynamistically' oriented science arises precisely where it lays claim to solving everything 'in principle'. In fact, every subject of research, or – as Nicolai Hartmann puts it – every 'stratum of existence', requires its own appropriate methodology. Very significant here are the words below from Alfred Gierer, which can be seen as the outcome of his research as biophysicist at the Max-Planck Institute for Developmental Biology:

> Philosophical limits to knowledge exist in the field of brain research primarily in relation to questions of 'consciousness' or 'the soul'. There are good reasons to assign every formally and precisely measurable information processing activity to physical and chemical processes in the neural network. But it remains questionable whether all properties of the brain are actually accessible to full, formal description. The terms 'inner' or 'emotional', especially, create serious problems from the scientific perspective, since they have no satisfactory objective definition. This is why there has been no end of attempts to repudiate the body-soul problem as a false one. But to do so would only be to suppress the deepest question of the limits of science. Conceptual acrobatics alone can, it is true, shift the problem elsewhere, but cannot resolve it. Inner or psychological experience is an immediate given, without knowledge of the physical brain processes that accompany it. Naturally there is a close connection between the two… but the validity of physical processes in the brain does not mean that we can entirely fathom the corresponding state of consciousness by using the methods of physics.

At the end of his article Gierer emphasises that 'consciousness is not fully encompassed by a physical account of the brain'.[45]

In so far as we are speaking here of inner experience of the sense world via the senses – and we can recall again the phrase of Empedocles that only like can perceive like – this means that only psyche can enquire into psyche, in the same way that 'physical' means must be used to investigate physical matters. What, therefore, does our sensory organisation comprise in so far as we experience its outcomes?

Let's think of a typical sensualist experience, such as all of us repeatedly have in springtime. Life is stirring everywhere in nature – things are sprouting and burgeoning. The woods cover themselves in fresh green, all the birds are busy and singing, anemones are flowering on the forest floor, and the grass is growing again. The somewhat mouldy smell of the woods in winter gives way now to a fresher scent. The weather grows warmer, we shed clothes and we suddenly feel the intensity of countless fragrances, the birdsong, the warmth, the breeze, transporting us into sensory communion with nature. No wonder that this is the time of pairing in the natural world. Or think of being beside the sea in summer, surrounded by warmth, fresh air and water, when we can experience a mysterious strengthening and renewal of our sense of life. Precisely by immersing ourselves in our sense experience, in the manifold interplay between inner and outer world, in a refreshing deepening of our breathing rhythm, we may well say of such moments, along with Faust, 'O stay I beg you, in your loveliness.'

The phenomenalist says, 'The senses do not deceive', while the sensualist emphasises that 'The senses give me the feeling I exist – they make me strong and healthy'. Cultivation of the senses is indispensable, especially in childhood, if we are to find our way into reality. Sensory loss is loss of reality. I'm not thinking now of the misfortune of being deaf or blind – for there are many ways to live a fulfilled life – but of the laming and suppression of a range of senses due to our one-sided technology and media-oriented civilisation. The grave harm to health arising from this has called forth various therapies over the past three decades, especially for instance the 'sensory integration' developed by A. Jean Ayres.[46]

Back at the beginning of the twentieth century, Rudolf Steiner was already repeatedly emphasising the key importance for childhood, and consequently for life as an adult, of developing and properly cultivating the senses. Specifically, in 'Waldorf education' in 1919, Steiner pioneered the view that cultivation of the senses was a central concern.[47] And it is good to see that over the years other researchers have also studied this complex in depth, in particular as far as educational therapy and practice are concerned.

Whilst editing Goethe's scientific writings, Steiner himself was already not only acknowledging and valuing Goethe's phenomenalism – praise widely echoed in the world, interestingly, in 1999, in celebration of the 250th anniversary of Goethe's birth – but also giving it a firm epistemological foundation by clearly demonstrating, among other things, the objective aspects of our sensory experience. Since this issue should not be underestimated when fully evaluating both sensualism and phenomenalism, I would like to cite the whole of a passage from Steiner's

'Introductions to Goethe's Scientific Writings'. While the line of reasoning is more comprehensive and differentiated in the larger treatise, the key perspectives are evident in this passage:

> If we could trace the whole sequence of occurrences in any sense-perception process, from the peripheral ending of the nerves in sense organs to the brain, we would never find the point where mechanical, chemical and organic processes – in other words temporal, spatial ones – cease, and what we call the actual sense perception arises, for instance the sensation of heat, light, tone etc. The place cannot be found where the causative motion might be seen to pass into its effect, the perception. Can we even speak at all of the two things as being in a cause–effect relationship?

Steiner continues:

> Let us examine the facts very objectively for a moment, and consider a certain sensation arising in our awareness. In doing so it simultaneously points us to some object in which it originates. When I have the sensation of red, then through the content of this thought I usually connect with it a particular, spatial location, or the surface of a thing to which I ascribe what expresses this sensation. This is only not so if, through an external action, such as a blow to the eye, the sense organ itself responds in its own inherent way, in this case a light sensation. Let us leave aside these special instances in which, it must also be said, sensations do not arise with their usual precision. As exceptional cases they cannot instruct us about the nature of things. If I have the sensation of red, originating from a specific locus, I am initially directed to some object in my surroundings as the medium of this sensation. I can of course now ask myself what spatial-temporal processes are occurring in this thing while it appears to be endowed with the colour red. It will become apparent that my question is answered by mechanical, chemical or other processes. But now I can go further and investigate the processes that have occurred en-route from the object to my sense organ, my eye, so as to mediate to me the sensation of the colour red. Again, I can only discover such mediators to be processes of motion or electrical currents or chemical changes. The same findings would inevitably arise if I could study the further path of transference from the sense organ to the central locus in the brain. *What* is mediated in this whole process is the perception of red under discussion here. *How* this

> perception is embodied in a particular thing on the path between stimulus and perception depends only on the nature of this thing. Sensation is present at every locus, from the exciter of the stimulus to the brain, but not as such, not explicitly, but in a way corresponding to the nature of the object at each locus.

And finally,

> But a truth emerges from this, one that can shed light on the whole theoretical foundation of physics and physiology. What do I learn from studying a thing encompassed by a process that arises in my consciousness as sensation? I learn nothing more than the manner and mode in which this thing responds to the action issuing from the sensation, or, in other words how a sensation *expresses* itself in a particular object of the spatial-temporal world. Far from this temporal-spatial process being the *cause* that triggers the sensation *within* me, the opposite is true: the spatial-temporal process is the *effect* of sensation in the spatial, temporal dimensions of an object. I could intrude as many things as I like on the path from the exciter of the stimulus to the organ of perception: in each will occur only what can occur by virtue of its nature. For this reason the *sensation* remains what expresses itself in all these processes.[48]

The reality of this 'sensation' is thus entirely psychological in character. In diverse forms or metamorphoses, therefore, the element of sensation becomes apparent in the object, in the media of the intervening space and in a person's own physiological organism. Sensory qualities therefore turn out to be objective *elements of existence* appearing in our subjective human organisation. And here, from two different sides, phenomenalism and sensualism meet in so far as we consider them in their archetypal nature. For study of art, too, and for religious experience, the examples cited in the previous chapter apply, as long as we regard them with the appropriate differentiation.

On the one hand, the boundaries between phenomenalism and sensualism are fluid, for the two outlooks are mutually determining; on the other hand, precisely in their ultimate conclusions, they turn out to be twofold: there is a huge difference depending on whether the world is as I perceive it to be, or whether it is only the product of my sense organisation. To ground my life, with its cares and hopes, in a deeper reality, a deeper meaning, the way I see the world – my worldview - is of key importance.

We can think here of Goethe's poetic rendition of the deeper experience of true sensory mysticism, as we find it also in Jakob Böhme:

> If the eye were not sunlike by nature
> How could we see light shine?
> If God's potency did not live in us
> How could we delight in the divine?

As mentioned earlier, sensualism can develop a strongly religious aspect. Even some views of a realm beyond the earthly bear a sensualist character, for instance when paradise is described as a place of sensory delights: 'They who obey Allah and his emissary, them he leads into gardens rich with waters, and eternally he will dwell there. This is a great felicity.'[49] Or:

> See therefore the picture of paradise, that is promised to the god-fearing: there flow rivers of water, that never cease; rivers of milk whose taste never alters; rivers of wine, to delight its drinkers; also rivers of purified honey. There will they receive all kinds of fruits and absolution from their Lord.[50]

Of course we can interpret these suras from the Qur'an as pictorial accounts of an unearthly realm overflowing with life, and all the more so if we sense that sensualism and a world of spirit ought never to be mingled. On the other hand, the Qur'an, specifically, has passages so redolent of the material world that a metaphorical interpretation becomes difficult. As an example, here is a sura where reference is made to the just:

> They will be closest to Allah and will dwell in gardens of bliss... they will rest upon cushions adorned with gold and precious stones and lie opposite each other. Young men, in the eternal blossom of youth, will encircle them to wait upon them with cups, vessels and bowls full of flowing wine... and with the flesh of fowls, as plentiful as they may wish. And virgins with great black eyes, like pearls still hidden in their shells, will be given them as reward for their deeds.[51]

Thus we see the Qur'an and its images of sensory felicity in the after-death world. With thoughts of flesh, fowl and virgins as reward for a just life, we have certainly entered a realm of materialistic spirituality, one that is not uncommon in the history of religion. Modern reports of weeping or bleeding statues fall into the same category.

If we cast a glance at the history of philosophy, we find that a narrow sensualism arises relatively late – not until the modern era – with the English sensualists or empiricists. The philosophers of Greek antiquity did not regard sense existence very highly: for them, the sense world, because of its continual fluctuations, did not have the enduring character of being. Paramenides, who lived in the sixth century BC, said, 'These two are the same: thinking and being.' This was his ontological creed! Plato thought similarly, albeit in somewhat more nuanced fashion, as we will see in Chapter 8 on idealism. There is a strong sensualist aspect in Epicureanism which must, though, be seen in a differentiated way, for its principle of happiness and enjoyment is not restricted to merely sensory pleasure. Spiritual pleasure, it holds, is more enduring and therefore ultimately promises more and greater happiness.

In today's vernacular we speak of an 'epicurean' as someone who unthinkingly enjoys the material pleasures of existence. In philosophical terms the gourmet is also a sensualist, and, in general, true sensualists often have a life-affirming, warm and 'full-blooded' character.

The principle of sensory empiricism as the foundation of knowledge, of enquiry into truth, was instigated very strongly, if not solely, by English philosophers. Francis Bacon writes:

> There are and can be only two ways of searching into and discovering truth. The one flies from the senses and particulars to the most general axioms, and from these principles, the truth of which it takes for settled and immovable, proceeds to judgment and to the discovery of middle axioms. And this way is now in fashion. The other derives axioms from the senses and particulars, rising by a gradual and unbroken ascent, so that it arrives at the most general axioms at last.[52]

And Thomas Hobbes states:

> Concerning the thoughts of man, I will consider them first singly, and afterwards in train or dependence upon one another. Singly, they are every one a representation or appearance of some quality, or other accident of a body without us, which is commonly called an object. Which object worketh on the eyes, ears and other parts of man's body, and by diversity of working produceth diversity of appearances.
>
> The original of them all is that which we call sense (for there is no conception in a man's mind which hath not at first, totally or by parts, been begotten upon the organs of sense). The rest are derived from that original.[53]

> [*Translator's note*: This passage is a re-translation of the German text, as we were unable to locate the English-language original.]

Our modern sensory physiology is, if not exclusively, philosophically rooted in Bacon and Hobbes. And it is characteristic that David Hume, who lived in the eighteenth century, is quoted verbatim in the introduction of a modern text on sensory physiology (see the text p. 28 by Josef Dudel): 'Man is nothing other than the sum of his experiences.' Indeed, no objection can be made to the relative justification of this phrase!

During his own enquiries and research, albeit from a different point of departure, Rudolf Steiner took up this theme and gradually developed a holistic view of the senses which has proven itself in many ways in educational and art therapy practice. For instance, in his 1919 lectures on *The Foundations of Human Experience*,[54] he expounded on a human organism of twelve senses, all rooted in the physical body but with differing degrees of involvement in the threefold dimension of the human being – body, soul and spirit. These senses are: the sense of touch, of life, of movement, balance, smell, taste, vision, warmth, hearing, word, thought and I. In modern literature in this field we usually find that nine senses are mentioned.[55] As yet unrecognised are the sense of word or language, the sense of thought, and above all the sense of I – the perception of the *other* person as an I-endowed being. Our capacity to increasingly respect the autonomy of the person standing before us is primarily rooted in the sense of I – which, like every sense, can be greatly enhanced and refined. The study of biographies, for instance, can help us further develop this sense, as can, above all, what Goethe in his fairy tale speaks of as being 'more glorious than gold' and 'more enlivening than light' – which is conversation.

It is precisely in dialogue that the sense of I can develop an ever-deeper strength. Films, TV and 'virtual reality' experiences are problematic in children's education, and later also, because there is no tangible interlocutor present to be directly addressed by the sense of I. For the care and development of the senses it is always true to say that life needs life; the pulsing life in my senses needs the tangible life of nature.

This example serves only to underline the practical significance of sensualism. Each of the twelve worldviews naturally has a practical aspect, in that it determines our impulse for action, the way in which we actively engage with life.

Seeing the human being as 'answer to the world's enigma' also involves the basic tripartite structure already referred to: with our body we experience the world; in our psyche we internalise it; and with our spirit, in wakeful, conscious cognition, we not only participate in the spiritual cosmos but are ourselves also part of it. Thanks to this threefold structure of our being, we can develop various worldviews. The two so far discussed, as well as materialism, are evidently native to our body. But then come worldviews that take their starting point more from powers of soul and spirit, and not only those bound up with our senses. Thus, the factors that lead someone to a particular view of the world must also include their overall constitution, with all the socio-cultural influences to which they have been, and are, exposed from childhood onwards. It is therefore an enormous enrichment of our inner life to engage in lively cultural contact with others, especially when they have a different outlook from ours.

During the course of our life we naturally need to find and stand up for our own standpoint, but always with a gesture of opening to others – for we, like the world, conceal infinite depths within us, and so every encounter can become a further step in our quest for an ever-fuller realm of truth. This does not of course preclude rejecting a worldview of a particular hue. Our ability to discriminate and our capacity for judgement should always retain their integrity. What matters is that we become learners in these things, and precisely in a multicultural society that we never forget to stay true to ourselves.

I will end this chapter with a passage by Hugo Kükelhaus, who has written important things also in connection with the development of the sense organs, and given many people new and deeper perspectives. The words cited here are like meditative phrases. First he speaks of the experience of an eclipse of the sun, and then he says:

> My gaze falls upon a rose. Can I not relate to it in the same way I experienced the sun when it was eclipsed? My ear hears the chirrup of a bird. Can I not hear its song in the same way as the world came close to me when it fell silent? The sun is shining on my skin. Can I not feel its warmth in the same way I felt it when it grew cool? See its light the same way I saw it when it lost its lustre? Taste the water as if springs and rivers had dried up? Eat bread as if there were no more grain? Eat fruits and meat as if there were no more plants or animals? Breathe the air as if it were a rare thing? Speak to my neighbours and play with children as if neighbours and games were faded legends? But yes! Surely this 'as if not' is a description of what has already long since occurred, is long since true?[56]... We need to safeguard the organs' original potential to develop towards global realisation, and, where this potential remains undiluted

> – in the infant – to let it unfold fully. Here, in particular, it is important to prevent all that can obstruct and inhibit life[57]... No God... can save us. We cannot save ourselves. What can save is sight of God. Our organs are the foundations for perceiving God. It is necessary, because possible, to develop the organs into what they are by fulfilling the conditions of their functioning.[58]

This passage emphasises the importance of our senses for a humane and dignified existence. Sensualism thus reveals itself to be a view of the world and life that is as valid as phenomenalism, and the other worldviews.

5

'Earth Goes on Standing Firm' – Materialism

PROMETHEUS (*bearing a torch in his hand*):
… And thus I loudly invoke you brazen powers:
Lift your strong arms lightly, so that, in moving measure
A mighty chorus-dance of hammers quickly
Provide us with much useful molten metal.
(*Several caves yawn open, and fires begin to burn*)

SMITHS
Kindle the fire's flame!
Fire is chief of all.
He who the fire stole –
Great deed – shall have the highest name.
He who has kindled it,
Into alloy rendered it,
Forged it and plied it,
Crown now his head.
…
Earth goes on standing firm,
Lets herself be tormented!
How she is dug and rent!
How she is torn and bent!
We'll drag it forth.[59]

The earth goes on standing firm! Goethe succeeded masterfully here in conveying in sound a sense of the dense solidity of the earth. It is almost as if we're hearing Cain's hook plough as he tears open the now hardened earth to wrest food from it. In its origins, the earth was by no means so hard and solid as we know it today – something about which science and religious tradition, despite their very different perspectives, are in relative agreement. The myth of the world's origins in Genesis (Chapters 1–3) can of course be interpreted in different ways. But if one lives with these stories long enough, the increasing density developing through the process of creation comes to seem like a narrative thread running through the wealth of enigmatic images. Right at the beginning we hear of the 'waters' over which the spirit of God moves; and then these primal waters are divided:

> And God said, Let there be a firmament in the midst of the waters, and let it divide the waters from the waters. And God made the firmament, and divided the waters which were under the firmament from the waters which were above the firmament: and it was so. And God called the firmament Heaven. And the evening and the morning were the second day. And God said, Let the waters under the heaven be gathered together unto one place, and let the dry land appear: and it was so. And God called the dry land Earth; and the gathering together of the waters called he Seas: and God saw that it was good.

To understand the pictures in Genesis we need primarily to think in terms of huge dimensions of time. We move here from a primal condition of undifferentiated fluidity to a division between the waters over the heavens (!) and waters beneath them, from which, over the course of aeons, the 'dry land' emerged. This process came to an interim conclusion after the Fall. Before this, the virginal earth, at God's command, endowed a Tree of Knowledge and a Tree of Eternal Life, and the whole Garden of Eden was watered by a fourfold river. Growing there was 'every tree that is pleasant to the sight, and good for food'. But with the Fall – which did not occur in a moment, but instead embodies a long process – human beings sundered themselves increasingly from bright, divine worlds. The land was 'accursed', and henceforth people had to nourish themselves from it by the sweat of their brows. 'Thorns also and thistles shall it bring forth to thee', cries God to the despairing children of humanity, in this image indicating matter's increasing hardness.

And finally the metaphor of the 'coat of skins', that God gives to Adam and Eve before they leave behind them the garden with the Tree of Life, may also be a further reference to the hardening of human nature in these early times, arising through their endowment with something of animal nature. The last scene of the third chapter of Genesis tells us, though, that we are not yet in a purely physical earthly realm: 'So he drove out the man; and he placed at the east of the garden of Eden Cherubims, and a flaming sword which turned every way, to keep the way of the tree of life.'

This condition of an earth that is still soft is also described very strikingly in a creation myth of the Cherokee Indians. Here again we witness a progressive process of hardening, whose ultimate purpose is to provide a solid earth upon which humans and animals can dwell:

> When all was still water, the animals were above in Galun'lati, above the dome of the heavens. But there it was very narrow and they wished to have more space for themselves. They asked themselves what might lie beneath the water, and at last Dayuni'si invited the waterbeetle, 'grandchild of the beaver', to set forth and find out. He shot hither and thither over the water's surface but found no solid place to rest. So then he dived below to the bottom and rose up again with soft mud which grew and expanded on all sides until it became the island which we call earth. Only then was it attached to the heavens with four ropes. But no one can remember who it was who did this.
>
> At first the earth was flat and very soft and wet. The animals were restless, they wanted to descend, and sent many birds out to see if it had dried yet. But the birds found no place to land, and returned to Galun'lati. At last it seemed to be time. So they sent forth the buzzard and told him he should make everything ready for them. This was the 'Great Buzzard', the father of all buzzards that we see today. He flew over the whole earth, close to the ground, but it was still very soft. When he came to the land of the Cherokees, he was very tired. His wings began to droop and touch the ground. Wherever they did so, a valley was created, and wherever they rose again, a mountain. When the animals above saw this, they were seized with fear that the whole world might become mountain, and so they summoned him back. But to this day the land of the Cherokees is full of mountains.[60]

It is a fundamental law of evolution that the solid crystallised out of fluidity, and that in turn – as other creation myths suggest – this fluid state was preceded by an airy or gaseous one. But the whole order of creation is founded on the element of which the great Heraclitus of Ephesus said, 'This world order, the same for all, was made by no God and no man, but fire ever was, is and will be, and lives eternally, kindling in measure, and extinguishing in measure.'[61]

This key dynamic of all evolution, which we can also call a fundamental law of cosmogenesis, is found also in human physical development from the early embryonic stage through to the 'skin and bones' of a very old person. We can also put it like this: all life is fluid, mobile and changing; at the moment death forces start to work, density and rigidity arise, through to rigor mortis, utter immobility. There is good reason why Father Time or the Grim Reaper was always depicted as a skeleton.

Such aspects are not foreign to modern cosmology research. True, it speaks a different language and, as already suggested, starts from a different outlook, one we will consider in detail in the next chapter. Representative of a series of similar accounts are a few passages we will quote here from Klaus Strohbach's *From the Big Bang to the Earth: The Evolution and Transformation of our Planet in the Cosmos.*[62] We are less interested now in the question about the reliability of the big bang hypothesis than we are in the evolutionary stages of the cosmos described here, from the point of view of the condensing of primordial substances – here in line with particle physics – and their concentration into foci. This is connected with gravity, one of the 'elementary forces of the universe' as they are called today, which is of fundamental importance for understanding materialism and materialistic experience.

Here are the relevant passages, which follow an account of the explosion of an unimaginably hot, dense core and its disintegration:

> The following period, which lasted a million years, was marked by the predominance of radiation... this was the irradiation era or the 'fireball'. The fireball began of course already a second after the birth of the world. Gamov[63] therefore referred to the primordial matter from which the world evolved, in this view, as ylem. Today we speak of the big bang or the fireball. The image of a fireball can tell us more than the ideas of the lepton or hadron era, which primarily represent mathematical findings, and are really only comprehensible to nuclear physicists.... After about a million years, the radiation mass density diminishes below material density and increasingly gives way to matter. The era of the fireball is over, and the material cosmos has begun.
>
> Initially matter is only present in the form of its lightest elements, hydrogen (around 90 per cent) and helium (around 10 per cent). These gases form areas of changing density and turbulence. The formation of galaxies begins at the latest once the universe has expanded to roughly

> a thirtieth of its present dimensions, through the process known as gravitational instability, and this occurs initially only as a lenticular accumulation of the gases referred to... whereas the universe expands unceasingly, matter on the other hand consolidates into galaxies and stars.

This consolidation became possible through forces of gravity. If one sought to understand this mighty process with the help of the Aristotelian categories, one would have to speak of substance, time and space. Aristotle developed the ten categories as an 'organ' for self-orientation in the manifold nature of the world. These ten core statements about the world, which could be enlarged to twelve,[64] offer us purely philosophical access to an understanding of world phenomena, and remain useful modes of enquiry. In the sense of these categories, too, we can speak of a 'primordial substance' that consolidates in the course of time, increasingly filling space as 'matter'. Matter is thus what fills space. Since roughly the seventeenth century it has been regarded primarily as having the property of corporeality and impermeability. Only at the beginning of the twentieth century did this prevailing view slowly give way to the other, according to which the world is constituted of atoms, built up of the tiniest, microscopically invisible, elementary particles. If we consider that a single atom has a diameter of around 1/10,000,000 mm, we are really seeing here the predominance of a worldview that initially relinquishes pure materialism so as to understand the world on the basis of mathematical calculations. This is the worldview of mathematism, which we will consider next in Chapter 6. In connection with materialism, it is important to recognise that the mathematising view does not, in the larger context and experience, overturn the reality of matter in its enduring stability, solidity and impermeability. It only offers a different view of things, and, in a certain sense, even atomic physics holds on to matter's relative stability. Niels Bohr says of this:

> For me, the starting point was the stability of matter, which is after all a pure miracle from the perspective of previous physics. By the word 'stability' I mean that the same substances with the same properties continually recur, that the same crystals are formed, the same chemical compounds arise etc. This must surely mean that even after many changes arising from external influences, an iron atom is ultimately again an iron atom with exactly the same properties.[65]

What we are interested in here is not the possibility of transformation or the emergence of new elements in the subatomic field, or the attribution of matter to energy, for the latter also belongs to a different worldview that we will be discussing later, i.e. dynamism (Chapter 13). Specifically on the subject of the emergence and disappearance of materiality, the physicist Hans-Peter Dürr will later have some very interesting things to tell us. But in this chapter we are concerned with a primal experience of 'matter' in its density and solidity, such as all human beings have had since the dawn of time thanks to their sensory organism, and from which classical materialism originates.

In sensualist terms we could assign the primal experience of matter, weight and solidity to the sense of touch. In infancy this already gives us significant experiences. I find security in the physical world and sustaining strength. The gradually developing solidity of the skeleton gives me a stable support. In relation to the world's gravity and solidity, I try out and develop the power of my muscles, and through my delineated corporeality, enclosed in my skin, I can feel myself increasingly to be a solid individual. As 'I', ultimately I experience myself at the centre of my whole constitution, with a 'standpoint' both in space and in judgement. I owe all this largely to my physical body amidst a world of metals, stones, woods and other solid substances.

Thus, we can sense the key importance of material experience in and through the world for us human beings. The 'material' structure of the world, as we perceive it by virtue of senses corresponding to it, is an intrinsic property, and thus is part of what 'helps the world most inwardly cohere'. But it is not this alone that does so. The problematic nature of materialism and similar views related to it, such as positivism and pragmatism, is not their clear justification but their claim to exclusivity when explaining universal phenomena. Pure materialism by no means leads inevitably to an atheistic position. In the very midst of the Enlightenment's triumphal march, Friedrich Christoph Oetinger, a profound theosophist and alchemist, uttered this heartfelt cry: 'Corporeality is the end of the ways of God.'[66] But in the twentieth century too we find important physicists who are very close to a spiritual view of the origins of matter, such as James H. Jeans, who, in 1930, based on his research into the emergence of new elements in the subatomic field, wrote of envisaging the creation of matter in a not indefinitely distant time, and of matter not existing before it becomes or has been called into existence. This perspective brings us 'very close to those philosophical systems that regard the universe as a thought in the spirit of a Creator, rendering all discussions of material creation pointless'.[67] [Translator's note: This is a translation of the German text, as we were unable to locate the English-language original.]

In consequence of this, Walter Schubart, author of the book *Spiritual Transformation*, concludes:

> 1. Matter is not – as mechanistic physics has claimed – the absolute that has been and is at all times, but it was created; it is transient, and has its periodicity. 2. It must have emerged from a supra-material, thus spiritual sphere. The radiations... can be interpreted as emancipations of a divine, spiritual creator will.[68]

However we may relate to the phenomenon of materiality, any ultimate answer to the question of what matter actually is becomes hugely more difficult owing to an easily ascertainable fact, formulated as follows in the nineteenth century by the epistemologist and theologian Aloys E. Biedermann: 'We cannot easily say what the mode of existence of matter is, or in other words express it in thought, which would mean transforming it into a thought.'[69] A significant realisation! In Chapter 14 on realism, this question will be taken up once more.

However we approach such thoughts and considerations about the origins of matter, they will certainly not diminish our daily experience of the world's materiality. Materialism itself, as a one-sided worldview, is actually relatively young. It originated primarily in the modern era, reaching its culmination in the nineteenth century, the century of classical materialism, before partly ceding the field, as we indicated, to mathematising and dynamistic outlooks. While materialism as a theory is currently fading away in the thinking of modern physicists, it has nevertheless taken hold of broad areas of our lives. The possession of material goods above and beyond immediate needs has become the aim and purpose of countless people's lives. Since the 1960s, the term 'prosperity' has applied to a form of society based on superfluity, a materialism of daily life that has gained a strong grip on our minds and hearts. Materialism does not halt even before questions whose answer ought to come from a spiritual view of things. We have already referred at various points to the problem that arises from generalising the application of a single worldview.

I recall a brief, intense discussion I had many years ago with a childhood friend beside my father's open coffin. He had known my father for a long time and liked him a great deal. We hadn't seen each other for many years, but by chance met each other again in the hospital. We were both standing in silence, with a brother of mine who was also there, when suddenly my friend said, with a deep sigh, 'Do you know, death is something quite different for me from what it is for you' – and he looked at my father. 'It's like an engine that has stopped working. It just isn't functioning any more.'

Naturally, this conversation made no difference to our friendship. With admirable consistency, my friend had drawn the final conclusions of a deep conviction. Thinking about this today, I am reminded of an interview that appeared in the *Süddeutsche Zeitung* on 25 August 2000. There too, the human being is described, ultimately, as a machine. The interview in question concerned a head-transplant project. Robert J. White is a professor of neurosurgery at a US university, and is the only physician who has so far successfully transplanted monkey heads. In addition, he is a member of numerous science committees, including the Pontifical Academy of Sciences. Although the problem involved in this is evident, I would still like to cite the whole text of the interview. The crassness of outlook that becomes apparent here is an extreme testimony to general trends in our time, which of course include genetic manipulation, bioethics and the whole field of cloning, as no less relevant examples.[70]

> ***What is the purpose of such interventions?***
> I wonder how you can ask this! For many gravely ill people, this operation is the only chance of survival. Think of a patient whose whole body has succumbed to cancer. As long as your brain is still tumour-free, a head transplant could save you. But to be precise, we should speak of a whole-body transplant, since the whole of the sick body is replaced.
>
> ***And the new body would function properly?***
> No, the person concerned would be paralysed from the neck down. We're unable to reconnect the separated spine. Although in the meantime it has proven feasible to heal injured spinal nerves in rats. I hope and pray that in the next ten years scientists will have similar successes with human patients. Then it might actually be possible for paralysed people to walk again one day, also head-transplant patients.
>
> ***Could one at least still speak after a head transplant?***
> We will try to implant in patients electronic prostheses that facilitate speech. A similar apparatus supports Christopher Reeve, the Superman actor who had a terrible accident. And as we know, he now even gives lectures.

Hand on heart, Dr White: when will you undertake the first human head transplant?
The problem is that this operation would be very expensive – too expensive to do here in Cleveland. It would cost around five million dollars. That's why I'd like to operate in the Ukraine, at the Neurological Research Centre in Kiev. The costs there can probably be kept down to two million dollars.

Another advantage is that in the hospitals in Kiev I saw a great many brain-dead patients, so it won't be difficult to get a body for transplanting. Decisions like that are not hampered by too much bureaucracy. I would need three to four weeks to train up my team. And I'd have to sort out the formalities with officials in Kiev. We haven't yet discussed a head transplant but I imagine they'll be very keen. I have already done operations in Kiev in the past.

Dr White, do you believe that people have a soul?
Certainly. I'm a Catholic.

The interview continues:

In many places in the world, people regard body, soul and spirit as a unity.
The Christian philosopher Thomas Aquinas also held this view. But it is mistaken – and modern transplant medicine is the proof of it. Head transplants are a slap in the face for eastern religions and Thomas Aquinas! Consciousness and memory have their seat in the brain, and therefore the soul does too. The body is only a machine that keeps the brain alive. In recent times, psychologists, philosophers and theologians have anyway been talking far too much about the brain. I always ask myself whether these people have ever even seen a brain. Have they cut it open and looked at what is there, as I have done for four decades now?

One might also turn the argument on its head: the brain is your field, and that's why you locate the soul there.
Hang on a moment. I studied general medicine at the world's best universities.

And so?
I am an internationally acknowledged expert on ethical questions in medicine, and even advise the Holy Father on these matters.

Yes?
Certainly. Back in the 1970s I had a very lively discussion with Paul VI about brain death. And under John Paul II my contact with the Holy See continued.

Did you tell the Pope that you wished to do head transplants?
No, but I did express my conviction that the brain is the seat of the soul. No doubt I was somewhat impetuous in doing so – John Paul II flinched a little. But that is my view, and I keep to it. It's simply the truth: you and I are our brains. My thoughts on the matter go further than this: where, for example, is the centre in the brain where sin originates?

No idea.
Let's assume you want to murder someone. You're planning to kill them. Who is planning this? Your brain, of course. So where is the region in the brain where such thoughts arise – the desire to kill or equally your adulterous desires for your neighbour's wife? I don't know if we will ever find this place but if we do, we might one day be able to cut it out. Do you have any more questions?

Do you like Frankenstein?
I love Dr Frankenstein and I'm fascinated by Mary Shelley's novel. She was far ahead of her time.[71]

And in the book *Man a Machine* by Julien Offray de la Mettrie, published in 1748, we find the roots of this form of practical materialism. Here are several sentences from it:

> The human body is a machine which winds its own springs.... Everything depends on how our machine is wound up.... Let me say in passing that, in my view, the better and more trustworthy of two doctors will always be the one well-versed in the physics and mechanics of the human body, who leaves to one side the soul and all anxieties which this chimera causes fools and the ignorant, and concerns himself only with the pure sciences.[72]

In reading these sentences, I recalled lessons that well-meaning teachers gave us as schoolchildren to explain important bodily functions – such as: the brain is a switchboard, the heart a pump, the respiratory tract a chimney and the kidneys a sewage works. Or the famous sentence by Carl Vogt, that our thoughts relate to the brain in exactly the same way as bile to the liver and urine to the kidneys.

As science increasingly emancipated itself at the beginning of the modern era from medieval theological outlooks, and, in simplified terms, began to investigate the miracles of the sense world by sight and the powers of reason, the worldview of materialism nevertheless took a long time to put down deeper roots in the general population. And yet, in a humanity still largely holding to religious belief, a huge longing awoke to travel the globe and explore the physical world. Whereas in medieval cathedrals the angelic hierarchies soared aloft in paintings and depictions, people now sought the *breadths* of the oceans and distant lands.

Conquest and awareness of geographical space became the first decisive step towards materialism, since space and matter belong together, after all. The great artists – we can think of the paintings of Giotto and Masaccio – studied the laws of space, while Columbus finally demonstrated that the earth is round, thus dispelling ancient ideas of its flatness. At the same time the heliocentric cosmology of Copernicus confirmed the beginning of a new era. The Enlightenment, taking shape above all in eighteenth-century Europe, increasingly assumed importance. The goddess of reason became *the* predominant faculty, and the French encyclopaedists, all contemporaries of de la Mettrie, created with their 'Encyclopaedia' a new form of intellectual knowledge that would give the strongest impetus to the many developing branches and fields of materialism.

Naturally, there had been many enlightenment movements since antiquity, but never before had the attention of scientific thinkers and enquirers become so focused on investigating the sensory, material world as in these centuries: never before was so much effort directed at elaborating a technical, material civilisation. From this perspective, materialism, phenomenalism and sensualism belong together, and are mutually enhancing, however different and diverse their approaches. Although the next worldview to be considered, mathematism (Chapter 6), is also largely founded on empiricism, it draws quite different conclusions about God and the world from those we have been exploring thus far.

Sigismund von Gleich very aptly characterises the ontological aspects of these three worldviews: 'We are concerned here', he says, 'with a characteristic of visible manifestation (graphic vividness or *phenomenality*), with sensory perceptibility (*sensuality*) and with the tangible thusness of things and existence (*materiality*).'[73]

To conclude this chapter, I want to look briefly at a very subtle form of materialism. In the previous chapter we looked at sensualist-materialist ideas about life after death. To this we can add views of an ultimately still material world of 'finer substance' that is thought to constitute a deeper stratum of our reality. In the theosophy of the nineteenth and twentieth centuries, and also in Victorian spiritualism and related movements, concepts became widespread that had formerly been the preserve of smaller circles. For instance, a common pseudo-spiritual view of the purely spiritual forces of etheric life is in fact just materialism in disguise. The spiritual sphere of the etheric world underlies all phenomena of organic life and the psyche and is accessible only to a purely spiritual method of enquiry, never through orthodox scientific models that posit such things as 'etheric atoms'. Wilhelm Hübbe-Schleiden, for instance, was a prominent proponent of this 'materialisation' of the spirit.[74]

The spirit cannot be photographed, either. Kirlian photography was developed by Semyon D. Kirlian between 1938 and 1958. In an interesting book that excited great interest in the 1970s and 1980s, and was republished numerous times – *Psychic Discoveries behind the Iron Curtain*[75] – there is much talk of this materialism disguised as pseudo-spirituality. The book devotes many pages to Kirlian photography. Semyon D. Kirlian and his wife developed a specially constructed high-frequency spark generator and a procedure that creates 75,000 to 200,000 electrical vibrations a second.

> The generator can be connected to various clamps, plates, optical instruments, microscopes or electron microscopes. The object to be investigated (finger, leaf, etc.) is inserted between the clamps with photo paper. The generator is switched on and a high frequency field is created between the clamps which apparently causes the object to radiate some kind of bio-luminescence onto the photo paper. A camera isn't necessary for the photography process.
>
> The very first photographs were 'a window on the unknown', say the Kirlians. A leaf torn from a tree, when placed in the field of a high frequency current, revealed a world of myriad dots of energy. Around the edges of the leaf there were turquoise and reddish-yellow patterns

> of flares coming out of specific channels of the leaf. A human finger placed in the high-frequency field and photographed, showed up like a complex topographical map. There were lines, points, craters of light and flares.[76]

The authors wondered whether such phenomena could be the energy body that clairvoyants refer to as the 'aura', which has always previously been thought of as a spiritual emanation. One cannot render the etheric visible; only its *effects* can sometimes acquire a certain visibility, for instance in sensitive crystallisation. This realm can only be directly investigated by spiritual means.

Thus we find three aspects of 'matter', with many intermediate stages and much interplay between them:

- the element of dense, solid, firm and impermeable matter as the starting point for materialistic experience;
- a complex of effects that are explained by ideas of mechanics, statics and dynamics, such as de la Mettrie's 'machine man' or also Newton's 'heavenly mechanics'; and finally
- a 'spiritual' level, which is nothing other than an, albeit still enigmatic, aspect of matter itself; the latter underlies various phenomena with which the modern New Age movement has been preoccupied. We will return to the related complex of 'energy' in Chapter 13 on dynamism.

Materialism turns out, therefore, to be a fully justified worldview, albeit with diverse aspects and nuances. It has validity within the world of matter and its laws, and embodies a very significant human experience. On our quest for the essential nature of existence, we cannot overlook the enigma of 'matter', whether we regard it from a religious, material, mechanistic or 'semi-spiritual' perspective. The idea that all matter evolved from a process of contraction or consolidation is thus certainly allowable. That it developed from a spiritual element is something, as we saw, that Rudolf Steiner, amongst others, expounded on many occasions.[77] Goethe himself came to this view fairly early on. It enables us to see materialism in harmony, or if you like in creative opposition, with spirituality. This comes to exemplary expression in a poem that Goethe wrote in old age, in 1826, when he was looking at Schiller's skull, at a time when Schiller's bones were moved from the crypt of St James graveyard to the ducal library. We will conclude this chapter on materialism with this poem.

Within a gloomy charnel-house one day
I viewed the countless skulls that lined the walls
And of old times I thought, that now had faded.
Close packed stand they who once so fiercely hated,
And hardy bones, that to the death contended,
Lie intercrossed now that the breath's abated.
What held those crooked shoulder-blades suspended?
No one now asks; and limbs with vigour fired,
The hand, the foot – their use in life is ended.
But peace is not yet theirs, for now they're raised
Back into daylight; though not to general praise,
For none can love the dried-up husk, however
glorious, noble once its living core.
And yet within this crowd of rigid bones
A glorious script, a precious, holy form
Was granted to my sight: and shone
So that within this vault, so cold, forlorn
I felt a sudden rush of warmth and joy
As if from death a source of life rose up.
What strange delight! What rapt devotion!
That form preserving such a godlike trace!
A look transporting me towards that ocean
Whose rolling billows mightier shapes embrace!
Mysterious vessel! Oracular – I am unworthy
To hold you in my hand. Unless to bear
Your form, O greatest treasure, from this mouldy
Prison back to the free air, to sunlight clear.
Can there be knowledge of any greater worth
Than God in nature revealed to us?
Than learning how nature, from solid forms of earth,
Lets the spirit issue; how, long-tended,
It preserves what spirit first engendered?

6

Measure, Number and Weight – Mathematism

Mathematism is a fascinating worldview. As old as humanity, one might almost say, it accompanies the whole course of cultural history. Always current, we find it to be deeply bound up with humanity's quest for knowledge. If we trace the Greek etymology of the word – 'mathesis' – it means knowledge as such. Kant famously said that 'in any distinct doctrine of nature only so much real science can be found as there is mathematics there'.[78] In this exclusive focus, Kant was, among other things, an outstanding successor to the great Galileo Galilei, one of whose mottos was: 'Those who seek to solve scientific questions without the help of mathematics, undertake something impossible to execute. One must measure what is measurable, and make measurable what cannot yet be measured.'[79]

A direct line leads from these statements testifying to the importance of mathematics for enquiry into the material world, to modern scientists such as the late astrophysicist Stephen Hawking, and his quest for a universal formula to explain everything.

This trust in the ability of mathematics to lift the veil on the world's secrets is founded on the comprehensibility and soundness of mathematical principles. Here, too, there are two schools of thought. Kant, for instance, starts from the premise that mathematics is a subjective product of human consciousness overlaid by human beings on a world that cannot actually be grasped. In other words, reason does not draw its laws from nature, but imposes them upon it. This hypothesis of Kant's stands in opposition to the other fundamental mathematical outlook, such as Novalis formulates it: 'The whole of mathematics is really a grand equation for the other sciences. All sciences therefore ought to become mathematics. True mathematics is the real element of the magician.'[80] The moment we consider mathematical relationships in the world as objective, the step to religion is at hand. Novalis again: 'Mathematics is the highest life. The life of the gods is mathematics. Pure mathematics is religion. We only arrive at mathematics through theophany. True mathematics is at home in the Orient. In Europe it has degenerated into mere technology.'[81]

We can feel in these lines the enthusiasm that this science of all sciences kindled in him. His disposition for universality also led him to the following comment: 'Poetics of mathematics. Grammar of mathematics. Physics of mathematics. Philosophy of mathematics. History of mathematics. Mathematics of philosophy. Mathematics of nature. Mathematics of poetry. Mathematics of history. Mathematics of mathematics.'[82]

And: 'In music it appears positively as revelation.'[83] Thus, Novalis.

But what can all this signify for us in our daily life? Apart from at school and work, when am I a mathematist? Although not everyone can become a mathematician, our cultural milieu and, above all, our schooling system has in some respects made us all into mathematists. It has done so in two ways, with differing degrees of intensity and quality, of course. First, though this is something of a simplification and generalisation, the basic gesture of every process of cognition is a mathematising one. When we seek a *single* common denominator in mathematics, when we conduct a conversation or a negotiation in such a way that we summarise the problem and seek a *single* agreed solution, or if we even perhaps seek a single formula to explain the world and all its phenomena, mathematism is always involved. A primary capacity of our thinking consciousness is that we treat questions and solutions according to a unifying principle. We usually look for the one fulcrum of a problem where our understanding can give us leverage.

This type of quest for knowledge and discovery of truth was developed in particular by the great Aristotle, who primarily lent it scientific status in his writings on logic where he developed his doctrine of syllogism – that is, of right conclusion or right thinking. Every judgement, he says, is composed of 'concepts', and from judgements logical 'conclusions' are drawn. Here it is very noteworthy that Aristotle regards the truth of a judgement to depend on thinking first according with reality. The following classical syllogism is famous: (1) All people are mortal. (2) Socrates is a person. (3) Thus, Socrates is mortal. We can see that this involves a kind of conceptual categorisation of things and situations. The ten categories or conditions that we mentioned in the previous chapter (see p. 43) are pure mathematism from the perspective of the cognitive process. Thus, Aristotle writes of the diverse 'modes of being':

> Every word spoken that refers to one thing alone signifies either substance or quantity or quality or relation, place, time, position, state, action or suffering. To give a rough and general idea, examples of substance are 'man', 'horse'; of quantity: 'two cubits' or 'three cubits'; of quality: attributes such as 'white', 'grammatical'; of relation: 'double', 'half', 'larger'; of place: 'in the Lyceum', 'in the market-place'; of time: 'yesterday', 'last year'; of position: 'lying', 'sitting'; of state: 'being shod', 'donning armour'; of action: 'cutting', 'burning'; of suffering: 'being cut', 'being burned'.[84]

We continually discover these categories in Aristotle's basic texts, and their many applications have been a major contribution to the fundamental structure of our modern thought and debate. Today we more or less imbibe such thinking with our mother's milk. When it awakens in adolescents, it goes hand in hand with the development of a subtle potential for power. It is a thinking that gives one support and security in argument, and thus also strengthens self-awareness.

When I was teaching middle and upper school classes I often discovered this first-hand in discussions and question sessions with pupils! In adults, stubbornness and polemical intolerance can go on thriving, the more people embrace and delight in a purely intellectual element. During a seminar based on the theme of this book I once had to make strenuous efforts to soothe an academic who could not contemplate the idea that anything apart from mathematism could offer a reliable answer to the 'enigma of the world'.

Such trends, growing since Descartes and his 'I think, therefore I am', are certainly understandable. As the modern era dawned, and people turned to earthly and material things, mathematising thought developed. To name one further example, we can think here of the great thinker and mystic Nicholas of Cusa who, more than almost any of his contemporaries, represents the transition to this new age. On the one hand, he is a Christian mystic, but on the other he also knows that Christian knowledge of God must now seek new ways. By developing and pursuing this path himself, he became the forerunner of modern scientific enquiry.[85] This is particularly apparent in his short book *The Layman on Experiments Done with Weight-Scales.* Johannes Hemleben describes this new approach to knowledge in a very telling passage:

> In his introduction, Nicholas of Cusa refers to Solomon, the wise king of Israel, who expounds on how God so gloriously 'created the world

> according to number, weight and measure'. Rabanus Maurus referred to the same passages too in his widely read book *The Universe* (also known as *The Nature of Things*). Both see Solomon's laudatory statement in terms of a divine harmony that underlies all creation as measure, number and weight. But Nicholas Cusa goes a radical step further. Without hesitation he urges those who seek to know nature to grasp all visible phenomena as far as possible through number, to weigh them with the scales, and measure them with the rule. While absolute precision, he acknowledges, cannot be obtained in the realm of knowledge, nevertheless all experience confirms that weighing with scales has very useful results for coming closer to the truth. Thus, the 'layman' conducting the 'discussion' desires a chart – which, to his regret, does not yet exist – in which would be compiled all differences of weight that can be discovered. This desire points unmistakeably towards something that would be achieved only very much later in the 'periodic table' devised by Mendeljeff. The layman says: 'I believe that by considering the differences of weight one may come closer to the mysteries of things, and can come to know much with the aid of probable inferences.' Clearly, Nicholas of Cusa has a glimpse here of determining what we nowadays call the specific weight of substances, and thereby arriving at well-founded knowledge of their properties.[86]

However, it is also worth mentioning that in Islamic culture a relatively long time before this, a highly developed analytic and experimental mode of enquiry had taken root. In general, it is interesting to find that important mathematicians and scientists emerged from the cradle of monotheistic religions – Islam, Judaism and Christianity. This is scarcely surprising if we think that a mathematising form of enquiry, focused on finding 'one common denominator', can *only* acknowledge one God if it concerns itself with religion or God. This is precisely what we have in these religions, with Christianity of course embodying a trinitarian monotheism: the unity of God is divided there into the active trinity of Father, Son and Holy Spirit, whose action is both historical and beyond time in the reciprocal interplay of the three-in-one.

We could also put it like this. Of the three, the 'Father' is the foundation of existence; the 'Son' – also called the Logos – is the divine power that kindles Creation: from within the 'Father' he penetrates the world through to the profoundest depths of the human heart, and can also be experienced personally. The 'Holy Spirit', finally, is not only *being* and *becoming* but also *consciousness*: both of the earthly realm and of the divine in the human being and the cosmos.

Many thinkers have resorted to the most varied images to express this unfathomable and, in fact, ungraspable reality. St Patrick, the great Irish saint, clothes this mysterious trinity of God in the picture of a three-leafed clover: unity in trinity. In a grandiose doctrinal poem, a profound twelfth-century thinker and theologian, Alanus ab Insulis, known as the 'Doctor Universalis', because he 'knew everything that could be known', compares the trinity with the threeness of spring, brook and river. Here is his view, as expounded in the *Anticlaudianus*, after he has first expressed more speculative theological musings on the theme:

> Thus the spring produces the brook,
> and the brook with the spring
> then gives rise to a river, of the same taste
> as the brook and the spring.
> Whereas brook, spring and river differ,
> yet in one thing they accord
> entirely since all three are of
> the same substance,
> and in them is a unified nature, *one* colour, *one* gleam,
> *one* and the same taste, and their countenance
> equal in quality:
> spring of suns, whose light outdoes the sun.[87]

This too is mathematism!

In the Qur'an of Islam, this corresponds to the following passage: 'Allah is Allah, and there is no God but him.'[88] And in the Hebrew Bible, when Moses receives the Ten Commandments in thunder and lightning, we hear: 'And God spoke all these words, saying: I am the Lord thy God, who have brought thee out of the land of Egypt, out of the house of bondage. Thou shalt have no other gods before Me' (Exodus, 20, 1f.). Mathematism! – or monotheism, here in contrast to Egyptian polytheism (though this is not to say that this passage in the Bible excludes the possibility of the existence of other divine beings).

The philosophical-mathematical character of this religious outlook comes to expression in the biblical prohibition on images: 'Thou shalt not make unto thee any graven image, or any likeness of any thing that is in heaven above, or that is in the earth beneath, or that is in the water under the earth' (Exodus, 20, 4). In Islam, too, it is not permitted to depict living creatures – which is why we find the fascinating geometric arabesques of Islamic art, and the beautifully designed script in which, among other things, the verses of the Qur'an were written. Nor does music belong to Islamic worship, though by contrast Islam achieved magnificent things in architecture: clear lines and multi-faceted surfaces of great purity. It is remarkable that the principle of purity, of cleansing, plays a key role in the religious practices of Islam, as it does also in Judaism! Clear thinking can only be pure thinking. And it is said that 'Allah is swift in calculation.'[89]

It is not my aim here to engage in comparative religious studies, however appealing that idea might be. The examples cited here are only to direct attention to the mathematist principle in religion, since no religion can be comprehended in terms of one principle alone. If Goethe had been focusing only on religions in his poem 'The Mysteries', he would have found it difficult to establish twelve distinct and separate religions. When he speaks, as quoted earlier (see p. 2), of the 'most diverse modes of thought and feeling', or of the 'love of God' manifesting in 'every religion', he certainly means a view of the human being and the cosmos that in a sense encompasses the trinity of science, art and religion, in close accord with the well-known and widely quoted verse by him:

> He who possesses science and art
> Possesses religion also;
> He who does not possess these two
> Will need to have religion.[90]

Goethe was unable to complete 'The Mysteries', but, as we have suggested (p. iii), his whole oeuvre is basically an answer to the question it throws up about a harmony of different outlooks. It must be apparent by now that we could have quoted him in support of each of the worldviews so far discussed. This is true too of mathematism, as we will see below.

In our brief historical digression, we started with Nicholas of Cusa after quoting René Descartes, the important mathematician. We referred to the fact that Nicholas prefigured some of the later methodologies of science. Mathematist thinking itself is very ancient; it is only relatively new as an *exclusive* method of research or enquiry in our modern, Western world. This change – a paradigm change, it could be called – is expressed very clearly by no less a figure than Werner Heisenberg. In his essay 'Recent Changes in the Foundations of Exact Science', he states:

> I have tried here to explain how physics and chemistry – driven by we know not what power – have continually developed towards a mathematical analysis of nature subject to the principle of unity. The claims

> of our science to knowledge of nature in the original sense of the word have increasingly diminished as we have done so.[91]

As we saw, Stephen Hawking – like other figures – sought a 'universal formula'. His first book *A Brief History of Time* was published in 1988 and swiftly became a bestseller. The German news magazine *Der Spiegel* devoted a leading piece to him and conducted a thought-provoking discussion with the physicist and cosmologist. A few passages from the conversation will help illumine further aspects of the mathematical, mathematising outlook.[92] In connection with what has been said here about the importance of phenomenalism, sensualism and materialism, it is interesting and also symptomatic to read what the reporter writes in his introduction:

> Only as a student, and never again afterwards, did Hawking examine the universe through a telescope. He only did so a couple of times, and what he saw there, as he later stressed, did not in the least impress him. Nevertheless, in the view of many colleagues in his field, he is more profoundly versed in the riddles of the cosmos than any other researcher, and in the dizzying calculations that aim to help us understand the universe.

Then, after a further introductory article, follows the discussion on 'God and the Universe':

> SPIEGEL: Do you believe in God, or in the idea of some higher power?
> HAWKING: I do not believe in a personal God.
> SPIEGEL: Does that mean you believe in an impersonal God?
> HAWKING: If you like, you can say that God is the embodiment of the laws of physics. But that is only confusing, since most people think of God as a being to whom one can have a personal relationship. The laws of physics have little of the personal about them.
> SPIEGEL: But if something as fleeting as energy or even time are eternal in your opinion, what about other phenomena of similar transience, such as our mind or consciousness? Might they not also be eternal in some way?
> HAWKING: For me, a human being is more or less comparable to a computer. Certainly somewhat more complex than the computers we have today. But I do not think that anyone would conceive the idea that a computer possessed an immortal soul.

...

SPIEGEL: The question about our place in the universe seems one that hugely preoccupies you. Have you found an answer to this?

HAWKING: We are just a somewhat advanced breed of apes on a little planet orbiting a very average star. But we can understand the universe, and that does make us into something very special.

It's worth dwelling on these words a little since, they are symptomatic of the worldview of a highly gifted mathematician and scientist, someone who naturally deserves our great respect, irrespective of whether he subsequently retained this thinking or revised it. But life means change, and only narrow-minded thinkers remain fixed for decades in an immovable outlook. Dogmatically holding to a position you have once adopted – a danger for all of us – is the ideal breeding ground for a long list of social dangers: dogmatism, nationalism, racism and sectarianism, to name but a few. These are the threads from which all developmentally obstructive fundamentalisms are woven today, whether religious, artistic, political or scientific in nature.

Nevertheless, I still maintain that every worldview is justified. When and how a particular worldview offers the greatest resolution to particular aspects of the 'world's enigma' is another question. Inner development that integrates different and divergent outlooks has nothing whatever in common with a levelling plurality. It involves, rather, an art of logical reasoning attuned to a particular reality, and not that form of logic called symbolic or mathematical logic, a kind of logical thinking that calculates with symbols. The danger of this formalisation certainly lies not in the 'mathematical' clarity that is sought, but in an alienation from everything actual and real in the natural world around us, to which our concepts belong as integral and integrating constituents of it. We referred to these matters in the first two chapters. In Aristotelian logic, or in appropriate application of the categories, we are concerned, as already mentioned, with a syllogism that remains valid, or with a handling of *categories of worldview* which, if they are to lead to the truth, must likewise proceed logically.

The comparison that Hawking makes in the interview between the human being and the computer is untenable even in terms of traditional syllogistics. Of course he is free to think about God in any way he likes. But it is another thing to assert that the human being does not have an immortal soul *because* a computer does not have a soul, and to conclude this based on the premise that a person is comparable to a computer.

Let's examine the computer for a moment, with this in mind. Can it create its own software in a free process of cognition, and programme itself accordingly – let us say, in order to understand the world? Can it – unprogrammed – intuit itself as an 'I'? Can it love, hate, reproduce, experience beauty, develop religious feelings? The more we list human qualities, the more grotesque does the comparison appear. But it is quite a different matter if, instead, we say that the computer's various processes can, certainly, be compared to particular, isolated accomplishments of our brain.

Nor is it acceptable to equate understanding with mere combinatorics. We would refer here to the cultural philosopher Theodor Litt, who describes understanding as the 'integration of a meaningful act into the totality of a tangible context of experience'.[93]

To say 'We are just a somewhat advanced breed of apes on a little planet orbiting a very average star' involves overlooking the wonders of this world that meet us every day, without regard for the many 'natural' or 'universal' constants that, in the view of modern science, underpin the whole structure of the cosmos: wonderful interactions at the level of both microcosm and macrocosm which work together in nature like the finely balanced weights of a mobile. Surely the spiritual mathematism of Kepler, one of the great architects of the new worldview, is not only more comprehensive in scope but also closer to the truth?

Amongst the proponents of a worldview there are, as we have seen, not only differences of intensity but also differences in understanding its content. For instance, there is a 'pure' colour-circle, and accordingly also 'impure' colours. To say that the particular shading of a worldview is one-sided or not in full accord with the truth is no more 'intolerant' than to claim a particular colour is garish, strident or dull. The important thing is to ascertain a set of facts and circumstances *sine ira et studio*, as the Romans would say: 'without anger or fervour'.

Kepler's inspired mathematism is in some respects related to the high prizing of mathematics as expressed in the world pictures of Plato and Pythagoras. The fundamental idea is that the world originates and endures in God's creative mathematising. Here are a few representative passages from Kepler's work *Mysterium Cosmographicum* (*Secret of the Universe*):

> For what appears, in the quest for truth, as arduous and lofty to the uninitiated, can, by mathematical concepts and with the aid of images, be convincingly, clearly and irrefutably presented. These show the revelations of super-creaturely (= supersensible) properties in numbers, and

> allow the forces of intelligible (= spiritual) forms to manifest in intellectual ones (i.e. in the mind's thoughts). For this reason, with the help of mathematical concepts, Plato gives us many wonderful doctrines about the divine. And behind the philosophy of Pythagoras is concealed, as behind a curtain, an introduction into the mysteries of divine teachings.... Mathematics makes the greatest contribution to reflections on nature by revealing the well-ordered fabric of thoughts according to which the universe is formed.... Mathematics perfects us ethically, by implanting order and harmony in the customs of our life. It offers bodily stances that accord with virtue, along with melodies and movements... so that all those who from youth onward strive for virtue may come at last to perfection. It spreads before us well-ordered virtue, doing so differently in numbers, in figures and in musical harmonies. It shows us also in what way vices are constituted of too little or too much. Through all this it lends us harmony and regularity of character, and ethical grace.[94]

But such ideas are not confined to him. A whole series of twentieth-century scientists or physicists have said similar things, albeit in a somewhat different 'shade' of formulation, and will no doubt continue to do so. For the world is not only composed of *phenomena* comprehensible through the *senses,* but is truly shaped according to measure, number and weight. In fact, adherents of mathematism perceive a creative mathematising and geometrising of infinite diversity, and wonder at its harmonious accord as a sign of cosmic intelligence. Max Planck, for instance, states in his lecture on 'Religion and Science':

> The most varied and diverse measurements, all concurring with each other, have now led us to the conclusion that all physical occurrences are without exception attributable to mechanical or electrical processes elicited through the movements of certain elementary particles such as electrons, positrons, protons and neutrons, and that both the mass and also the charge of each of these elementary particles are expressed by a very particular tiny number, one that can be determined all the more precisely, the more these measuring processes are refined. These small numbers, known as 'universal constants', are in a sense the immutably given cornerstones upon which the whole construct of physics is raised, and of which it is composed.... The universal constants were not invented for utilitarian purposes, but they irresistibly urged themselves upon us through the concordant results of all relevant measurements;

> and – the important thing – we know in advance very precisely that all future measurements will lead us to the same constants again. In summary therefore we can say that the science of physics requires an assumption of a real world that is independent of us, one that we never directly perceive but can always only perceive through the spectacles of our empirical senses and the measurements mediated by them.... And yet an actual wealth of successes in scientific research lead us to the conclusion that we will, through tireless furthering of our work, at least continually come closer to an unattainable goal, and will be strengthened in our hope of increasingly deepening insights into the omnipotent power of reason holding sway over the natural world.[95]

Every small plant, tree, animal reveals the miracle of an actively geometrising and mathematising intelligence, ceaselessly ascending from species to species in manifold manifestations to the most complex of all creations, the human being. From the magical geometrical forms that we find, for instance, in the depths of the ocean – we might think of starfish, the skeletons of radiolarians, or jellyfish – a direct line can be traced to, say, snow crystals. And plant forms – from the forget-me-not through to orchids, from daisies through to a blossoming rose – everywhere display a kind of applied geometry. But in caves and subterranean caverns too, where, since time immemorial, crystals and metals are to be found, we are surrounded by pure mathematics: cubes and dodecahedrons, prisms and pyramids – a world rich in forms and substances.

Goethe was well acquainted with this world. Although he himself was no mathematician, he esteemed mathematics very highly. In his direct observations of nature he demanded of himself the rigour of the mathematician. Rudolf Steiner very aptly characterises this aspect of Goethe:

> Although he modestly admits that he has never acquired skill in handling mathematical concepts and outlooks, he requires one thing nevertheless, a *phenomenalism* as he practised this in his scientific writings. He demands that one work back from secondary phenomena as we initially encounter them in the surrounding world, to the primal or *ur*-phenomena. But of what kind is this work? Goethe demands that we return to these archetypal phenomena in the same way a mathematician proceeds when he starts from a complex form of something outwardly perceived but works his way back to an axiom. *The primal phenomena are to be empirical axioms, experiential axioms.* And thus, in a truly mathematical spirit, Goethe demands that we *inwardly*

> *interfuse phenomena with mathematics.* He expresses this by saying the following: 'We seek the primal phenomenon with an awareness that in doing so we could, in the most rigorous sense, account for it to the mathematician on his own terms.' Thus what Goethe is seeking is a modified mathematising, an interfusing of phenomena with mathematising endeavour. He demands for scientific enquiry a phenomenology thoroughly imbued by the mathematising outlook.[96]

Even in Goethe's search for the archetypal plant, we see his mathematising approach. Thus, on one occasion he wrote:

> The changing nature of plant forms, whose idiosyncratic course I had long been observing, now awoke in me increasingly the thought that the plant forms around us are not predetermined and fixed but that rather, with stubborn, generic and specific obstinacy, they are endowed with a happy mobility and flexibility so as to accommodate themselves to so many different conditions that affect them across the globe, and accordingly form and reconfigure themselves... it became ever clearer to me that the way in which they are all subsumed under one overarching concept could be enlivened in a higher fashion – a requirement that at that time hovered before me in the sensible, yet not sense-perceivable, form of an archetypal plant.[97]

Before we end this chapter and move on to a further worldview that involves a *thinking* grasp of reality – to rationalism – let us cast a brief glance at the world of art. Since this book primarily aims to offer stimulus and food for thought rather than to present a 'totality' of these contexts, this survey will remain cursory.

The worlds of music and mathematics are known to be inseparable. Pythagoras's cosmically oriented mathematism also encompassed the music of the cosmic spheres. This experience is one often recounted in cultural history. Novalis said that mathematics is 'positively made manifest' in music, and Beethoven said something similar. On 28 May 1810, Bettina Brentano wrote to tell Goethe that Beethoven had said this to her:

> Speak to Goethe about me – tell him that music is the sole unembodied entry to a higher world of knowledge which, while encompassing the human being, is not comprehensible to him. Rhythm of the spirit is required to grasp the essential nature of music; it gives intimation, inspiration of heavenly sciences, and what the spirit experiences of it through the senses is the embodiment of spiritual insight.

In the pictorial arts, too, especially as they developed in the twentieth century, we see an increasingly mathematistic quality. Great mathematicians of the Renaissance sought mathematically correct perspective, or a human form that accorded with ideal proportions. Here we need only think of Leonardo da Vinci, or of scholars such as his friend Luca Paciola, whose 1509 work *De divina proportione* Leonardo illustrated. But this is not what I mean. I refer here, rather, to the constructivism of Vladimir Tatlin, who confined himself to the pure harmonies of simple geometrical forms, or, especially, the Stijl Group of Piet Mondrian and the whole development of abstract art. Further instances are Cubism, from Cezanne to Picasso, Braque and others, or American 'minimal art'. Seemingly very abstract mathematism conceals a great many possibilities that become apparent primarily when this principle actively and creatively manifests in the cosmos and the human being.

To conclude, a comment by Albert Steffen at the end of his deeply reflective booklet *Pilgrimage to the Tree of Life*. The poet here connects a poetic, spiritual mathematism with an existential experience in the realm of psychism (which we will also discuss later in the book). He starts from Goethe's perception:

> Now I suddenly understood the archetypal plant. I saw how a plant germinates, grows, blossoms and bears fruit, and repeatedly arises anew from the seed, throughout a whole aeon, by natural necessity; and how in doing so it connects the earth with the heavens. In the arrangement of the leaves, in the shape of flowers, in the rising and evaporation of water, in the blossoming and fading of colours, I discovered a manifold rhythm: tones, counterpoints and harmonies, the dancing of countless spirits... a secret eurythmy that, in tune with the harmony of the spheres, brings about growth and dying, configuring from below and dissolving in an upward direction, turning towards the sun, a search for the earth's centre, a spiralling to the course of the planets, ceaseless changes of colour and shape: I could only accompany this if I surrendered myself as a being that has understood itself to be similar to the archetypal plant, that is, as an eternal entelechy beyond birth and death.[98]

7

'And Behold, It Was Very Good' – Rationalism

'And God saw every thing that he had made, and, behold, it was very good. And the evening and the morning were the sixth day. Thus the heavens and the earth were finished, and all the host of them' (Genesis 1, 31 to 2, 1). Thus ends the first account of the Creation in Genesis. Once the work has been accomplished, God rests on the seventh day, which henceforth is sacred.

Reading of these six days of the Creation, with its five repetitions of 'And God saw that it was good', one might wonder whether God in his omnipotence really needed to appraise his works in this way. But no doubt that is too human a thought. Rather, we are here shown a characteristic in the totality of Creation, to whose truth and reality the worldview of rationalism can penetrate. Of all properties of the world and the human being, this outlook, with its close affinities to mathematism and idealism, perceives what is morally sound or also rationally meaningful: the 'good'. Whereas mathematism focuses primarily on the quantitative nature of Creation, rationalism is concerned with the qualitative. But the boundaries between them are of course fluid, especially as this mode of reflection does not exclusively start from, or aim at, the phenomenological, sensualist or materialist view. Rather, its field is morality and purposefulness, as these come to expression for instance in the many symbiotic relationships in nature, also described in biology. Symbiosis means, after all, a community of different living creatures for mutual benefit, though this can be seen in the broadest terms. We should avoid applying moral standards in our observations of natural relationships, as it were 'moralising' them, for instance imposing on plants and animals our categories of good and evil; but we can nevertheless perceive a quality in Creation which can, as already stated, be defined as a purposeful accord of all natural interactions and relationships.

What Max Planck experienced as the 'omnipotent power of reason holding sway over the natural world' can be understood in mathematical or mathematistic terms, as we examined in the previous chapter. But it can also be studied from the aspect of meaningfulness, of reason – and then we have rationalism, as this book conceives of it. Only this kind of rationalism is meant here. Rationalism is otherwise generally understood as a conviction that reason – *ratio* – is the source of knowledge, in contrast to sense experience. We characterised this outlook as an aspect of mathematism, but it could also be called intellectualism. The meaningfulness of the Creation, this reciprocally attuned interplay of all the realms of nature may certainly be called 'good'. We also say, do we not, a good apple, good earth, good water, good honey; or a good film, a good piece of furniture, a good opportunity, a good idea, a good book. There are countless uses of the extraordinarily manifold concept 'good'. Or we can think of the 'natural constants' already mentioned, without which no life would be possible; and above all of primary ecological equilibrium. Albert Einstein said something very beautiful:

> But the investigator is imbued with the causality of all phenomena. The future is no less necessary to him and definable than the past... his religiosity lies in a rapt wonder at the harmony of natural laws, in which is manifest such superior reason that all meaningful human thinking and classifications are, by contrast, an entirely worthless reflection.[99]

Yes indeed: Creation can be called intrinsically 'good' in its original condition. In this sense, rationalism includes a conviction that the human being is also fundamentally good. At any rate, God ascertained that the whole fabric of Creation was not only good but – after the human being was created in his image – actually 'very good'. Let us take this in not too human terms but *sub specie aeternitas* – from the perspective of eternity.

What has been said about the good in other cultural contexts?

Plato, the teacher of Aristotle, identifies the good with the divine. In the human being, says Plato, all thoughts and concepts lead something like a shadowy existence. They possess their luminous, creative reality in the realm of ideas in which every human soul tarried before birth. Every earthly thing corresponds to an idea in the pure world of ideas, which is seen as a higher form of existence, as divine. This is a rough and very abbreviated survey of Plato's doctrine of ideas, and it would need much more elaboration and differentiation. Now Plato compares the idea of the good, the highest of ideas, *to agathon*, to the sun. Just as the sun is the source of life and vision, so likewise is the idea of the good the source of being and perception. In Book 6 of his *The Republic*, Plato, in the voice of Socrates, gives especially clear expression to this view. It represents a summit of ancient rationalism, which of course later entered Christianity via Roman culture – as we can see in the Stoics.

Over the centuries it emancipated itself from Christian theism and underwent a further intensification as a cultural determinant in the age of the Enlightenment, regarded as the classical era of rationalism. This rationalism was of course also concerned with ethical questions, but in an already very abstract, intellectual form. It then culminated in very diverse schools of thought in the nineteenth and twentieth centuries, and continues to this day. In Plato's work the 'good' is thus not yet – as we will see later – an outcome of ethical individualism, but, as it were, a star that, though never reached, we can orient ourselves to like a lonely sailor.

Here are a few passages from this noteworthy dialogue between Socrates and Glaucon. Plato wrote substantial parts of his philosophy in the form of dialogues. Aristotle also composed dialogues but, characteristically, his major works were written in prose – which is why he is regarded as the founder of scientific prose. But now back to Plato:

> 'What,' he said, 'is there any knowledge higher than this – higher than justice and the other virtues?'
>
> 'Yes there is a higher knowledge, and we ought not make a shadowy outline of it only but seek the fullest clarity and precision. It is ridiculous, surely, to strive for the greatest clarity and purity in relation to things of small value, but to relinquish it when it comes to describing the very highest things.'
>
> 'That is something to ponder. But what is the highest study, and what is its subject?'...
>
> '... you have often heard that the idea of the good is this highest study. Only through it do justice and the other virtues first acquire their value and benefit. You also well know that I have this good in mind, and at the same time I also want to say that we have no clear knowledge of it. Do you think that the possession of all other things is of any value if we do not possess the idea of the good? Or do you think that it is of any use to us to possess all possible things but not the good? Or to understand everything else but not what is beautiful and good?'

> 'Assuredly not.'...
>
> 'By the idea of the good you can now conceive of something that endows perceivable objects with truth and the perceiving soul with the power of knowing. Set it there as the cause and origin of our knowledge, and as the cause and origin of the truth we acknowledge. But you will do well to regard it as something other and higher than those two great things, knowledge and truth. Just as we reasonably consider light and vision to resemble the sun but not themselves to be the sun, so here too we have the right to declare that those two things, knowledge and truth, resemble the good but neither of them is the good itself. The good must be placed above them.'
>
> 'That is incomprehensibly lofty! The good facilitates knowledge and truth but stands higher than either!

Plato continues:

> 'But our study teaches us that there exists in every human soul both the capacity and means to assimilate spiritual things. Yet in the same way that the eyes cannot by themselves turn to look backwards but the whole body must be turned from the dark to the light, so, by our capacity for perception and insight the whole soul must be turned away from the world of becoming until it can endure sight of the true world and ultimately that of the most luminous objects in this true world. This object is the good, isn't it?'[100]

A later dialogue, *Timaeus*, takes its point of departure from *The Republic*. Both are among Plato's most influential works. In *Timaeus* we also hear about the creation of the world. The world-creator, whom Plato calls 'demiurge', creates out of the infinite substance of his goodness or benevolence:

> TIMAEUS: Let us therefore say what cause moved him who assembled this universe, the realm of becoming, to embark on this work. He was good, and in a good person envy never arises, whatever its object might be; and, since he was free of this, he also wished that everything should be made to resemble himself as much as possible. This starting point for the developing world is therefore surely something that we men of insight should acknowledge as being the most intrinsic. Since God desired that as far as possible everything should be good and not bad, and yet

> everything visible was not tranquil but in unregulated and disordered motion, he conducted it from disorder into order, because he believed that this condition was better than the other. But it was and remains true that the highest and best creator should bring forth nothing other than whatever is most beautiful; and, in his pondering he found that amongst the things that are by their nature visible no work devoid of reason could ever be more beautiful than one endowed with reason if one compares them in their entirety, but that, in turn, reason without soul could not possibly be imparted to any creature. In these considerations he imparted reason to a soul and the soul to a body, and from these forged the edifice of the universe in order to see the loveliest and best work naturally perfected. And so we are justified in expressing the fact that, in all probability, this world arose as a truly ensouled and reason-endowed entity through the providence of God.[101]

In Stoicism, a widespread and diverse school of ancient philosophy, named after the *stoa* or hall of pillars in Athens where Zeno of Citium, its founder, used to gather his pupils, much of this quotation reappears, albeit in somewhat altered form. At the time of the Roman Caesars, Stoicism had even become an ethical religion of the Roman people. Caesar Marcus Aurelius also testifies to it in his famous *Meditations*:

> You must always reflect upon what kind of nature the universe possesses, and what your own nature is, and in what relation the latter stands to the former, and what kind of part it is and what kind of whole; and there is no one who could prevent you from doing and uttering whatever is in harmony with nature, of which you are a part.... Whatever you do, do it with the endeavour of being good, 'good' in the true meaning of the word. Follow this precept in everything you do.... Always take the shortest path! The shortest is in accord with nature; all our action and speech will then be perfect.'

A core dictum of his rationalism states:

> The substance of the entirety of the world is pliable and easily mutable. But reason, which holds sway throughout it, contains no intrinsic cause to do evil, and no thing is harmed by it. By this reason everything occurs, and comes to its proper goal.[102]

Epictetus, a refined Greek Stoic and older contemporary of Marcus Aurelius, once wrote as follows of the fundamental goodness of human nature:

> The ethically good person is preoccupied with his rational soul; his body is the domain for the physician and teacher of gymnastics, as the fields are for farmers. The task of an ethical, good person is to make use of thoughts in a way that accords with nature. But in the nature of every soul lies the predisposition to approve what is true, to reject what is false, and to remain reticent about what is uncertain.[103]

These testimonies from the world of religious and philosophical tradition have allowed us to form a fairly adequate picture of rationalism, as an outlook that sees universal reason permeating and shaping the world. Thus, evil would be the virtual negation of this originating entity of primal goodness and truth, to which, according to Plato, beauty should also be assigned. Without yet touching on issues of freedom, therefore, human beings have a capacity to find the truth or to succumb to error, to acknowledge what is true or to disseminate lies. We can either pursue our sun-like nature or darken our being. The roots of all evil, and the origins of all sin, are here seen to lie in our sundering from the Summum Bonum, the highest good. The action of Adam and Eve, too, did not correspond to the laws established by God and holding sway in the Garden of Eden!

It can be said, really – although with a pinch of salt – that rationalism is, or should be, the guiding star of lawyers. Justitia holds a pair of scales in her hand to gauge whether people's actions correspond to the harmonious equilibrium of cosmic–earthly powers. At any rate, the whole realm of ethics – seen from both a heavenly and an earthly perspective – is the true domain of rationalism. Whereas the mathematist focuses on the quantitative and calculable aspect of the world, and on the cognitive process that involves finding a 'common denominator', the rationalist is concerned with ethical and rational quality. It probably does not need stating that both outlooks – and more than these – can live in one and the same person. We need think only of Einstein, in whom both these elements were very highly developed. After all, as human beings we have the predisposition for all twelve worldviews.

If a person is strongly rationalist in character, then we have a detached individual who is averse to anything emotionally exaggerated, who always has themselves in hand, and usually has a good eye for the sensible unfolding of interpersonal dynamics – for instance, in conversations. In a team of colleagues – a faculty of teachers, say – such people are usually a blessing. Whereas the detailed focus of the mathematist can sometimes tend to single-track thinking, whether they are materialistic or spiritual in outlook, rationalists can repeatedly find ways to rediscover the golden mean. Aristotle, after all, who enduringly forged our ethical concepts, defines 'virtue' as the right centre between two extremes.

We find in Gautama Buddha a distinctive form of this kind of rationalism. Five hundred years before Christ he developed an ethics that has still not lost its glory today. At the age of 29, Shakyamuni, son of a king, left his palace and embraced homelessness. Burning questions about the meaning of human life and suffering led him to the schools of the best-known brahmans, or into the loneliness of the forests. But neither the teachings of wisdom nor the rigorous deprivations of the hermit brought him the enlightenment for which he hoped. Only in deep meditation did the true light dawn, whereupon he founded an order and, as it is said, set the wheel of his teachings going. Nowadays Buddhism is a world religion. The core of his teaching includes the eightfold path, which testifies to a pure rationalism already in its emphasis on what is right and true:

1. Right view
2. Right resolve
3. Right speech
4. Right conduct
5. Right living
6. Right exertion
7. Right awareness
8. Right reflection[104]

At the heart of his pronouncements is universal compassion, world-encompassing love. This is a path of meditation. The remarkable thing about it is that it dawns *inwardly* in the secluded meditant. Rather than hearing a 'Good' enthroned in a distant heaven speak to him, it is as if his inner soul is opened. With this gesture of internalisation, quite new tones resound in the historical development of ethical values.

In the Gospels we find an ethics that, albeit differently focused, has affinities with this. In the Christianity whose cultural and religious influence started about 600 years later, what speaks in human beings is the actual ground of meaning of the world, the Logos. The goal of Christian mysticism is the indwelling of Christ in the human soul. The great St Paul expresses this mystery succinctly but profoundly: 'nevertheless I live; yet not I, but Christ liveth in me' (Galatians 2, 19). Christ is at the same time annunciation, thus an appeal to interiority, and also fulfilment. Here are three examples:

> And also when you pray, do not do it as the hypocrites do. They love to stand in the synagogues and on street corners when they pray, to make an appearance before people. Yes, I say to you, they make mockery of their own reward. When you pray, enter into your inmost chamber and close the door, and thus send up your prayer to the Father Ground of the world, to the realm that is hidden from the senses. (Matthew 6, 5f.)[105]

This prompting occurs in the context of the Sermon on the Mount, which is really a unique appeal to individual responsibility to seek the kingdom of God *within*. This internalisation comes to especially clear expression in the Gospel of St Luke:

> The Pharisees asked him when the Kingdom of God should come. And he answered, 'The Kingdom of God does not come in a form outwardly visible. Nor does it come such that one could say, it is here, or it is there. For behold, the Kingdom of God is within you.' (Luke, 17, 20f)

Concerning our relationship to the sense world, Buddha already tells us that the path of wisdom involves liberating the heart from all attachments that bind it to the world of sensory things, until the state of Nirvana is attained, which tradition describes in these terms:

> Here all forms of existence have entirely vanished. Whoever has recognised this realm of non-form, his spirit is delivered and released; and whoever has annihilated the path to existence has, glad of this annihilation, attained the goal of the teaching and has relinquished all forms of existence. This too the sublime one said, as I have heard tell.[106]

The final words of the high-priestly prayer that figures in St John have a different emphasis. The disciples of Christ should not depart from this world. The goal of the indwelling of the Logos in the human soul is an unfolding of powers towards redeeming and transforming earthly nature, as this occurred archetypally from Easter Sunday onwards. Here are the words that Christ addresses to the 'Father':

> I do not ask that you should take them away from the earthly world but that you preserve them from evil. They are not of the earthly world, as I too am not of this world. Sanctify them through the truth. Your word is the truth. As you have sent me into the world, so have I now sent them into the world. And I sanctify myself for them so that they may be sanctified in the truth.
>
> And I do not ask you only on their behalf but also on behalf of those who shall unite with me in their pronouncements, that they all may be united as one; just as you, Father, are within me, and I in you, so let them be in us, so that the world can come to believe that you sent me. I have given them the power of revelation which you gave to me, so that they may be one, as we are also one. I am in them, and you are in me, and thus they will be dedicated to perfect unity, so that the world perceives that you sent me, and that you love them as you love me.
>
> Father Ground of the world, my will is that they whom you gave me will always be with me and that they may see the revelations of my being that you gave me before the world was. Sublime Father Ground, earthly human beings have not recognised you; but I recognise you, and these have recognised that you have sent me. I have revealed your name to them, and I will continue to reveal it, so that the love with which you have loved me may be preserved in them, and thus my I may be revealed in their I. (John, 17, 15–26)

This modern translation gives especially clear expression to the promised presence of the Son of God within the human being. The 'Word', the Logos, which, as we read at the very beginning of the Gospel of John, was the origin from which all came forth – the Greek term in fact means both the word as thought and utterance – is the creative *meaning* intrinsic to the cosmos, through to the tiniest creature, since everything in God's plan has meaning and intention. Naturally this is a rationalist interpretation. The word 'Logos' can also be differently interpreted, as we will see in the next chapter.

Now this meaningfulness of the cosmos, which emerges directly from the meaningful utterance of God, and further unfolds, was not an unknown concept in antiquity. For this reason a Church Father with a Platonist outlook like Augustine was able to say that it existed already before the advent of Christ.

Whatever one's position on these interpretations and contexts, it remains a fact that in the course of history the creation of ethical values increasingly became a purely human rather than a divine affair. The

Commandments of Moses lost ever more of their orientating power for a great part of humanity.

In the Renaissance, the first great epoch of the modern era, a great gulf opened up between these two worlds, the divine and the human. Morality either succumbed to the yoke of an uninhibited lust for power, as witnessed in the enigmatic personality of the Florentine Niccolò Machiavelli, whose text *The Prince* became required reading for all tyrants through to our own era – a stock-in-trade of totalitarian dictators; or else it was assigned to human freedom, as for instance in the high-minded contemporary of Machiavelli's Giovanni Pico della Mirandola, whose principles, as set out in his book *On Human Dignity*, became likewise renowned. Between these two poles are all sorts of other positions. Below are two passages from these two books. It is worth mulling them over and sampling their flavour, for together they reveal a kind of hither-and-thither in the human psyche which still lives on in the unconscious depths of every modern person. First, Machiavelli:

> Many have formed ideas of free states and autarchies of which in reality no one has either seen or heard anything; for between life as it is, and life as it should be, there is a difference so huge that he who looks only to what ought to be will be far more likely to ruin than sustain his life. A person who seeks always only the good will inevitably go under amidst so many people who are not good. A ruler, therefore, if he wishes to assert himself, must acquire the capacity to act not only according to moral laws, but to make use of them, or not, as necessity requires.[107]

And then, Pico della Mirandola: here he is conveying what God speaks to Adam:

> We lent you, O Adam, no particular dwelling, no power of sight, nor any other special gift, and this was so that you might have and possess any dwelling, any vision, and all the gifts you desire entirely according to your own will and your own opinion. The other creatures received their nature through laws preordained by us, and thereby are kept within confines. You are not constrained by any insurmountable barriers but it is intended that you predetermine even your nature according to your own free will, into whose keeping I have placed your destiny. I have placed you at the centre of the world so that you may gaze around you comfortably from there, to see all that exists in the world. We created you as neither a heavenly nor earthly being, as neither mortal nor

> immortal, so that you may determine yourself, as your own, completely free and honorary sculptor and poet, what form you desire to live in. You are free to degenerate into the underworld of the beasts. Likewise you are free to raise yourself into the higher, divine world through the resolve of your own spirit.[108]

In humanism, in the primary aim of educating humanity to develop all valuable potentials, lives a rationalist ideal that runs like a golden thread right through to modern times. Here freedom is also the clear air in which human goodness can really thrive. We might recall here Wilhelm von Humboldt's noteworthy book *On the Limits of State Action*. The beginning of Chapter 2 immediately announces a kind of programmatic appeal in which we rediscover familiar tones:

> The true purpose of the human being – not the one which changing fashions dictate but which immutable reason prescribes – is the highest and fullest development of his powers as a whole. For this education and development, freedom is the first and indispensable condition.[109]

These ideals lived very strongly in many contemporaries of Humboldt's – not least in Goethe who, in this respect, was a thoroughgoing rationalist, albeit quite different from the usually atheistic Enlightenment thinkers of earlier decades. The nineteenth century was not only the century of classical materialism, but a period of great social upheavals, triggered by the industrialisation introduced in England in the last third of the eighteenth century as the consequence of inventions such as the steam engine and the mechanical loom.

This first Industrial Revolution also gave rise to Marxism, which is rightly regarded as historical materialism but can also be seen as a particular brand of ethically oriented rationalism. To put it simply we might say that Marxism places human beings into a natural context in so far as it considers them governed by natural drives and the quest for possessions. In a sense, occupying the space between Machiavellian anthropology on the one hand and Freudian psychology on the other, Marxism began to impel the masses. The revolutions that followed later released in a devastating fashion the aggressive potential that culminates in Marxist dialectics, i.e. in its concept of class warfare. The violent release of fanatical emotions will preoccupy us again later, in Chapter 13 on dynamism.

But humanistic rationalism did not of course vanish in the subsequent period, not even during the Cold War period. Here we could name many figures; but something said by George F. Kennans, a high-ranking diplomat who was awarded the Peace Prize of the German Book Trade Association in 1982, is representative of this stance. In passing, let us remember that true diplomats are usually rationalists. Not seldom, like Kennan, they have a fundamental trust in human beings' innate powers of reason. He was well versed in Russian affairs, and the following quotation from him – Glasnost was not yet in sight – could be interpreted as the expression of great naivety, especially from the point of view of the 'hawks' in the world's parliaments. Towards the end of his address, given in German in St Paul's Church, Frankfurt, he said

> ... that a new attempt must be made, far more seriously, realistically, consistently and decisively than anything so far done, to make war in Europe completely inconceivable in future; that is, to create conditions in which a new European war becomes so improbable that we could at last be liberated from this terrible and unquantifiably dangerous paroxysm of military suspicions and preparations that at present has us in its clutches; then we could turn ourselves to positive tasks that, on both sides of the ideological divide, so urgently and insistently await our action.
>
> Please do not think that I am unaware of the enormous difficulties of this undertaking. I realise that nothing less is needed here than to get a whole range of nations and governments to realise that, for them, war – this oft-sung institution of our European past, the centuries-old acceptance that national interests or desires can be sanctioned in this way – is no longer a realistic method of influencing other governments, and in fact not even a meaningful form of defence; to realise that we must instead learn to raise ourselves above all ideological or political obstacles, and confine ourselves to other means of influence. Is such a thing feasible? My answer may surprise you, for this is my answer: why shouldn't it be?[110]

This is a truly rationalist stance!

In a true realpolitik – which should not be confused with the practice of mangled compromise, examples of which are sadly legion – a relatively pure rationalism does of course come to expression. Not least in 'values philosophy' or also 'values ethics' as developed in the twentieth century and represented by figures such as Max Scheler and Nicolai Hartmann, we see further aspects of rationalism. In Hartmann himself we find a mind that conveys the idea that human beings can discern moral values in a kind of inner, clairaudient sense – as if a higher aspect were 'speaking' within us:

> The mind's contact with the realm of values lies in its connection with the other world, as it were a *clairaudience for the call* that resounds from there into the world, for the promptings that emanate from values. The sense of values has the form of an inner *hearing*, and is closest to the *primary meaning of 'reason'*. And it certainly makes good sense to regard practical reason as a *hearing of values*.[111]

Surely it is but a stone's throw from here to the idea that the Logos speaks within us?

The unmistakeable dangers implicit in our cultural and military race for dominance can only be diminished by a sense of global responsibility. With his important 'World Ethos Project', the theologian Hans Küng initiated an attempt to find a basic stock of common ethical values that could offer practical ways of realising this responsibility. As E. Wolfgang Bödefeld writes, this responsibility 'must be borne by religions, and all religious and non-religious people'. In his innovative book, Küng initiated this project in 1990, and it has since received global recognition and affirmation. Based on his draft, in 1993 the World's Parliament of Religions agreed its 'Declaration of a Global Ethic'. Thus, the representatives of all religions agreed upon the content and principles of an ethic common to all humanity.[112]

This is important and illuminating in two respects. First, it makes possible really fruitful dialogue between the hemispheres: a consensus on some common basic ethical values as a cornerstone of intercultural collaboration. And, secondly, a confluence of all the different cultural currents in the world is only going to be realistic in the foreseeable future in relation to ethics. As far as ideology or doctrinal differences are concerned, a kind of babel of confusion will continue to reign for a long time to come, and to demarcate groups against each other. The latter owes to the written texts of religious faiths, *tenets of faith* to which all believers of a particular religion or church must subscribe. Of course this does not apply to all religions – for instance, neither to Hinduism nor to Buddhism. But, as we saw in the previous chapter, this unifying of religious doctrine under one formula is the outcome of mathematist thinking. It initially precludes any different truth. Thus, mathematism is a Janus-headed figure: clearest knowledge, on the one hand; repudiating dogma, on the other. The era that Goethe heralds in his 'West–East Divan' has not yet arrived:

> To God belongs the Orient!
> To God belongs the Occident!

To North and South, the spreading lands
All rest tranquil in his hands.

He, the only just and true,
Wills for each person what to each is due.
Of all his hundred names let this
Be given the highest praise.
Amen.

And yet in the world today there are ever-greater numbers of people looking in this direction: a clearly positive force at work.

To end with, I'd like to quote a poem by Goethe, the practical value of which should be reconsidered in the light of very recent history. A range of issues that we have considered in this chapter are here made tangible in an authentically 'Goethean' manner:

May the human being
Be noble, helpful and good!
For this alone distinguishes him
From all other beings
Whom we know.

Hail to the unknown
Higher beings
Of whom we have an inkling!
May the human being resemble them!
Let his example teach us
To have faith in them!

For nature is unfeeling:
The sun shines
Equally upon evil and good;
And moon and stars
Gleam as brightly upon
The criminal as on the best of men.

Wind and rivers,
Thunder and hail
Rush in their course
And in their passage

Take no account
Of whom they seize or batter.

Happiness likewise
Taps blindly in the crowd:
Sometimes inhabits
Curly-headed innocence,
Sometimes also the bald
Skull of the guilty.
By eternal, iron laws,
All of us must
Complete our life's cycle.

But only the human being
Can do the impossible:
Can distinguish, choose and redress;
Can lend to the moment
A long duration.

He alone may
Reward good,
Punish evil,
Heal and redeem,
Beneficially connect
All that errs and goes astray.

And we, we honour
The immortals,
As if they were of our human kind,
As if they did on a larger scale
The little that the best of us
Does or would like to.

May the noble human being
Be helpful and good!
May he tirelessly create
What is useful and just,
Be an exemplar to us
Of those beings whom we intimate!

8

The Logos that Was at the Beginning – Idealism

Evening had arrived and the first stars gently began to gleam. Great tranquillity seemed to spread over the ocean, out to the far horizon. The group of people who had been happily eating and conversing also grew quieter. The sun had gone down – for, after all, the whole earth needs its warmth and light.... While not forgetting the striking experience of yesterday evening, they had not yet discussed it at any length, either.

What had they witnessed? For the first time in their lives they had seen that rare and wonderful light phenomenon known as a 'green flash'. When the last part of the sun sinks below the water's surface, an intense, cone-shaped, turquoise-green ray shines out, stretching almost to the eastern horizon, and remains hanging in the air for a few minutes like a visible trumpet fanfare. It is as if a rainbow, issuing from one point, managed only to spread out in a narrow, green triangle. You no longer see the sun, and the whole sky above the horizon takes on a very delicate and subtly shaded pink-blue coloration, which still remains when the green flash has become no more than an echo in your retina. This is what they had seen the evening before. From a terrace with a view in all directions, the small group of students had witnessed this enigmatic spectacle at the very beginning of their weekend together. Now, suddenly, one of them began to speak:

> Strange, really, if you think that the sun is just a ball of fiery gases, and that such phenomena arise through simple light refraction. If the Egyptians had known this, it seems to me they would have been hard pressed to worship the sun as a god. A ball of gases, in fact in principle a

> nuclear reactor! But I suppose that back then, as now, the masses needed some kind of 'opium' so that their rulers could maintain power – and without power, where would we be?

Speaking these words, he looked pointedly at a history student, a woman, who promptly replied:

> You and your gas balls and your chatter about matter! All you can ever do is trot out your materialistic prejudices, but you're unable to actually look at anything and see it! Every phenomenon of nature, if we see it truly, points far beyond itself – it's like a person's face. We've often talked about this. What do you see when you look Lisa in the eyes? Do you say, 'I love your accumulation of molecules?'

Her spiritedness, and her arguments, which went right to the heart of the matter, and not least her comical comparison of his lovely Lisa with a heap of molecules, caused a welcome lightening of the mood. While another of their party was surprised that, whether seen as phenomena or matter, they had not recognised that everything is only neural experiences in the brain, another of them, a mathematics student, began to speak:

> No, it's not as simple as that. If I start from the premise – daily reconfirmed by science – that our whole world is actually founded on mathematical laws, I would say that the green flash arises in this case through a rare dispersion of sunrays refracted in the atmosphere, which more strongly accentuates the image of the sun in the short-wave region of the visible spectrum than in the long-wave – yellow-red – part of it.

The group grew somewhat restless. In their first conversation the evening before, Lisa, the philosophy student, had tried to explain that our deeper ethical awareness is only really comprehensible if we regard it not, as Freud does, as the expression of a societally overlaid superego, but as part of the totality of cosmic reason. They had gathered this weekend because they wanted to support the 'World Ethos' project at their university. Only yesterday, Lisa had been quoting Plato, comparing the sun to the light of the highest good. The physics student, who had just started going out with her, and had spoken about a ball of gas a moment before, had kept quiet as she said this.

The conversation was at risk of turning in a quite different direction from the one that had brought them all together. But the evening was rescued by another of their companions, who simply said, 'The sun is the sun is the sun. Enough of that! And now let's return to our original intention, to work practically in support of Küng's project.' In the end it turned out to be a good, fruitful weekend.

The reader will have recognised here some of what has already been discussed in earlier chapters of the book. If, like the author of this book, you have been involved in all kinds of study groups and faculties over the past 40 years, you may well recall many such discussions – on other themes too: for instance, on pedagogical or artistic questions, and, not least, practical questions about life. This was why I felt moved to find means of communication and mutual understanding, above all ways of enlarging my own views. It was primarily the actual *practice* of immersion in this twelvefold totality of worldviews, over some decades, that opened up for me a broad field of research and study. I had found my path. And so I hope that readers of this book will find similar stimulus for their own study.

But now let us move on, into the realm of a worldview that, though one of the best known, is nevertheless also one of the most deeply misunderstood: idealism.

What is the pure, primary experience of idealism, beyond ideals, ideologies and ideologues? Plato is usually the figure seen as the originator of idealism, and this is no doubt correct. In the last chapter we elaborated on this a little, entering as it were through the gateway of ethically oriented rationalism into the 'world of ideas'. I will now look at this more closely.

For Plato, *ideas* are the truly real element. For him, they are eternal, unchanging essences that cannot be encompassed by our senses. The things of the sense-perceptible world are only the reflections of ideas whose last glimmer leads a shadowy existence in our concepts. These are subject to mutability and decay, whereas the world of ideas shines in eternal clarity above all earthly life. In its life before birth, the human soul perceived the wealth of the world of ideas, but it forgets this at birth. We can develop a conceptual knowledge of sensory things because with every perception the soul – unconsciously – remembers its pre-birth vision (*anamnesis*). Plato himself was really a poet-philosopher, full of religious enthusiasm and yearning for beauty, harmony and pure humanity. At this level we encounter 'Platonic love', which is likewise misunderstood. In reality this is a love relating to the whole of existence. Plato's Eros is primarily a soul-spiritual concern, as are human beings themselves. The physical expression of love is only its transient reflection.

We can say that Plato's view of the creation of the world sees it as descending from 'above' down to the dark matter of corporeality. God creates sensory things according to the blueprint of ideas. The immortal soul has an eternal yearning for the true light: it seeks to flee the sensual bonds of the body and to turn to the better, purer world of ideas. Having a pre-existence, it naturally also has a post-existence, whose quality is determined by the life we lived while on earth. Although Plato's philosophy really culminates in his ethics, truth and beauty are equal qualities of the *agathon*, the primordial good, in its substantive ideality. Seen overall, this doctrine has a strongly artistic element, and has appealed to artistic souls from time immemorial. But philosophically too, through to our own time, Platonism has provided a fundamental outlook in many fields. Even in particle physics it plays a highly significant role, albeit one that primarily accentuates its mathematical aspect.

When Plato speaks in the idiom of a mythical seer, he goes as far as calling the ideas 'gods'. Basically, Platonist philosophy – though it has multiple aspects – is a unity of science, aesthetics and religiosity in an idealistic context. No wonder, then, that it acted like a ferment in the development of Christianity, more or less throughout. Not until the rise of medieval Scholasticism does a strong dose of Aristotelianism – though this was never entirely absent – enter the mix. Together they create the rich soil upon which humanism and the Renaissance were able to develop. At that point, above all in the natural sciences, developmental tendencies arose that we have already referred to in the earlier chapters of this book.

Let us now take a closer look at this complex in its entirety. What is it that distinguishes idealism from rationalism, and from mathematism, even though all three are the outcome of purely thinking consciousness? Or to put the question in a different way – what is the quality of being, or the ontological substance of which calculable measures and numbers constituting the cosmos consist? And of what material is the 'good' woven? Out of its primary experience, idealism states that these consist of the actual and real substance of ideas. Although this is an experience that we can also gain today, it is likely to be unknown to many contemporaries, even if they think of themselves as idealists. (In German vernacular speech, after all – though this is an extreme example – people refer to an extremely small quantum of something as 'idea' – equivalent to using the word 'shade' in English. When hanging a picture on the wall, for instance, they will say, 'Move it just an "idea" [shade] more to the left.') This illustrates the small significance accorded to 'idea'! Plato would probably turn in his grave at such diminution of its value.

In his Viennese period, the student Steiner offered fine testimony to an ontological understanding of the world of ideas. He was 26 when he wrote this:

> The *world of ideas* is the primary spring and principle of all existence. It contains infinite harmony and blissful tranquillity. Anything it did not illumine with its light would be a dead, denatured existence with no part in the life of the whole universe. Only what draws its being from the *idea* has significance upon the universe's tree of creation. The idea is the intrinsic clarity of spirit that is sufficient *within* and *to* itself. Each separate being must have spirit within it, for otherwise it falls like a dead leaf from that tree, and its existence would be vain.... There are four spheres of human activity in which a person dedicates himself wholly to the spirit and annihilates all self-involvement: knowledge, art, religion and loving devotion to an individual in the spirit. Anyone who does not live in at least one of these spheres is not alive at all. *Knowledge* is devotion to the universe in thoughts; *art* in perception; *religion* in the mind and soul; and *love* a devotion with the entirety of all spiritual powers to something that appears to us as a precious being within the world's totality. Knowledge is the most spiritual and love the most beautiful form of selfless devotion. For love is truly a heavenly light within daily life. Pious, truly spiritual love ennobles our being in to its inmost fibres, and exalts everything that lives in us. This pure, pious love transforms our whole life of soul into something else, that has an affinity with the world spirit.[113]

It is striking here that a person must have this spirit *within* them. Thus we meet an element that, strictly speaking, diverges from idealism in so far as, for idealists, ideas are like always unattainable stars which can, nevertheless, guide us. We used this image earlier. Steiner departs from such transcendentalism. It is an approach that will later prove a central preoccupation when we encounter realism in Chapter 14. Here, first, we are concerned to define an idea that is not found in mathematism, since it is primarily a formal science, or in rationalism with its eye for purposeful reason – that is, the wise *arrangement* and *ordering* of things in space and time. Quantity and quality – as Aristotle understands them – are reflected in these two worldviews. But Steiner gives the following answer to the question of what the idea consists of, and what it is: 'The idea is the intrinsic clarity of spirit that is sufficient *within* and *to* itself.' This sentence is a very fine meditation to help us reach the core of idealism.

In fact, what does our *own* reality consist of? Surely of our thoughts, feelings and will impulses. And of what substance are these? Are they the same 'stuff' that dreams are made of? That wouldn't be wrong, though not yet clear enough. Let us for a moment intensely imagine a dear person or a beautiful place that we loved being in. This gives us a colourful, vivid picture, which may also awaken longing in us. It is an experiential reality for us. But of what does it consist? Really, of the light of consciousness. Consciousness and light are merely two aspects of the same phenomenon. We speak, do we not, of a clear head, or a 'light going on' for us. On the other hand, we are also familiar with expressions such as 'benighted', a dulled mind, unclear or muddy thinking. Then there is the lovely phrase, 'to shed light on something'. The true idealist does not live in cloud-cuckoo-land but, rather, is ontologically convinced of *this* reality. That is one side of it. The other is that ideas are for him active realities, corresponding to a more or less inherent quantum of energy to realise them. True idealists are always people of action, just as Plato's demiurge is a 'master of works'. Dreamers or utopians are as different from this as a model engine is from a real one.

Idealists experience the driving force of ideas in science and history. Fichte, who it is true was not merely an idealist, once said, 'All the world spread around us is the reified material for the fulfilment of duties.' A sentence like that speaks volumes! Kant's 'categorical imperative' is also connected with idealism, as are the mighty thought-worlds of Schelling and Hegel. In the history of philosophy, German idealism appears as its most pronounced form. But in twentieth-century Italy, too, we find influential proponents of an idealistically conceived worldview – for instance, in Giovanni Gentile and Benedetto Croce. Turning to England in the first part of the eighteenth century, we could name George Berkeley, although England was above all the cradle of important sensualists and empiricists.

Basically, idealism is a world movement. Its danger is its own grandeur: it often has little understanding of more sense-orientated worldviews such as sensualism and materialism – though this is, of course, at least partly mutual.

As we have seen, idealism is culturally and historically rooted in Platonism, and in a certain way also in Aristotelianism. The Aristotelian categories as ideal statements can be seen as ontological in scope. But it was the important figure of Plotinus, above all, who, around 700 years after Plato, more or less systematised Neoplatonism as the 'last form' of Greek philosophy. Although Neoplatonism arose over time through the mingling of Platonic, Aristotelian, Stoic and other teachings, it can nevertheless be seen as an autonomous albeit very complex movement. It is said to have been founded by the rather historically nebulous figure of Ammonius Saccas, who came from Alexandria – a site of universal intellectuality that also played a significant role, through the Church Fathers Clemens and Origenes, in the development of Christian doctrine. An important aspect of early Christian Gnosis can certainly be seen in this light. Once one has formed a living, true idea of idealism, this becomes a kind of magic key to unlock understanding of its many variations, from antiquity through to the modern day. In the context of this book, we can give only a few examples, which can be usefully extended by reading a cogent history of philosophy.

For this reason we will pass over the great Platonists from the School of Chartres, and also the Platonism of the Platonic Academy in Renaissance Florence – all wonderful expressions of idealism, with a deep connection to an undogmatic and artistically tinged Christianity.

We will turn instead to later centuries. Rudolf Steiner, who emerged in his time in Vienna and Weimar as a scientifically trained Goethe researcher, created a true memorial to Platonism in his book *Goethe's World View*. The first part of this book, which marked the culmination of around 14 years of study of Goethe's world, is at the same time a critical evaluation of Platonism, which we can here equate with idealism. He addresses aspects of idealism that are highly important in our context, and to which we will return in Chapter 14 on realism. First – as a prelude – some words by Goethe:

> *Ur*-phenomenon: ideal-real-symbolic-identical.
> Ideal, as the ultimate thing that can be known;
> real, as known;
> symbolic, because it encompasses all instances;
> identical, with all instances.
>
> Concept is the *sum* and idea the *result* of experience; drawing the former becomes understanding, grasping the latter requires reason.
>
> Reason is dependent on what is developing, understanding on what has become….
>
> The idea is eternal and unique; that we use the plural too is not good. Everything we become aware of, and of which we can speak, are only manifestations of the idea; we express concepts, and in this sense the idea is itself a concept.[114]

And now an account by Steiner from *Goethe's World View*:

> Plato became aware what an important part was played in the human being's worldview by the fact that the world reveals itself to us from two sides. Through insightful evaluation of this fact he recognised that the sense world, seen on its own, cannot be accorded reality. Only when the world of ideas is kindled within the soul, and a person, when observing the world, can contemplate both idea and sense observation as a unified cognitive experience, do they have true reality before them.... Platonism is the conviction that the goal of every quest for knowledge must be the acquisition of the *ideas* that sustain the world and form its foundation. If someone cannot awaken this conviction within them, they fail to understand the Platonic worldview. But in so far as Platonism has influenced Western thought, it reveals another side as well. Plato went further than merely emphasising the insight that, in *human perception*, the sense world becomes illusion if the light of the world of ideas does not shine upon it: in his account he prefigured this with an assertion that the sense world itself, separate from us, is an illusory world, and that true reality is only to be found in ideas.[115]

Here Steiner points to the historical fact that the true kernel of Platonism has been understood in a one-sided way. Steiner goes on to say that Goethe felt this separation of idea and reality to be an unhealthy element in human thinking. While he did not clearly express this in words, nevertheless in his sensibility, and as a shaping impulse in his own worldview, lived the sense that healthy human feeling teaches us continually how the languages of direct observation and of thinking come together to reveal the whole of reality, and that cogitating thinkers have usually failed to consider this. Instead of empirically looking at how nature speaks to us, they have developed artificial concepts about the relationship between the world of ideas and human experience. To fully understand the deep significance this kind of thinking had in the worldviews Goethe encountered, which he felt to be unhealthy and which he sought to question, one has to consider how the Platonist stream, which makes the sense world evaporate as illusion, thus distorting its relationship with the world of ideas, was reinforced by a narrow philosophical understanding of Christian truth in the development of Western thought.

Steiner then describes the division between the element of thinking in the philosophical sense, and religious feeling. Here I would like to add that Plato himself knew that our thoughts are a reflection, are shadows of reality, and themselves have no living character, but that, manifesting as memories when we regard the sense world, these shadow-pictures point to the source of light where they originate. We need to shift our attention and raise ourselves to this light to encounter the sun of the world of ideas. We could also speak of a shifting of what has interposed itself *between* the light and our thinking, and engendered only a shadow in it.

Steiner's further comments run as follows:

> Due to a one-sided grasp of Platonism, the human soul is then sundered from the relationship between idea and 'reality'. The soul projects its justifiably conceived relationship to the divine world order upon the relationship that lives *within* it, between the world of ideas and the illusory world of the senses. Through such a mode of thinking Augustine comes to views such as this: 'Without any hesitation we hold that the thinking soul is not of one nature with God, for he allows no commonality, but that the soul can be illumined through its participation in the nature of God.' When this type of thinking is one-sidedly accentuated, the human soul loses the ability, in observing nature, to experience the world of ideas as the essence of reality. And that mode of experience is interpreted as unchristian. A one-sided view of Platonism comes to encompass Christianity itself. As a philosophical worldview, Platonism remains more in the element of thinking, while religious feeling immerses thinking in our feeling sensibility and in this way anchors it in human nature. Thus, the unhealthy aspect of a narrowly conceived Platonism was able to take root in the development of Western thought and gain greater traction than it would have done as a merely philosophical outlook.... And this Goethean worldview inevitably finds not only that the effects of a narrow Platonism live in Christian thinking, but that it also feels alienated from true Christianity when it encounters it in a form so imbued with this Platonism. In many of the thoughts that Goethe conceived to better understand the world lived a rejection of the Platonist stream that he felt as unhealthy. At the same time, though, as we see in many aphorisms, he did have a clear sense, with Plato, of how the human soul can raise itself to the world of ideas. He felt within him the living reality of ideas in his observations of, and enquiries into, nature. He felt that nature itself speaks the language of ideas when the soul unlocks this language. But he could not acknowledge the world of ideas as something separate and distinct, and in consequence he was able to say of the plant world that it was not empirical experience but idea. He felt that his mind's eye saw this idea as reality, just as the physical eye

> sees the physical aspect of a plant. In Goethe's worldview, therefore, the school of Platonism was recreated in its purity in respect of the world of ideas, overcoming the narrower interpretation of it which had diverted attention from reality.

I will now turn to a branch of cultural studies – aesthetics, or the study of the laws and foundations of beauty, primarily in art – which, while encompassing various different approaches, basically has only two starting points. There are countless books on this subject – from Plato's outlook through to information aesthetics, which attempts to establish a value-free statistical and semiotic account of given or possible artworks. In the eighteenth century, Alexander Gottlieb founded aesthetics as an independent philosophical discipline. In its various forms, it naturally reflects the worldviews and respective questions with which enquirers approach it. Thus, we have materialistic, idealistic, existentialist and formalist schools, to name but a few. This is scarcely surprising if we consider the multiplicity of worldviews that we have been examining in this book.

I want to briefly reflect on the two core elements in every artistic endeavour. Once we have firmly established these, each person can use their own individual key of understanding from instance to instance. I am referring to *content* and *form*; or, to put it another way, the *material* that is used – stone, colour, tone, word, one's own body, etc. – and the *form* created as outcome of the artist's activity, in the finished artwork. Someone with an idealistic outlook who does not share Goethe's view – according to which the artwork, similarly to creative nature, merges idea and substance in an inexpressible, higher unity – will always tend to see the intrinsically artistic element in the idea, the concept, the 'inspiration', or possibly in the *intention* to provoke or to edify. Whether the flute emits a shrill piping, or a single line appears on the canvas, or even the image of a blood-smeared hand, in this view of art the artist's philosophical-intentional element is central. This is why we often find in museums and exhibitions that a scholarly explanation is mounted alongside these works.

This kind of symbolism is a variant of idealism, or sometimes the expression of a particular ideology. A different trend involves working as little as possible on the material, or arranging it in space – for instance, as an installation – to create an artwork. This, too, makes a philosophy visible. Or natural rocks are set up somewhere in a particular way in the landscape. Phenomenalists would see only rocks, and likewise the Reichstag in Berlin covered in material as nothing other than a giant, package-type object. Anything they could not phenomenologically experience they would transpose into the realm of transcendental art theory, which naturally also has its significance. In my view, some of Joseph Beuys's works should be seen and evaluated from this perspective. Here, too, in principle the work needs 'explaining'.

Modern art unfolds between these positions – only the thought 'behind' the work is important, irrespective of whether it's a fat corner or a honey pump; and the material itself, what is 'foremost' and palpable, should speak. This range naturally also encompasses the Goethean approach to art, to which we will return later, since it actually inhabits realism. For now we are just outlining the aspect of idealism, since the realm of aesthetics is hugely more manifold and we have only begun to touch on it. Here we share Steiner's view that, strictly speaking, we should not seek some kind of *generally valid* aesthetic, which would entirely overlook the worth of an individual in their unique, creative endeavour. This view, which already to some degree embraces monadism (see Chapter 12) has, in my view, lost none of its actuality in the twenty-first century. Steiner writes:

> Just as every true artwork is the individual, personal expression of an individual person, so any critique can only be a very individual reflection of the feelings and thoughts that rise in the soul of the reflecting critic as they attend to the artwork in question. I can never say whether a poem is objectively good or bad, since there is no norm for good or bad here.[116]

Let us now draw together the threads of what we have explored in this chapter. Our starting point was Plato's doctrine of ideas in so far as the ontological aspect also applies to the substance of ideas themselves: the light of ideality, we might say, is the tangible substance of ideas. The sentence by the young Steiner, formulated in what we might call his idealistic phase, about the world of ideas as the primal fount and principle of all being, exemplifies the depth of such a worldview, of which there is of course a whole spectrum of possibilities. A young person who visits a school or wishes to train for a career will be quite naturally idealistic, for they are seeking something that, while it lives in their thoughts, still waits to be realised. There are political, religious and other ideals that can kindle great power within us – not to mention narrow ideologies that are often implemented with an exclusive, mathematist focus, in a fundamentalist and brutal way. Our past and present sadly offer plenty of examples of this.

In the vernacular, 'idealism' refers to any way of life that is marked by ideals and their realisation, often in the sense of charitable actions. This would be practical idealism. We have already spoken of metaphysical and ontological idealism. In Chapter 7 on rationalism we also touched on the area of *ethical* idealism. And in the preceding passage just presented, taking the example of art, we discussed something of *cultural* idealism. Yet so much more belongs to idealism that a detailed and to any degree complete account of it as a 'power in the world' would far exceed the scope of this book.

Nevertheless, as we end this chapter I wish to focus briefly on an interesting development in the field of particle physics with regard to what is known as 'symmetry'. In the chapter on mathematism we encountered researchers who wonderingly acknowledge the mathematical and geometrical laws at work in the cosmos. In this present chapter our starting point was primarily the question of what 'stuff' constitutes concepts, ideas and ideals. We also asked the same question for measure and numbers.

Now from the field of nuclear physics surprising perspectives are arriving. Franz Herwig Schopper, former director general of the CERN European Research Centre near Geneva, wrote an article for the journal *Bild der Wissenschaft* ('Science Update')[117] in which he described new findings relating to the smallest foundational constituents in nature. The atom, originally thought to be indivisible, increasingly turns out to be a kind of complex of the most divergent nano-particles and anti-particles, which are given the most diverse names. In relation to the big bang theory in the chapter on materialism, we have already heard about leptons and hadrons (see p. 42). Based on the four primary forces at work in the cosmos – gravity, electromagnetism and strong and weak nuclear forces – Schopper writes, 'In physics, "understanding" no longer means reducing phenomena to mechanical models – to levers, clockwork and screws – but trying to unite the known four forces into a single *ur*-force, which explains all phenomena.' (In passing, let me point out the mathematist procedure here. Schopper is speaking of a *single* primary force. Thus the concern is not with a universal formula, even if the one continually becomes the other; characteristic here is the focus of enquiry.)

Then Schopper continues:

> The properties of these forces are – as physicists see it today – ultimately determined by the symmetry property of space and time.... The combining of two forces corresponds to the discovery of a higher symmetry that contains them both. The transition from the higher to the lower symmetries (symmetry rupture) occurs at a particular temperature, that is, at a certain energy density. We are therefore concerned

> with a kind of melting point, above which a unified force exists, and below which the forces manifest separately.
>
> The following is a grandiose concept, and perhaps only a dream that physicists are chasing: they are searching for a super-symmetry from which all natural laws could be derived – separate forces from the primary force, and from them in turn the elementary particles. This super-symmetry is thought to hold sway above the unimaginably high temperature of 10^{32} degrees. At the transition to lower temperatures it is thought there will be several 'melting points' whose temperature we can roughly calculate today. As we pass each melting point, one force is separated off from the primary force: first gravity, then strong nuclear force and finally weak nuclear force, leaving electromagnetism.
>
> These ideas are leading to a revolution in our scientific outlook. Since Democritus, people have been trying to trace natural processes back to ultimate, indestructible foundations of matter and to the forces active between them. Advances in the last 200 years have consisted primarily in the discovery of ever-smaller material particles.
>
> Modern physics now teaches that we must relinquish this over-tangible picture: the 'ultimate principles' to which we seek to attribute the dizzying multiplicity of natural phenomena are no longer indivisible clumps of matter but abstract symmetries and their fracturing. In this sense we are departing from Democritus and coming closer to Plato, whose 'ideas' are far closer to our symmetries than the atoms of Democritus – a change whose importance has not yet been fully fathomed, either within or outside physics.

An extraordinary conclusion! – and all the more so if we consider that the creative Logos we mentioned in the previous chapter is constituted of speech and thought – in other words, ideas. Thus, in idealism, too, we would find an expression of the Logos that was at the beginning.

9

I Am an I – Psychism

At this point we have covered half of our journey through the different worldviews. We first described the three outlooks that draw their content and reality from the world of the senses: *phenomenalism* as manifest appearance; *sensualism*, which allows reality to consist only of sensory impressions; and *materialism* as primary experience of matter in its density and solidity. There then followed worldviews that take primary account of the thought element in the world and the human being: *mathematism* focuses on quantities, *rationalism* more on ethical qualities, and *idealism* on the existence-engendering world of ideas. In all three of these we were able to find, in principle, the cognitive approach of mathematism in its quest for the *one* linchpin of knowledge.

The following worldviews draw their powers of knowledge from the depths of the soul. Feeling and will enhance and complement our assimilation of the world through the senses and thinking. Harder to pin down than the previous outlooks, they also offer us a far deeper insight into the human soul on the one hand and into the world soul on the other. In the same way that material perception experiences material things, and thinking experiences thought, so soul-spiritual perception experiences soul and spirit. As an image we might say: the temple of truth and reality has twelve equally large doors and towers that all lead us into the inner sanctum, albeit by different paths and through different rooms. Very individually configured, and constructed of manifold materials, a kind of architrave connects the different motifs on each gateway into an architecturally meaningful whole. This also reveals reciprocal interlacing as an expression of multiple levels of interrelated meaning.

Especially when we come to psychism we discover interesting connections between the different worldviews, and as it were a key to understanding them. If we draw a clock face with phenomenalism at one o'clock, in a sense we find psychism in opposition to phenomenalism:

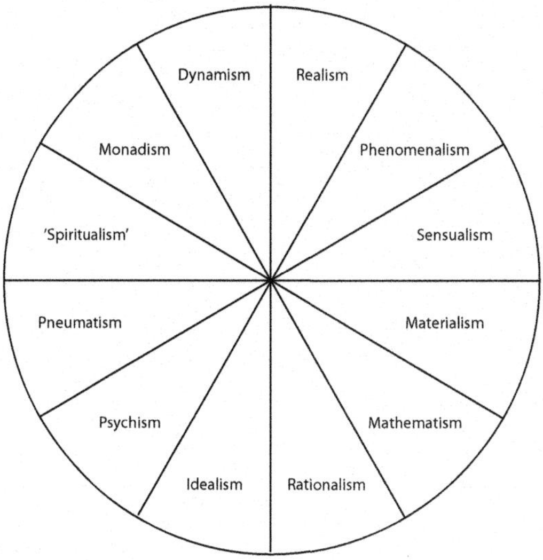

Thus, in the same way, every worldview has a direct connection with one other. The interesting thing about this schema is that it expresses a particular fact: each polar worldview is, on the one hand, a genuine opposite, but, on the other hand, also a true enhancement of the other! This means that the worldviews described below can already initially be understood simply by reversing one that has already been described. In this sense, psychism is initially a phenomenalism of the psyche, or of our whole inner world. It encompasses psychology, epistemology, mysticism – in other words the whole realm of self-knowledge, all that constitutes human interiority. The true psychist, who does not succumb to the materialistic error that the soul is *only* the product of bodily processes, will assume, in line with Empedocles' dictum that like only perceives like, that a kind of world soul exists in nature too, extending all the way to the stars. However, the psychist's primary interest is focused on their own inner processes, whereas that of the phenomenalist turns outwards to world phenomena.

The realm of psychism comprises, for instance, memories, experiences, dreams, moods, will impulses, feelings, thoughts and suchlike. The question arises here, as an epistemological one, about the participation of our being – of our I – in the origin of thoughts; and, ultimately, all psychist questions culminate in the question of the true essence of the human being in so far as our 'I' encompasses it. What we may call the ultimate questions of psychism lead us into the broad current of authentic mysticism.

Questions of this kind have accompanied us for long ages, albeit embedded in many different cultural, historical and religious milieux. From Heraclitus's phrase, 'I set out, questioning, upon the path to myself,'[118] through to key questions in the existential philosophy of the modern era, we can trace the different answers that have been given to the central issue of the nature of the self. At the same time we can recognise that, as in aesthetics, a *general* answer is inconceivable. In the realm of mathematist thinking and deduction, *one* answer can of course be given – which is why communities can gather under the umbrella of *one* common credo, or a *single* party programme, or *one* common scientific or artistic persuasion. In psychism the only valid answer is the one that existentially rises, repeatedly and ever anew, from the depths of the individual soul. Here each person is alone. Whether the answer is ultimately an immanent or transcendental one is initially of secondary importance. The abyss of our own being is one each of us must ourselves sooner or later endure, if not decipher! Below are a couple of examples of psychist questions and issues. From ancient China:

> I, Chuang Tzu, once dreamed I was a butterfly who fluttered here and there – in every respect I was the butterfly. I was aware of my butterfly existence and not of my human existence. Suddenly I awoke, and found myself lying there, once more as my usual self. But now I do not know if I was a man dreaming I was a butterfly, or whether I am a butterfly who dreams he is a man.[119]

And here, again, the Roman Marcus Aurelius:

> In what condition is my thinking soul now, and what do I make of it? And to what use do I put it? It is not, surely, void of spirit, not sundered and torn loose from a feeling of community? It has not, surely, grown one and merged with 'flesh' so that it is entirely ruled thereby?… What use does the thinking soul make of itself? For all lies enclosed therein. Everything else, whether dependent on your will or not, is dust and smoke.[120]

Then, in the realm of Christian mysticism, as represented by Hildegard of Bingen:

> The human being already has the heavens and the earth, and all creatures within him, and yet is a complete form, and within him everything

> already lives concealed.... The soul speaks: I am called to be the fellow of angels, for I am the living breath that God sent into the dry clay. Therefore I should know God and sense him.[121]

We find a deep philosophical foundation for psychism in the works of Johann Gottlieb Fichte. In his first introduction to his book *Science of Knowledge*, he immediately strikes a programmatic tone and homes in swiftly and directly to the nub of the matter: 'Regard yourself: turn your gaze away from everything that surrounds you and look inward: this is the first requirement that philosophy makes of her pupil. Nothing that is outside you is of concern here, but only yourself.'[122]

Since psychism ultimately leads us into deeper strata of the I, I will cite here a classical testimony to the most active I experience. This is Fichte's account of the 'fact-act' in his book *The Vocation of Man*:

> The I posits itself, and exists, by virtue of this mere positing, through itself; and also *vice versa*: the I *is* and posits its existence by virtue of its mere being. It is simultaneously the actor and product of its action.... Action and fact are one and the same thing, and therefore the 'I am' is the expression of a fact-act.[123]

It is interesting that one branch of existentialism points us in exactly this direction, though this is not to say that the philosophers who will briefly be cited here feel themselves to be following in Fichte's wake.

Let me also again mention in passing one characteristic of this present study. We are not concerned to, as it were, nail individual figures in cultural history to a fixed point, but rather to use the twelve worldviews as an aid or key for a more comprehensive understanding of what constitutes the world and how this comes to philosophical expression in different individuals. In the book's introduction I wrote of the developing multicultural society in our time, and of the possibility of making our thinking more flexible so that it can grow beyond its narrower confines – not an easy undertaking, but a rewarding one.

Karl Jaspers, one of the great existentialists of the last century, writes, 'In my existence I am fundamentally different from the existence of all things, because I can say: I am.'[124] Jean-Paul Sartre, in turn, touches on another aspect of existentialist questions:

> Atheistic existentialism declares that if God does not exist, there is at least a beingness whose existence precedes essence, a beingness that

> exists before it can be determined by any thought; and that this beingness is the human being or, as Heidegger says, human existence. What does it mean here to say that existence precedes essence? It signifies that human beings first exist, find themselves present, appear in the world, and that only after this do they acquire a particular essence. If we human beings, as existentialism sees it, are indefinable, this is because we are initially nothing. We only *become* later, and we become what we make of ourselves. Thus there is no human nature because there is no God who conceives of it in thought. Human beings are not only as they regard themselves as being but as they intend to be; we understand ourselves after existing in the way we desire in accordance with this urge to exist. We are nothing other than what we make ourselves into.[125]

These are all burning questions of our daily existence. Intrinsic to psychism, also, is a kind of conflict situation; for the 'fact-act' of active self-registering is the outcome of an inner conflict, as well as of a deep suffering. This becomes especially apparent in places in the works of Sören Kierkegaard, where he vehemently rejects what he calls abstraction and pure thinking. Below are two passages about true subjectivity and existence:

> In the language of abstraction, what constitutes the difficulty of existence and of those who exist never really manifests, and far less are its difficulties explained....
>
> In pure thinking we sit in profundity up to our ears, and yet sometimes one gains the impression that something distracted abides over it all because the thinker does not recognise what it means to be an existing human being.
>
> Every knowledge of reality is possibility; the only reality about which a person who exists is more than knowledgeable is their own reality, since they are present in it; and this reality is their absolute interest. Abstraction requires us to become devoid of interest so that we can know something; ethics requires us to be infinitely interested in the nature of existence.
>
> The only reality that there is for an existing person is their own ethical one; of all others they only know, but true knowing is transposition into possibility.
>
> The reliability of sense perception is deception. Greek scepticism has already sufficiently proven this, and modern idealism likewise. The reliability that knowledge of history seeks is also only deception, since

> the knower only knows about a historical reality after dissolving it into possibility.... Abstraction is possibility, either preceding or subsequent. Pure thinking is a phantom.[126]

How would idealism, rationalism or mathematism answer such questions? In all these passages one has a clear sense of inward-looking phenomenalism. But the polarity is still more far-reaching – as is the need for their mutual complementarity. Whereas the phenomenalist seeks the greatest objectivity, we find here a very strongly pronounced subjectivity. Where the phenomenalist intimates and discovers ever deeper strata of the phenomenal cosmos, a psychist intimates and discovers ever deeper strata of their own self. Where the phenomenalist attends outwardly, the psychist does so inwardly, and so on.

It does of course require a good deal of self-knowledge to understand the world, and a sound knowledge of the world – with our human surroundings too – to grasp ourselves better, and above all more clearly.

Goethe once said, 'If I know my relationship to myself and to my outer surroundings, I call that truth. And so each person can have their own truth, and yet it is always the same.'[127] It would, however, be quite mistaken to see in this saying of Goethe's a defence of a shallow and arbitrary pluralism. We should see his words here only in the light of his poem 'The Mysteries'. This is demonstrated by the seriousness of his enquiries and the rigour of his view of knowledge. We have already heard what he has to say about the dividing line between reason and understanding (see p. 87). While his works are an almost inexhaustible cornucopia of psychological insight – one need think only of his *Faust* – his relationship to epistemology is more problematic. He had a deep disinclination for all merely theoretical thinking: 'Theory in itself is of no use except in so far as it makes us believe in the complex of phenomena.'[128] Nor did he have any interest in accounting for the source of thinking itself. Thus, in one of his *Zahme Xenien* ('Tame Invectives'), which he wrote after 1824, thus after the age of 75, he says:

> How on earth did you get so far?
> They say, what you did was well done!
> My child, by taking very good care
> Never to think about thinking.

By contrast, a genuine, deep mysticism comes to expression in many of his writings. We can recall here the quotation, cited in the chapter on sensualism, about the deep affinity between the sun and the human eye. The first part remains more in the domain of a sensualist inwardness, while the second part leads us into the realm of clear religious mysticism:

> If the eye were not sunlike by nature
> How could we see light shine?
> If God's potency did not live in us
> How could we delight in the divine?

This aspect of Goethe becomes beautifully apparent in one of his *Proverbs in Prose*:

> Kepler says: 'My highest desire is to perceive the God whom I find everywhere in the outer world also within me.' This noble man felt, though unaware of it, that at this moment the divine in him was most closely connected with the divine in the universe.[129]

But the paths of psychism are so deeply and closely interwoven that it is hard to find an Ariadne's thread through the labyrinth. In this quest we should always remember the words of Conrad Ferdinand Meyer, which he puts in the mouth of his character Ulrich von Hutten:

> I'm not a book ingeniously spun
> But just a person full of contradiction.

To be a little abstract for a moment, a survey of the approaches and scope of psychist experience shows us two poles between which different schools move. At one pole we have a primarily *descriptive* phenomenology of inner experiences, as it were an inventory of the soul; at the other an effort to grasp the creative moment where these experiences *emerge* – not in the sense of tracing causes, as often in psychoanalysis, but with the question of how certain contents are engendered within me. Both poles are, really, two distinct circles, but can be joined in a lemniscate.

Edmund Husserl can be seen as a representative of inner phenomenalism. I will quote a passage from the second volume of his now classic *Logical Investigations,* where he is concerned with 'Investigations into the Phenomenology and Theory of Knowledge', and more particularly with the 'need for phenomenological investigations as epistemological preparation and clarification of pure logic':

> These are... accounts of that most general of modes that belongs to the further sphere of an objective theory of knowledge and, intimately connected with this, a purely descriptive phenomenology of experiences of thinking and cognition.... This whole sphere must be examined as epistemological preparation and clarification of pure logic; our immediate investigations will therefore relate to this domain.
>
> Pure phenomenology represents a realm of neutral enquiries in which diverse sciences have their roots. On the one hand it serves as preparation for *psychology* as *empirical science*. It analyses and describes (specifically as phenomenology of thinking and perceiving) the experiences of thinking, judgement, perception that are to find an explanation of their origin, an enquiry into their nature, through empirical, lawful means. On the other hand, phenomenology accesses the 'sources' from which 'spring' fundamental concepts and ideal laws of *pure* logic, and to which they must be traced back in order to establish for them the 'clarity' required for a critique and understanding of pure logic.[130]

If we start from a purely descriptive phenomenology of inner experiences – here those of thinking and perception – a pure psychology based on the inner results of observation lies close at hand. At the beginning of the twentieth century the pioneers of psychoanalysis sought to achieve this: Sigmund Freud, Carl Jung, Alfred Adler, Roberto Assagioli and many others. However different their models of interpretation, they belong to the large number of researchers in the field of psychist enquiry. In fact, every person who practises self-observation is in this sense a psychist, too.

Now an almost exclusive phenomenology of the soul is not yet sufficient, although it can form the point of departure for astonishing findings, as apparent for instance in C.G. Jung's works. Fichte's experience, continued and carefully deepened, leads to other experiences. Both paths can enhance one another in so far as the one path, the descriptive, can illumine the many rooms and inhabitants of our soul, whereas Fichte's path discovers and investigates the actual house-owner – our I. Let us look at this more carefully.

Carl Gustav Jung, who founded complex or analytic psychology, is an outstanding way-marker in the history of psychist enquiry. Whatever one may think of his research results, as a physician who achieved wide-ranging success, he infinitely expanded the perspectives and complexities of psychology, above all in the realm of the personal and collective unconscious, in whose depths he discovered enigmatic archetypes. These archetypes, which as it were crystallise into the conscious mind in the ever-recurring motifs of fairy-tales, dreams, delusional ideas and so forth, include the *self* also. This is

> the central archetype of order. The totality of the human being. Symbolically represented as circle, square, the quaternity, child, mandala etc.'[131]… The self is a property superordinate to the conscious ego. It encompasses not only the conscious but also the unconscious psyche.[132]

Jung describes the archetypes as 'incapable of consciousness, that is, transcendent': 'One should not for a moment give oneself up to the illusion that an archetype could ultimately be explained and thus finished and done with.'[133]

Consequently, Jung pushes through a door usually locked and barred against the human activity of cognition. In our enquiries into the depths of the psyche, we resemble a wanderer who enters the world of their own dreams and inner images but there retains full self-awareness and can roam at will. Fascinating worlds open to us as, if you like, a participating observer. With this in mind it is worth reading Jung's autobiography, *Memories, Dreams, Reflections*, from which the above quotations are taken. It is moving to learn in his own words about the beginning of his own specific encounter with the unconscious. The experience described below came at a time when he was subject to intense, emotional images and fantasies:

> To grasp the fantasies that moved in my subterranean depths, I had as it were to let myself fall into them. I not only felt resistance to doing so, but also extreme fear. I was afraid of losing my self-control, and falling prey to the unconscious – and what that meant was all too clear to me as a psychiatrist. Nevertheless, I had to risk taking possession of these images. An important motif in these considerations was that I could not ask anything of my patients that I myself did not dare undertake. The excuse that patients had someone to help them did not wash. I knew that the supposed 'helper' – me, in other words – had not yet himself had direct perception of these matters, but that I possessed at best a few theoretical preconceptions of dubious worth. The thought that this adventurous undertaking in which I was becoming entangled was one I was embarking on not just for my own sake, but also for my patients, helped me hugely at several critical moments.

Jung continues:

> It was during Advent 1913 that I resolved to take the decisive step (12 December). I sat at my desk and once more reflected on my fears; and then I let myself fall. It seemed to me as if the ground literally collapsed beneath me, and I plummeted into dark depths. I could not avoid a feeling of panic. But suddenly, and at not too great a depth I found myself, to my great relief, standing upright on a soft, soggy mass. Yet I was in almost complete darkness. After a while my eyes accustomed themselves to the dark, which seemed now like a deep twilight. Before me lay the entrance to a dark cave, where a dwarf stood. He seemed made of leather, as if mummified. I pushed past him through the narrow entrance and waded knee-deep through ice-cold water to the other end of the cave. There, on a ridge of rock, was a red, shining crystal. I grasped the stone, lifted it and discovered a cavity beneath it. At first I could discern nothing, but at last I saw flowing water in the depths. A corpse floated by, a youth with blond hair, with a head wound. He was followed by a giant, black scarab; and then, rising from the watery depths, appeared a (red) newborn sun. Blinded by the light, I wanted to put the stone back on the opening, but as I did so a fluid pushed its way through. It was blood! A thick stream of it spurted forth, and I felt nausea. It seemed to me that the flow of blood lasted an unendurably long time. At last it ceased, and the vision ended.
>
> I was most deeply distraught at these images. Naturally I saw that the *pièce de resistance* was a hero and sun myth, a drama of death and renewal. The rebirth was emphasised by the Egyptian scarab. At the end, a new day should have dawned, instead of which came the unbearable stream of blood – which seemed to me an entirely abnormal phenomenon. But then I recalled my blood vision from the autumn of that year, and I relinquished all further efforts at understanding.[134]

Here we see the 'descriptive moment' mentioned before; and there are always two elements: the active observer and their surroundings. But on these and similar paths one cannot find one's I at all, though – to remain metaphorical – we may intimate the one who fashions our garment, which we refer to as 'self'. What is meant by this?

Our 'I' (a term used in clear distinction to the 'ego' of psychoanalysis) is our most essential core of being – though now I am prefiguring the realm of 'spiritualism' [see translator's note on p. 13). It is eternal and indestructible, a divine element of which we can gradually become aware.

To put it simply, it is embedded in the largely inherited dress of soul and body, which is therefore an expression of a genus. It is of this material that a huge part of our unconscious consists. While it is also divine in nature, it is not identical with *my I.* It is sub-individual, or also extra-individual. In my view, that is the nature of Jung's 'self', which he sought to approach by enquiring into the *collective* forces at work in us, and their relationship to myths and images of the past. In doing so, he was able to draw findings important for modern humanity's soul life from the mysterious cauldron of the archetypes – for instance, the presence of the 'shadow' as balance to our conscious soul life, or the psychological reality of 'anima' and 'animus' as 'personification of female nature in the man's unconscious, and of male nature in the woman's unconscious'.[135] And much more besides.

But nothing about the unique, true I of the human being, our core of being, which also survives after death and exists before birth, and passes through recurring lives on earth in ongoing, progressive evolution. Lessing acknowledged this, and Rudolf Steiner was able to study it in a strictly scientific manner. That Steiner, in addition, laid the foundation for a science of the spirit, which is in principle available to everyone,[136] is mentioned here only because it also belongs to the realm of psychism. Gerhard Wehr, a man deeply knowledgeable about cultural history, once attempted a 'Confrontation and Synopsis' of the works of both C.G. Jung and Rudolf Steiner. What he says about the theme of reincarnation seems significant to me because, in my view, this marks the sharpest point of division between the two investigators. Having written of Steiner's view of the 'dynamic of the self', he goes on:

> This dynamic aspect is what also enables him to transcend each respective human life on earth and keep in view the I that passes from one embodiment to the next. C.G. Jung does not share this movement of thought. Jung, from the very outset, accorded no place to the idea of reincarnation. This absence of the idea of recurring earthly lives represents an important point of difference between Jung and Steiner.[137]

This dynamic of the self grows only in the soil of I-driven 'fact-acts' or self-realising actions. At the level with which Jung was preoccupied – if we are considering the existence of the I – there is only an either–or. So we can ask where, according to Jung, the soul's individual uniqueness ends. Below is a revealing passage – though it should not be forgotten that this direction of enquiry naturally also belongs to the realm of psychism:

> With increasing depth and darkness, the deeper 'strata' of the psyche lose their individual uniqueness. They become ever more collective as we 'descend', or in other words approach autonomous functional systems, at last becoming universal and at the same time extinguishing in the materiality of the body, that is, in chemical entities. The body's carbon is precisely that – carbon. At the very 'deepest' level, psyche is altogether 'world'.[138]

That is, the 'world' in which the substance of our soul – and not the I – originates. These are two paths that do markedly differ from each other: the 'extinguishing' of individual uniqueness, on the one hand, and a conscious step into the I's 'super-consciousness', on the other, which relates to normal consciousness in the same way as waking life relates to deep sleep. Novalis tellingly expressed this experience. As is well known, he made a thorough study of Fichte's 'I philosophy':

> Imagination places the world of our future either in the heights, or the depths, or in metempsychosis. We dream of travelling through the cosmos, but is the cosmos not within us? We do not know the depths of our spirit. The mysterious path leads inwards. In us, or nowhere, is eternity with its worlds, the past and the future. The outer world casts its shadow into the realm of light. At present, of course, it appears to us so dark, lonely, shapeless, but how differently it will seem to us when this obscurity is past and the shadow-body has moved away. We will then gain more pleasure than ever, for our spirit has been deprived.... The highest task of education is to take possession of our transcendental self, at the same time to be the I of our I.[139]

Goethe regarded the idea of reincarnation as a self-evident truth. It encompasses also the experience of the indestructibility of one's own I-hood as a 'living form (humanly) configured and self-developing', as he writes in one of his 'Primal Words – Orphic' poems:

> As on the day that lent you to the world
> The sun stood by to bring the planets' greeting,
> You soon began to flourish and went on thriving
> According to the law that governed your arriving.
> And *thus* you must be, yourself never evading –
> As said the ancient sibyls and the prophets:
> For neither time nor any power can break
> The living form configured and self-developing.

Yet this awakening to one's own higher nature is accompanied by a kind of death process. Our awareness of self, or we might say 'ego', bound up with the sensory world and created in interplay with it – we can recall here the relevant comments in Chapters 4 and 5 on sensualism and materialism – has to undergo a profound transformation. This kind of 'existentialism', too, brings turmoil and pain that can only really be understood by someone who has experienced them.

The spiritual-scientific path of schooling inaugurated by Steiner is no exception here either. Intensive, independent study of spiritual-scientific content and meditation – these often play over into each other – do not primarily furnish exciting experiences, a kind of fast food to still one's hunger for higher worlds; rather, they establish the foundation for progressive transformation of our whole human nature, which must in a sense be ploughed over if something new is to enter it. Or take another image for the process: a new pipe is needed to conduct the new wine. That this process is arduous and painful is confirmed by all who have ever encountered their lower nature, with its 'shadow' formed of all our secret desires and illusions.

One of the indispensable conditions for progressing on the path of soul development is an unsparing perception of our own deficiencies. These experiences of our own subjectivity are usually accompanied by a more or less vivid sense of our powerlessness to perceive what makes nature and the cosmos around us 'most inwardly cohere'. We feel that our whole state of mind needs to change if we wish to gain further insight. And transformation usually begins with the first serious step on the path of knowledge.

A gradually developing enhancement of our perception of nature and strengthening of our own experiences in thinking are among the first and most important results of such work: sensory things and the thinking schooled in the sense world must first be thoroughly experienced before deeper spiritual experiences arrive. All practice of this kind that we do brings about a progressive strengthening of our whole configuration of soul – and thus, also, of our I nature. Through such experiences – as a kind of echo – an increasingly vivid experience can arise of the higher self, of what reincarnates time and again in an ever-new ego garment: this is without father, mother, gender, but is, rather, universally human. An image for this would be that of a flower that has grown from the ploughed soil of the soul. Its leaves are our past lives on earth, which can unfold stage by stage in our own awareness.

This is a process, in the Goethean phrase, of 'dying and becoming'. In one of Goethe's *Proverbs in Prose*, we find the striking sentence: 'Our whole artistry consists of relinquishing our existence in order to exist.'[140] The 'configured form' can then arise anew in the divine.

The many diverse experiences that can be had on similar paths are difficult to classify. What I have just described may happen, but there are also higher experiences of the self without any clear impression of past lives crystallising in our awareness. Besides this, the terminology used to describe such experiences varies, as does, in some circumstances, their nature, depending on the cultural milieu in which a person lives. There are also sudden influxes of knowledge that have not been preceded by any discernible 'death process'. But if we look a little more deeply at our own past biography, something of this is likely to become apparent to us.

Sufism, which originally developed from ascetic schools of Islam, also testifies to deep mystical experiences. Below are several passages from Islamic mysticism, followed by sayings of Christian mystics. But this is not to say that the same realities are being invoked here. Let us simply take them as further testimony of psychist wisdom, whose 'substance' prefigures the realms of pneumatism and 'spiritualism':

> The contemplative perceives that he can best grasp the roots of his 'I' if he extinguishes his usual idea of this 'I'. When it has become clear how the appearance of the secondary I obstructs our union, it becomes unendurable.
>
> Between You and me stands an 'I am' that torments me. Oh, through Your 'I am' rid us of my 'I am' that stands between us. (Divan)
>
> 'I liberated myself from my "I" as a snake sheds its skin,' says Bastami.

Here, two concepts overlay each other and stand in opposition, although they belong in an essential and ultimate unity: a derivative or secondary subjectivity and an absolute subjectivity in which the former originates and in which it remains rooted. The drama and the dizzying scope of mystical experience – which seeks to grasp and fathom the inexpressible secret of existence – lie in becoming aware of this encounter of two concepts.

> Is it You? Is it I? That would be two gods. How distant, how distant from You, to assume a duality. One being, Yours, always utters itself beneath my not-being. To wish to add my wholeness to Your wholeness would be a double deception. (Divan)

At the very moment when the contemplative risks this dangerous leap into the abyss, in which the last trace of his egohood goes under, and he relinquishes awareness of his separate existence, the secret of his soul – the immaculate virgin – becomes apparent. The guest, with whom he conversed when haunted by the overweening ego, now shows itself to be his true self.

> I am become the One I love, and He whom I love has become me! We have merged as two souls in a single body. To see me means to see Him, and to see Him means to see me. (Hallaj)
>
> I saw with the eyes of God. He asked, 'Who are you?' and I replied, 'You yourself.' 'Then how should I name you? I must name you my I.' (Vadan)[141]

And here is Meister Eckhart: 'There is a power in the soul that sheds what is most coarse, and is united with God: that is the tiny spark of the soul. The bowl must break, and what is within it must emerge.'[142]

In his own telling manner, frequently apparent in his *Cherubinic Wanderer*, Angelus Silesius says:

> I must be Mary and bring forth God from me,
> If he is to grant me bliss in eternity.
>
> If Christ in Bethlehem a thousand times is born
> And not in you, you're still forever forlorn.
>
> God dwells within a light to which no way is found;
> Except you become the light yourself, you'll stay eternally blind.

With these passages this chapter is approaching its close. One question remains unanswered, of course: about the source of thinking, in so far as it relates to our human I. Just as there are two poles in psychism, the *descriptive* and the *active*, so this holds true, too, in relation to thinking. The experience of passive thinking was called *intellectus patibilis* in medieval times, and that of active apprehension, *intellectus agens*. Long and bitter disputes were held about whether people themselves – actively – form their thoughts: that is, whether they are *engendered* in the depths of the soul, or whether thoughts are only imparted to them from without. The latter view was propounded by the Arab philosopher Averroes on the basis that only divine apprehension can be called active.

In the context of this book we can say, somewhat simplifying, that the I that experiences and embodies itself in the sense realm does experience thoughts as a given that it, as it were, spectates upon. But if we strengthen our interior life[143] through study, observation and meditation, then eventually we can discover how, out of the depths – or heights – of our true self, a radiant inner sun power, as the creative light of thinking, shines forth and permeates our whole existence: The smaller I becomes one with the greater I. And, since the human being and the world are interwoven with countless threads, someone who develops this practice experiences not only a marked intensification of their own thinking, but also a deeper connection with the whole cosmos: phenomenalism and psychism turn out to be ever more intrinsic to each other. The human being and world being find each other in a new unity.

It was an experience of this kind that gave rise to the words of Sigismund von Gleich which I will quote to end with. They form part of a longer poem[144] and can be regarded as a profound meditation that helps us increasingly render the dynamic aspect of psychism into personal experience:

> Man, know yourself, as *I* within the I!
> Lose yourself to find yourself as *I*!
> You err within as long as you do not say:
> 'I live, but not I: the Christ lives in me!'
> The I, the ray of thought from cosmic light,
> In thinking illumines the *I* of worlds;
> And it is God's *I* that speaks within I being,
> As soon as this I kindles the cosmic light.
> Only because the *I* is the universe
> Can I think the universe inwardly in me;
> And because it is love, the *I* unites
> Most intimately world *I* with my human being.

10

I Am the Universe – Pneumatism

In the course of our account so far, we have also noted the dangers that lurk in every worldview when it is taken too far in a single direction. For every worldview becomes one-sided the moment it claims to be the whole truth. Psychism is no exception. In the previous chapter, we tried to consolidate the overarching concept of psychism and then take this as the basis for discussing various subsidiary concepts. This showed diverse aspects of something that, at core, is probably the most mysterious and enigmatic power we possess: our I.

The saying by Heraclitus, 'I set out, questioning, upon the path to myself,' has lost nothing of its topicality in our present era, with its ego trips, self-discovery workshops and biographical counselling. No doubt there are many causes of this, both cultural and psychological in nature. The great demands on us of our work, along with the extroversion of our media culture, and perhaps also the many uncertainties attendant on an unstable employment market, repeatedly face us with the fact that we are looking for, and questioning, ourselves. No doubt the spiritual dimension of our existence plays a not insignificant role here, for it too urges its rights in a more or less insistent way.

Yet it would not be the right path to look only inward, or to judge the world situation only from a psychist perspective. Psychology, also, as a partial domain of psychism, cannot lay claim to being more than an auxilliary science. The danger of navel-gazing is great, for the depths of the human psyche are unfathomable! Here we need to practise the virtues of a middle way. Fundamentally it is fitting for human beings to find themselves in the interplay between self-knowledge and knowledge of the world. An important contribution is made here not only by the worldviews of external perception – phenomenalism, sensualism and materialism – but also by those of inwardly engendered *world perception*, starting from pneumatism.

Just as psychism and phenomenalism correspond to and complement each other, so also with sensualism and pneumatism. The action, or substance, of the worldviews of *pure thinking* is both dissolved and heightened as it passes through the 'inner' worldviews. The unifying principle of mathematism, the ethical stance of rationalism and the creative nature of idealism then help to develop inner eyes and ears, leading not only to the assumption of a world soul, as in psychism, but also to true perception of it. However disagreeable people with a more materialistic outlook may find the subsequent worldviews, they are fully legitimate in the multi-coloured circle of reality and truth.

When the I, through its 'fact-actions' or self-realising dynamic, has encompassed itself autonomously, it tends to start growing beyond itself. This I growth corresponds to a real inner birth in the soul. Just as a healthy child starts heading out into the world, so does the newborn I. Where the child is focused on experiencing the sense world, the I seeks to live its way into the world's spiritual life, through the unfolding of hidden and, in the Goethean sense, also unacknowledged senses. In the foreword to the didactic part of his *Theory of Colours*, Goethe tells us that we must conceive of colours and light 'as belonging to the whole of nature: for she it is, in her entirety, who seeks especially to reveal herself to our sense of vision'. He then continues:

> In the same way, the whole of nature discloses herself to another sense. One shuts one's eyes, one opens them, one listens attentively, and from the gentlest breath to the fiercest noise, from the simplest tone to the highest harmony, from the fiercest, most passionate cry to the softest, reasonable word, it is only nature who speaks – revealing her being, power, life and conditions, so that a blind person, denied the infinitely visible world, can encompass in hearing an infinite life. In the same way nature speaks down to other senses, to those both known and unknown or unacknowledged; thus she speaks to herself and to us through a thousand phenomena.[145]

This 'infinite life' is the focus of pneumatism, and is for it an unfathomable spirit within the universe, experienced somewhere between intimation and vision. In antiquity, pneumatism often manifested as pantheism, and it usually has a more or less ecstatic character. The pneumatist seeks the soul's communion, its merging, with the spiritual universe. Just as, say, in a sensualist experience of summer, we seek a sensory communion with the elements, so the pneumatist in us yearns for an intimate connection with the hidden powers of nature. The borders between these two realms of experience are, however, fluid. A certain loss of self within the elements is no doubt the danger lurking here, and quixotic people with a penchant for their own subjectivity are exposed to it. Once, when I was speaking about pneumatism in a seminar, and kept quoting from books as I was doing so, a participant suddenly said, loudly and with a note of quiet triumph, 'But for such experiences I don't need all these books in front of me!' I merely replied, 'True enough, if it's only a matter of myself – then I don't need these books with their outlooks. But if it's a matter of understanding my fellow human beings more profoundly, sooner or later I can't avoid engaging with them. And that is what this course is trying to help us do.'

And yet, in a way she wasn't completely wrong. The experience she was referring to, and knew, can sometimes engender a deep sense of our unity with the world and certainly initiate a change in our lives. This is also how we can interpret the legend of Hubertus, in Chapter 3 on phenomenalism – at which point all our books and all our knowledge are simply noise and mirrors. This feeling of participating in something larger than ourselves, something more all-encompassing, was very beautifully expressed by the American philosopher Ralph Waldo Emerson:

> In the woods, we return to reason and faith. There I feel that nothing can befall me in life – no disgrace, no calamity… the currents of the Universal Being circulate through me; I am part and parcel of God.[146]

We find a similar experience also in Hölderlin's *Hyperion*:

> I have raised myself above the patchwork made by human hands, I have felt it, the life of nature that is higher than all thoughts; if I even became a plant, would it matter so much? I will *be*. How could I lose myself from the sphere of life, wherein eternal love, common to all, holds all together? How should I be sundered from the bond that unites all creatures? This does not rupture so easily as the loose alliances of the age. It is not like a market day that brings people noisily together in a crowd before they all go their separate ways again. No! By the spirit that makes us one, by the divine spirit inherent in each person and common to all! No! No! In the bond of nature, loyalty is no dream. We divide only to be more inwardly united, more godly, in peace with everything, with ourselves. We die so as to live.[147]

The religious impulse that lives in this worldview is also striking, which is why we find traits of pneumatism in all religions that have a connection with the spiritual in nature. This does not, of course, exhaust the scope of pneumatism. When the psychist experience leads us beyond ourselves, it manifests, as we saw in the previous chapter, as mysticism of the soul or, as here, as nature mysticism. Deep experience of one's own core of being in the one case, and in the other an experience of the soul of the world. A feeling-imbued growing into my inner divinity *through my own willed I* in psychism, and a will-impelled growing out into a higher world through *my feelings* in pneumatism. Whereas the 'act-fact' frees the I from its bodily constraints, here the world of feeling is released from its ties to the world of the senses. It is lent wings, if you like, and by this means the ecstatic experience arises that we referred to. (The Greek word *ek-stasis* means, in fact, 'standing outside oneself'.) In religion this plays an unmistakeable role, although there are also other religious paths.

Recently I read the flyer for a dance workshop, written by the course leader herself. It expresses the ecstatic element in a very idiosyncratic and insistent kind of language. Here it is:

> In this workshop I will try to take a further step into the jungle of my heart – into this zone within, called the soul, that continually brings me into movement, even if I sometimes forget it.
>
> I am a surfer on the ocean of feelings, thinking they are my own when I ride the waves heroically, or thinking others have caused them when I fall and go under.
>
> Sometimes, in brief moments of ecstasy, I sense what feelings really are to me: the water out of which our souls are born, that sustains us all and unites us.
>
> I want these moments to expand in my life, like the rings made by a sinking stone in a great lake.
>
> I wish to follow the trail to the source they spread from.[148]

This too is pneumatism!

You can find further examples aplenty of this outlook on life, above all by looking back through history. It is certainly not only Christians with a mystical-ecstatic tendency who, as it were, merge with the universal divine. The wise seer and esoteric teacher Al-Ghazzali, an important representative of medieval visionary mysticism, even spoke of 'the soul being swallowed' by the divine Father of the cosmos. In one of his books he describes very telling connections between the world of the outward senses and the supersensible world. In the heart, he says, a window to both of them opens:

> *The Wonders of the World of the Heart*
> The wonders of the world of the heart are infinite in number. But the nobility of the heart rests upon one thing, and is above all wonderful, even if most people ignore it.
>
> That upon which the heart's nobility rests is a twofold thing: knowledge and power.
>
> The nobility that rests upon knowledge is in turn twofold. All people can understand one of them, but the other is more mysterious than the first, not known to all, and of very rare quality. The first, palpable to all, is this: that the heart possesses the power of all sciences and arts, through which we understand all arts, and can read and understand what is found in books, such as geometry, arithmetic, the art of healing, star-lore and jurisprudence. Although the heart is a unity that cannot be divided, nevertheless all these sciences have space within it; indeed, the whole world within the heart is no more than an atom in the ocean. In the space of a moment it raises itself in thought from the earth to the loftiest heights of heaven, and strides through the world from dawn to sunset. Bound to the world of earthly dust, humankind measures the whole span of the heavens, perceives the scope of every star and, through the arithmetical art, tells the number of a person's cubits. With cunning we entice the fish from the ocean floor, and the bird down from the realms of air, and make the strongest of beasts, the camel, elephant and horse, serviceable to us; and everything that exists in the world as wonderful sciences we make our trade and occupation.
>
> All this knowledge we gain by means of the five senses. Therefore it is an outward knowledge, and everyone knows the way to obtain it.

Al-Ghazzali continues:

> Yet more wondrous than all this is that window that opens within the heart towards the supersensible world of the heavens, just as five gateways open to the sense world outside the heart. This sense world is called the corporeal world, while the supersensible world is known as the world of spirits. Most people know only the corporeal world that is perceived through the senses, but that is shallow and unfounded; and as a path to knowledge they know only that of the senses, and this too is shallow.

> But do not believe that the window of the heart opens only towards the world beyond the senses in sleep and death. This is not so. Rather, when a waking person chastises themselves and cleanses their heart of anger and desire and all bad nature, and all evil in this world, and then settles in a secluded place, closes their eyes, quietens the senses, and connects their heart with the higher world by continually saying silently – not aloud with the tongue – 'Allah! Allah!', until they lose awareness of themselves and the whole world, and no longer know of anything but God, then, although they be awake, that window opens, and what others see only in sleep they perceive in waking.[149]

One of the profoundest of Angelus Silesius's sayings comes to mind here:

> Two eyes the soul has: one into time doth see
> The other turns towards infinity.

In another verse, he points to the enigmatic common root of both inner and outer senses:

> In spirit the senses are all one sense and view:
> Who sees God, tastes, feels, smells and hears him too.

This is not to say that both seers have experienced precisely the same thing. To determine this would require a detailed study beyond the scope of this book. But for now it is enough to recognise that pneumatism is at work in both, and at a very high level.

One motif that is almost ubiquitous, wherever this worldview governs experience, is love. Without the expression of the powers of love, pneumatist experience is scarcely conceivable. As examples of this, I would like to quote two figures in the twentieth century for whom love plays a key role. Then we will consider what it is exactly that, let us say, average pneumatists experience, located as they are between the world of the absolute I – in psychism – and the world of the absolute spiritual cosmos in 'spiritualism'. As mentioned earlier, the boundaries are fluid, but the hues of each worldview are nevertheless consistent. It is like two rivers uniting into a larger one: sometimes you can clearly see the differently coloured currents continuing side by side for miles.

The Egyptian Anwar El Sadat, a statesman who tragically lost his life, and the French scholar Jacques Lusseyran describe in their respective autobiographies experiences that clearly *also* point towards what we have been discussing. In terms of both human qualities and worldview, their experiences are very significant.

Sadat, who as a young officer had already played an active part in the political dynamics of his country, was not spared imprisonment. As the inmate of Cell 54, he gained an outlook that eventually led to him being awarded the Nobel Peace Prize in 1978.

> During my time in Cell 54, my material needs grew ever fewer, and at the same time, the bonds that chained me to the material world started to fall away from me, one by one. My soul, relieved of its earthly freight, was now free and rose aloft, like a bird that flies off into the sky, into the outer regions of existence, into infinity. As long as we have material needs – desiring to be this thing or that, hoping to possess this thing or that – nothing will ever belong to us, but we will, rather, be owned by these 'things'. A slave of things does not exist as a human being. Only when we cease to seek material values can we really become master of ourselves and so truly exist.
>
> Once liberated from the narrow confines of an existence of mundane sufferings and trivial feelings, a person can pass over into a new, hitherto unknown, broader and richer world. Their soul will enjoy absolute freedom, uniting with life in its entirety, will overcome time and space. Through this process of liberation, a person develops the power of love and all earthly powers. Even those that might confuse a person's thinking will contribute to the attainment of complete inner peace, and so lead us to absolute bliss.
>
> This is why I consider my last eight months in prison to have been the happiest period of my life. I was led into the new world of self-denial, which enabled me to merge my soul with all other beings, to expand it and enter into communion with the Lord of all existence.

Sadat continues:

> Without love a person may grow to a great old age, but will feel that they have never really lived. They will feel they have omitted something very important, and sense that, however great their achievements, in reality they have accomplished nothing.
>
> I have always felt these things. For me, love has always been a high, human ideal; but in Cell 54 I suddenly discovered that love really is the most beautiful of all. The moment the heavy chains – those that had bound me to my 'smaller self' – had fallen away, I began to enjoy the love of God. I

> felt that I lived within his love, that love was the law of life. Only in love did life – no, being itself – become possible. Without love, being ends.
>
> Love helped me to recognise myself. As my individual being united with the greater being of all creatures, my starting point, the love of homeland, that is, for Egypt, became love for all that is, the love for God. And out of the feeling of love, I embarked on the fulfilment of a duty (my responsibility), whether in those last months in prison, immediately after my release, as member of the revolutionary committee, or today, when I am President of Egypt.
>
> This is why I am a tireless advocate of love. Love is human certainty towards all social contingencies. If you live in love, you possess spiritual fertility. Loving means giving, and giving means building, while hatred, on the other hand, means destroying. The hatred that held sway for 18 years in Egypt before I became President was a destructive power that tore down everything, and we are still suffering its consequences.[150]

Jacques Lusseyran lost his sight as a child through an accident at school. But he found a different light that he continually perceived around him, and in which he always felt himself embedded. He discovered the world which Goethe, who called his enquiries into nature 'pantheist', described in the words we quoted at the beginning of this chapter:

> One shuts one's eyes, one opens them, one listens attentively, and from the gentlest breath to the wildest noise, from the simplest tone to the highest harmony, from the fiercest, most passionate cry to the softest, reasonable word, it is only nature who speaks – revealing her being, power, life and conditions, so that a blind person, denied the infinitely visible world, can encompass in hearing an infinite life. In the same way nature speaks down to other senses, to those both known and unknown or unacknowledged.

These inner senses, of which Goethe speaks, opened to Lusseyran. We particularly find the pneumatist element where he tells us that he 'bathed in light', and sense the special quality that lends wings to his words:

> Immediately, the substance of the universe drew together, redefined and peopled itself anew. I was aware of a radiance emanating from a place I knew nothing about, a place which might as well have been outside me as within. But radiance was there, or, to put it more precisely, light. It was a fact, for light was there.

I felt indescribable relief, and happiness so great it almost made me laugh. Confidence and gratitude came as if a prayer had been answered. I found light and joy at the same moment, and I can say without hesitation that from that time on, light and joy have never been separated in my experience. I have had them or lost them together.

I saw light and went on seeing it, though I was blind. I said so, but for many years I think I did not say it very loud. Until I was nearly fourteen I remember calling the experience, which kept renewing itself inside me, my 'secret', and speaking of it only to my most intimate friends. I don't know whether they believed me, but they listened to me, for they were friends. And what I told them had a greater value than merely being true; it had the value of being beautiful, a dream, an enchantment, almost like magic.

Lusseyran continues:

The amazing thing was that this was not magic for me at all, but reality. I could no more have denied it than people with eyes can deny that they see. I was not light myself, I knew that, but I bathed in it as an element which blindness had suddenly brought much closer. I could feel light rising, spreading, resting on objects, giving them form, then leaving them.

Withdrawing or diminishing is what I mean, for the opposite of light was never present. Sighted people always talk about the night of blindness, that seems to them quite natural. But there is no such night, for at every waking hour and even in my dreams I lived in a stream of light.

Without my eyes light was much more stable than it had been with them. As I remember it, there were no longer the same differences between things lighted brightly, less brightly or not at all. I saw the whole world in light, existing through it and because of it.

Colours, all the colours of the rainbow, also survived. For me, the child who loved to draw and paint, colours made a celebration so unexpected that I spent hours playing with them, and all the more easily now that they were more docile than they used to be.

Light threw its colours on things and on people. My father and mother, the people I met or ran into in the street, all had their characteristic colour which I had never seen before I went blind. Yet now this special attribute impressed itself on me as part of them as definitely as any impression created by a face. Still, the colours were only a game, while light was my whole reason for living. I let it rise in me like water in a well, and I rejoiced.

> I did not understand what was happening to me, for it was so completely contrary to what I heard people say. I didn't understand it, but no matter, since I was living it. For many years I did not try to find out why these things were going on. I only tried to do so much later, and this is not the time to describe it.

The world of tones likewise became a profound experience for him.

> Sounds had the same individuality as light. They were neither inside nor outside, they were passing through me. They gave me my bearings in space and put me in touch with things. It was not like signals that they functioned, but like replies.
>
> I remember well when I first arrived at the beach two months after the accident. It was evening, and there was nothing there but the sea and its voice, precise beyond the power to imagine it. It formed a mass which was so heavy and so limpid that I could have leaned against it like a wall. It spoke to me in several layers all at once. The waves were arranged in steps, and together they made one music, though what they said was different in each voice. There was rasping in the bass and bubbling in the top register. I didn't need to be told about the things that eyes could see.
>
> At one end there was the wall of the sea and the wind rustling over the sand. At the other there was the retaining wall, as full of echoes as a talking mirror. What the waves said they said twice over.[151]

In this last description we find pneumatism and internalised sensualism connected with a marked element of phenomenalism. It testifies to a great love of Creation. In later passages of his autobiography Lusseyran will also speak of the 'fact that the world is so clearly a unity'. To his friend Jean he said:

> There is only one world. Things outside only exist if you go to meet them with everything you carry in yourself. As to the things inside, you will never see them well unless you allow those outside to enter in.[152]

The character of this mobile and dynamic worldview should by now have become apparent, as well as what distinguishes it from psychism, though naturally the one can always slip over into the other. If the soul in psychism is comparable to a lake from whose depths 'I' experience rises towards the surface like a golden fish, pneumatists immerse themselves in the life stream of the world. Lusseyran 'bathed in light'; he put on light, as it were, like a garment. He says the tones 'went right through me', and he experiences light, tone and life as a unity.

Since every worldview is, indeed, a view, what is the gaze of the pneumatist really falling on? Let's consider this question more thoroughly. Whereas the mathematist regards the numerically comprehensible structure of the universe, and the rationalist, by and large, the realm of ethical meaning, the pneumatist initially regards *life* itself. Where the idealist has in view the ideal and purposeful substance of the world of ideas, the pneumatist primarily focuses on the diverse life and activity of nature in its growth and decay, in the rhythmic harmonising of all its powers. Not only in his botanical works, but specifically as a poet, Goethe was able to describe in masterful words this world of etheric formative forces, of spiritually creative powers that underlie all living processes in nature.[153]

The scene, part of which is reproduced below, comes from the first part of *Faust*. We should attend here to the effect that the sign of the macrocosm elicits in Faust, and the longing awoken in him by the earth spirit, above all where the latter appears to speak out of 'floods of life'. At the same time we are shown once again the great truth that Empedocles similarly formulated – that only like perceives like. In relation to the twelve worldviews, this means that one must, as it were, become *similar* to them in order to experience them. This is straightforward in so far as this twelve-fold quality resides in all of us; but it is in turn not straightforward to live our way into an element that initially feels alien to us. Life teaches us this at every turn, but it also shows that, by practice and never-failing goodwill, we can come ever closer to this goal.

> Was it a god who wrote this symbol here,
> That quietens the tumult in my breast,
> That makes this poor heart full of joy
> And with mysterious power
> Discloses nature's forces all around me?
> Am I a god? Such light is dawning!
> In these pure features now I see
> Nature at work before my soul.
> Only now makes sense what the wise recount:
> 'The world of spirits is not closed;
> Only your mind is shut, your heart is dead!
> Awake, O pupil, up, assiduously
> Bathe your earthly breast in dawning light!'

He looks at the symbol.
How everything is woven into one:
One element in the other acts and lives!
How heavenly forces rise and fall
And pass to each other golden pails!
On wings of fragrant blessing
From heaven they delve through earth,
harmoniously through the cosmos ringing!

What spectacle! But alas, no more than that!
Where do I grasp you, nature infinite?
Where are your breasts, your springs and founts of life
That nurse both heaven and earth, for which
The withered heart so longs –
You flow, you pour; and yet I pine in vain?
Reluctantly he turns the book over, and sees the symbol of the earth spirit.
How differently this symbol works upon me!
You spirit of earth are nearer to me; now
I feel suddenly my forces rally,
I glow again, as if from newer wine.
I feel courage to venture into the world,
To bear the woe and weal of earth,
To bluster, blow with tempests
And not to tremble in the shipwreck's havoc.
But clouds come over me –
The moon conceals its light –
The lamp's put out!
Steam rises. Around my head
Flicker rays of red – a shiver
Wafts down from above, grasps hold of me!
I feel it – you hover round me, spirit invoked.
Disclose yourself!
Ha! There's something brimming in my heart:
To feelings new
All my senses are stirred up!
My heart is wholly given to you, come what may!
You must! You must! Even if you should die!
He takes up the book and secretly utters the symbol of the SPIRIT. A red flame flickers and the spirit appears within it.

SPIRIT Who calls me?
FAUST (*turning away*) O terrible countenance!
SPIRIT You have drawn me to you powerfully,
Long sucking at my sphere,
And now –
FAUST Woe, I cannot endure you!
SPIRIT You pant and beg to see me and to hear
My voice, to see my countenance;
To your mighty appeal I bend
And here I am! What piteous terror
Takes hold of you, superior man!
Where is the loud, brave invocation,
Where is the breast that did engender
A world within itself, which it bore and fostered?
Where the heart, with leaps of joy
That proudly dared to raise itself to spirits?
Where are you, Faust, whose voice rang up to me
Who sought me with all his forces, urgently?
Was it *you* who now, from the tempest of my breath
Cowers in the depths of life, in dread alarm:
A fearful, crumpled worm?
FAUST Must I yield to you, a form of flame?
This is me. I'm Faust, and of your kind!
SPIRIT In streams of life, in a storm of deeds
I surge up and down,
Weave hither and thither.
Birth and grave
An infinite ocean,
A fluid weft,
A glowing life:
Thus I weave at the world's roaring loom
And weave the godhead's living cloak of time.
FAUST O busy spirit who puts a girdle round
The whole wide world, how close I feel to you!
SPIRIT You resemble the spirit that you comprehend,
Not me! [*vanishes.*]
FAUST [*collapsing*]. Not you?[154]

The ubiquitous 'spirit' of the earth is certainly no 'busy' spirit, as the despairing scholar believed in his 'inner tumult'. This world of soul-spiritually living agency, which has conjured visible nature before us since time immemorial, is an extraordinarily ramifying and interlinked interplay and mutual resonance of creative energies that gives rise to the living garment of the godhead: nature itself. If we break through the shell of positivist preconception, and through mathematism, rationalism and idealism clear a path towards the creative ideas, we have already come a long way. If we then complement what has thus been achieved with an experience of psychism and pneumatism – albeit only in a preliminary way initially – a truly new world opens before us: from the world of phenomena we slip, as it were, into the world of beings, from effects to agencies, from the I to the universe.

Usually, this all occurs very gradually. First the elements – earthiness, fluidity, airiness and fieriness – are experienced, as it were, as harmoniously forming and ever self-reconfiguring etheric agencies. Here we can start to perceive a manifold life and activity of elemental beings who increasingly manifest as the earth soul. The next steps require precisely what Goethe states in the saying quoted earlier (p. 107), that we 'relinquish our existence in order to exist'. We can say that from psychism onwards this 'dying to become' is the overriding motto for *existentially* penetrating these 'inner' realms of the human being and the world. Only then can the Jacob's ladder of simultaneously self- and god-aware angel beings gradually manifest, which would then lead us into the realm of 'spiritualism'. Whereas sensualism is primarily to do with a sensory experience of the world, pneumatism is concerned with its experientially supersensible nature. Whereas materialism shows us the material foundations of existence as indispensable for humanity's evolution, 'spiritualism' reveals its spiritual foundations. The ultimate ontological *question of substance* is posed by the interplay of materialism and 'spiritualism', whereas sensualism and pneumatism *primarily* have to do with the development and function of organs of perception. As we've seen, Angelus Silesius said:

> Two eyes the soul has: one into time doth see
> The other turns towards infinity.

The other eye is *initially* the mysterious 'third eye' situated roughly at the root of the nose in the centre of the forehead. In relation to the whole human being we also speak of chakras or of lotus flowers, whose motions within us creatively accompany the manifold movements of the soul-spiritual world, by uniting with them.[155]

It is now of outstanding importance that pneumatism not only has a past history but has further evolved as we have. Prior to the stage of psychistically conscious and powerful I experience, manifesting from the dawn of the modern era onwards for ever-broader swathes of humanity, ecstasy marked the highpoint of pneumatism. Already in the Pauline experience of the Christ-I, however, a new experience of the spirit is making headway, although initially attainable only by a few. I believe that even Peter, called the 'rock', had to wait a long time before the level of this new, pneumatist experience was granted him – perhaps only in the Ascension scene, as it is recounted in the Acts of the Apostles. There, the resurrected Christ was assumed into a 'cloud', or, in other words, united increasingly with the earth's elemental atmosphere. He himself had announced this: 'All authority has been given to Me in heaven and on earth… and lo, I am with you always, *even* to the end of the world' (Matthew 28, 18–20). Only *after this,* during the Whitsun event, did Peter grow into his full greatness. When Christ walked on the water (e.g. Matthew 14, 22f.) – which we can certainly interpret as a spiritual awakening – Peter had not yet achieved the inner stability to sustain himself in the 'ocean' of soul and spirit. We may assume that, in his spiritual openness, Peter, the fisher, was repeatedly granted a pneumatic experience, even if this did not intensify into ecstasy. Only slowly did he wrestle his way through to the I stability that is the precondition for modern pneumatist experiences.

The advancing from authentic psychism to a pneumatism of conscious, I-governed immersion in the soul-spiritual realm of the world should be counted as one of the primary tasks for alert people today, especially as we develop into the future. No later, at least, than the beginning of the very diverse New Age movement, as it developed in the 1960s and subsequently, have we known that increasing numbers of people find the world of spirit to be accessible to them and are attempting to 'walk' on its waters. In this sense, pneumatism finds its place within the twelve outlooks on humanity and the world, with its appeal, still quiet amid the noise of our externalised civilisation, to what can help us find our cosmic dimension anew. A poem by Manfred Kyber will round off this outline and at the same time lead us on to the next chapter:

Take me up into your unity,
single universe of life,
bathe me in the purity
of your ocean's crystal wave.

Give me the elixir to drink
that brings forgetfulness to me,
let the soul in its yearning sink
into the ring of eternity –

where in diamond distances
stars circle stars in the heavenly ether.
Star angels, towards the stars
guide my eternal spirit further.[156]

11

The Jacob's Ladder – 'Spiritualism'*

> And Jacob went out from Beersheba, and went towards Haran. And he lighted upon a certain place, and tarried there all night, because the sun was set; and he took of the stones of that place, and put them for his pillows, and lay down in that place to sleep. And he dreamed, and behold a ladder set up on the earth, and the top of it reached to heaven: and behold the angels of God ascending and descending on it. And, beheld, the Lord stood above it, and said, I am the Lord God of Abraham thy father, and the God of Isaac.

What does this dream image tell us? A hierarchically ordered dance of different orders of angels embodies the manifold agency of God for human beings and the earth: the ladder *stands* upon the earth, and Jacob obeys the word of God, who assures him of his presence and his aid:

> The land whereon thou liest, to thee will I give it, and to thy seed; and thy seed shall be as the dust of the earth, and thou shalt spread abroad to the west, and to the east, and to the north, and to the south: and in thee and in thy seed shall all the families of the earth be blessed. And, behold, I am with thee, and will keep thee in all places whither thou goest, and will bring thee again into this land; for I will not leave thee, until I have done that which I have spoken to thee of. And Jacob awaked

* This terms 'spiritualism' and 'spiritualist' could easily be confused with the 'spiritualist' movement, with which it has next to nothing in common. It refers, rather, to a 'spiritual' mode of apprehending reality. When the term is used in the text, it is placed in quotation marks to indicate this crucial difference.

> out of his sleep, and he said, Surely the Lord is in this place; and I knew it not. (Genesis 28, 10–16)

This is God as historical agency, who continually sends his angels – his messengers – to help humanity in its evolution. In the religious documents of all cultures and all ages there are countless testimonies to God's agency. And the godhead itself is, respectively, a tribal God, a national God and a God for all human beings. The hierarchically ordered divine realm corresponds to a pattern or structure of constituting bodies in us that has been named differently in every culture. Most simply we can call it 'trichotomy', owing to the three levels of body, soul and spirit, to which we can accord differing, and relatively clearly delineated functions.

To these factors Christianity adds the fact that at the beginning of the Christian era the Son of God – the Christ Logos – revealed himself to humanity as a human being. He overcame death and implanted in each person, along with the seed of individual immortality, the power, also, of transformation, of ongoing spiritualisation of the body. With the advent of the new human being, a new earth and heaven will eventually arise.

Acknowledgement of the divine world is one cornerstone of 'spiritualism'. Another is the assumption that the spirit simply is *everything*, and matter *nothing*. An ontological back-and-forth can arise between these realms, or we can say an interdependency: matter condenses from spirit, and resolves back into spirit again. On the one hand, matter is the 'end of the ways of God' (Oetinger – see p. 44), and, on the other, the spirit is the alpha and omega of cosmic evolution. The rhythm of ontological development would at the same time be a true equilibrium, or right relationship, between the extremes of 'spiritualism' and of materialism with their many variants and intermediate stages.

We find a wonderful example of 'spiritualism' in the Song of the Lord in the *Bhagavad Gita*, one of humanity's most ancient holy books. In the passage below we hear how Krishna instructs the hero Arjuna before a decisive battle. Arjuna catches sight of his near relatives in the enemy camp and wants to relinquish the fight. But the God Vishnu, as Krishna, who is serving Arjuna as his charioteer, explains to him the need for the battle. This 'Song' is a part of the Indian epic the *Mahabharata* and is doubtless the most widely read book of Hindu teaching. It was written down roughly between the third and second century BC.

Thus Arjuna spoke to the Lord of hearts.
'I do not wish to fight!' he sighed, and fell silent.
But, with a friendly smile, Krishna approached.
And there, in view of both armies,
Spoke as follows to the hesitant one:

KRISHNA
You sorrow where no reason for sorrow is,
And your words lack true wisdom.
The wise do not sorrow at what lives,
Nor at death. Never was there a time
When I was not, nor you; those too,
The rulers of the earth, have been always; nor will
The time ever come in future when even a single
One who is true will cease to exist.

Whatever is real lives for ever. As in the life of the body
Childhood is followed by youth, and then by age,
So birth and death follow always
For the vessels in which the spirit dwells.
What is immortal in human hearts
Will appear anew in bodies.
The wise know this, and sorrow not.
It is your sensory life alone
That binds you to substance, cold and heat,
That makes you feel joy and pain.
This life is brief and full of flux:
Bear it with patience. The human soul
Grown strong within itself
Raises itself above these things,
Remaining tranquil in pain and pleasure,
Enduring through eternity. What is true
Will always remain real, and what is not real
Can never be in truth. And he who knows the truth
Has the wisdom to distinguish
Between being and appearance.

Know, therefore: immortal is the spirit
That is the spring and potency of all life.
It cannot fail and die, and no one can

> Destroy the ground of being, which is eternal.
> Only the fleeting shadow bodies, that
> We call the temple of the spirit, which spirit
> Indwells and overshadows, die.
> So let them die, Prince! Battle bravely.
>
> He who says, 'I have killed', or thinks
> That he can be killed, is judging falsely.
> He does not perceive his true self, that never
> Can be killed, and does not kill either.
> It is never born, and never ends.
> Beginning and end, and change are only
> Dreams concerning temporal things.
> Forms fade away but the spirit remains.
> And they who know the nature of all things,
> Which is a nature uncreated and
> Imperishable, also know
> That even when the form passes away
> The essence never is destroyed.[157]

Let us compare the above with a few passages from the chapter on materialism. What would de la Mettrie say? Let's remind ourselves (p. 48):

> The human body is a machine.... Let me say in passing that, in my view, the better and more trustworthy of two doctors will always be the one well-versed in the physics and mechanics of the human body, who leaves to one side the soul and all anxieties which this chimera causes fools and the ignorant, and concerns himself only with the pure sciences.

Here we meet the crassest of opposites, and it is not all that easy to allow equally deep justification to both. Where the materialist digs himself ever deeper into the sand of the earth like a crab, the 'spiritualist' rises ever higher up the ladder of spirit. The risks are plain: earth obsession on the one hand and fleeing the earth on the other. It is well known that ancient cultures were spiritually oriented to a high degree.

The change towards a more materialistic view of the world started back in ancient Rome. And this is one reason why Gnosis – still a strongly spiritual outlook which, after its earlier forms, took hold in the second century of the emerging Christian Church – was so bitterly contested by the Church Fathers. They experienced it as a one-sided 'spiritualism', above all in Docetism, which refused to acknowledge Christ's actual embodiment as a human being and his resurrection. The accusation of one-sided 'spiritualism' also in some senses applied to the later Cathar movement, in which the Church likewise saw a danger for Christianity. In the high Middle Ages, as is well known, the horrific crusade against the Cathars destroyed countless human lives and a flourishing culture. In the Christian camp of those times the word 'tolerance' would have been inconceivable.

It is also interesting that in Gnosis, which transplanted itself through many channels, albeit often in modified form, we find a classification of human beings according to the degree of their *spiritual vision*. Here, the 'pneumatics' take precedence, followed by the 'psychists' – who are only able to raise themselves to belief. The lowest level is occupied by the 'hylics' or 'somatics', who remain caught up in 'hyle', or matter. Today the very reverse is the case through the broadest swathes of humankind: the seed planted by de la Mettrie has flourished in abundance. Nevertheless, since the late 1960s, more and more books with a spiritual content have appeared. Film-makers, too, have in recent years also, for instance, taken up the theme of 'angels' in various ways. Let us take a closer look at all this.

Dionysius the Areopagite, often called 'Pseudo-Dionysius' by researchers, imparted to Western culture a ninefold hierarchy of the angelic orders.[158] Rudolf Steiner's spiritual research both confirmed and substantially enlarged on this tradition, even to some degree updating it.[159] The spiritual hierarchies – from the angels upwards through the archangels, Archai, Exusiai, Dynameis and Kyriotetes to the Thrones, Cherubim and Seraphim who stand before the face of God – are like a 'levitating' periodic table of spiritual elements, in the same way that Mendelejeff's periodic table takes us increasingly downwards into gravity. And yet they work down into the depths of material substance, each hierarchy opening in love to the next higher level.

We are concerned here with diverse ranks and qualities of angelic being, and with an evolutionary plan according to which lower orders can grow to become ever-higher ones. Ecclesiastical hierarchies, such as we find in the Catholic Church, are supposed to reflect the angelic orders.[160] The choirs of angels are divided into three groups. The spiritual emanations of the highest triad, received from God, are taken up by the next lower order, which passes it on in turn to the lowest triad, which intervenes directly to shape world epochs and individual lives. While these spirit beings are individual and differ from each other, the 'One' holds sway over them all.

With inconceivable love they realise the plan of Creation – and do so in collaboration with the still somewhat intractable tenth hierarchy, that of humanity. They do not have the problem of freedom insofar as they do not wish to do anything other than to fulfil God's will.

The spiritual hierarchies also include the realm of adversarial powers, the 'fallen angels', so that 'spiritualism' really encompasses infinite worlds, along with the spheres in which human souls dwell before birth and after death in a process of continual transformation. Goethe, who has many spirit beings appear in his *Faust*, was aware of God's far-reaching 'educational' programme, whereby humanity, too, will ascend higher rungs of Jacob's ladder. On 11 March 1832, shortly before he died, he said to Eckermann:

> After the well-known six days of Creation, God certainly did not rest; he is still working continually as on the first day. To compose this gross world from simple elements and to let it roll year in, year out, in the rays of the sun, would doubtless have given him little joy if he had not also had the plan of establishing on this material foundation a nursery for a world of spirits. He is therefore now continually active in higher natures in order to educate the lesser ones.

Dionysius reveals himself also as a mathematist in the way in which he 'numbers' the spirit beings, and points to the unifying 'One'. The following commentary on the 'Perfect and the One' could also have found a worthy place in Chapter 6 on mathematism:

> Thus much on this subject! But let us now, if acceptable, proceed directly to the conclusion, to the *most important point* in our account! For divine revelation expresses, on the one hand, everything, and everything together at once, of the originator of the whole world and, on the other, celebrates him as the *One*. The perfection of the divine is not merely intrinsic perfection, uniformly determined for and by itself, and in every respect most entirely perfect, but is also perfect in so far as it is past all pitch of perfection in accord with its surpassing perfection. It encompasses everything limitless, is extended beyond all and every boundary and is not constrained or fixed by any being, but rather extends itself in its never-exhausted enrichments and infinite influences to everything and beyond everything. But it is named perfect both because it is capable of no growth and is forever perfect, and because it suffers no diminution, containing within itself, as it does, everything as

> prior possession, and overflowing in one inexhaustible and at the same time over-brimming and never-waning bounty, by virtue of which it perfects everything that is perfect and fills it with its own perfection.
>
> But the 'One' is named God because, through the surpassing excellence of the *one* unity, it is uniquely everything and because, without detaching itself from the One, it is the cause and origin of all. Nothing of all things is without participation in the One, but just as every number participates in the overall unity, so that we speak of *one* twofoldness and *one* tenfoldness, and *one* half, *one* third, *one* tenth, so the whole of the world and each smallest part of it has a part in the One, and everything only exists by virtue of the existence of the One. But it is the One that is the origin of all.[161]

'Spiritualism' is the life breath of religion and its highest expression. At the same time it does not always manifest in culture in its purest form. Like every other worldview it is not only saddled – as we can see in the above passage – with others, but mingled with other elements that can obscure its inherently crystalline clarity: materialistic visions of the other world, for instance, or the very widespread 'spiritualist' movement (see translator's note on p. 15. Audible or visible 'spirit manifestations' belong in the realm of materialism, which is in fact likewise far deeper and more complex than orthodox and so-called hard-nosed materialists believe. Even if outer and interior worlds, or earthly and spiritual worlds, are often divided only by a very thin veil, we ought not to confuse the contours and qualities of each world. In a holistic worldview, no doubt, spiritual and material beings and forces are in a mysterious accord and interplay, but – from the human perspective – matter is initially matter, with all its phenomenalistic, sensualist and materialistic constituents, and world spirit is world spirit, and as such can only be experienced through pneumatic and 'spiritualist' modes.

In the 'near-death' experiences that have become ever-more prominent in recent years, we usually see, for example, a strong materialistic quality. It is not that these experiences are inauthentic or that they may not change a person's life for the better, but they are nevertheless not spiritual experiences in the pure sense. They are, though, significant transitional experiences. If, for instance, I imagine the world of spirit inhabited by muscular angels, this opens the way to a worrying falsification of the truth.[162]

The following account by Betty J. Eadie clearly shows this coarsening of the spirit. In her book about an 'extraordinary near-death experience', she describes, among other things, certain angelic beings: 'I saw that [these angels] are giant men, very muscularly built, with a wonderful countenance about them. They are magnificent spirits. I understood simply by looking at them that to struggle against them would be an act of futility.'[163]

This is reminiscent, is it not, of the Masters of the Universe – muscular and armoured plastic dolls produced by the entertainment and toy industry.

This phenomenon (of near-death experiences) can perhaps be partly explained by the fact that these people experience a powerful divide between their soul-spirit and their body, but that they nevertheless remain connected with the spirit by a thin thread. In near-death experiences their core of being dwells de facto in the world of spirit. But their immersion in the material sense world continues to resonate in their soul-spiritual awareness, coarsening the perceptions they have of the spirit world. For this reason, though such accounts are often genuine, at the same time they can be misleading. They also acquire a tragic aspect because countless readers swallow them at face value. The real nature of supersensible experience is, after all, supersensible, and can only be perceived appropriately in a purely pneumatic and 'spiritualist' manner.

Given that it is non-spatial and supratemporal, the very concepts we form of it require something quite different of our consciousness than the three-dimensional world with which we are so familiar. Spatial distances fall away entirely, and the flow of time is raised into a higher unity in which past, present and future merge. Anyone who has had such experiences can confirm this. It is difficult to convey the character of this higher dimension without succumbing to an abstract conceptual acrobatics. Interior spaces, human-cosmic interiorities, open first of all, with beings and occurrences that are devoid of all external sensory form. The seer grows into these, as it were transforming into them. As suggested already, this is a process of creative penetration, and an expansion of awareness, by means of which the seer – the meditant – participates in the consciousness of higher beings. Even the first steps into these entirely new light dimensions require a fundamental transformation of our ordinary, waking consciousness: 'here' there are no muscular angels, like heroes from Star Wars, let alone 'space observation stations', as is reported in other accounts.[164]

Naturally, supersensible seers have to translate their experiences into images and words, into human language, in order to be understood, and in a certain sense this applies also to many near-death experiences. In the case of vivid, pictorial accounts, these first have to be properly interpreted – all the more so in the case of the greatly coarsened images in the experiences referred to here. If one takes them at face value – which is what usually happens nowadays – they are absolutely misleading. It is a key task of 'spiritualism' to awaken awareness that the post-mortem, spiritual world cannot look like the physical sense world that surrounds us here. A no less important task lies in interpreting or testing these images to see what truth they contain. Otherwise, what should we think of the following experience which is, on the one hand, to be regarded as thoroughly authentic and yet, on the other, in its *form of communication*, clearly reflects the materialistic structure of the narrator's consciousness? Because of this, the experience becomes simultaneously shockingly true and untrue.

Dannion Brinkley was struck by lightning through his telephone's receiver, and blasted across the room – after which he was declared clinically dead. Similar to many others in comparable situations, he reported seeing a being of light with whom he began to ascend, flying through

> energy fields that looked like prisms of light. Some of this energy flowed like great rivers, while some eddied like tiny streams. I even saw lakes and small pools of it.... Through the mist I could see the mountains the color of deep-blue velvet. There were no sharp peaks and craggy slopes with jagged edges in this mountain range. The mountains were gentle, with rounded peaks and lush crevices that were a deeper blue.
>
> On the mountainside were lights. Through the mist they looked like houses turning on their lights at twilight. There were many such lights, and I could tell by the way we swooped down and accelerated that we were headed directly for them. At first we moved toward the right side of this mountain range, which was enormous. Then we banked left and moved swiftly toward the shorter side.
>
> How am I moving? I wondered, looking around at the heavenly landscape beneath us.[165]

Here again, we see fairly earth-bound ideas. The strongly materialistic character of these experiences is especially apparent in the chapter 'Boxes of Knowledge': Brinkley experiences a kind of stage, upon which

> I was able to count the Beings as they stood behind the podium. There were thirteen of them, standing shoulder to shoulder and stretched across the stage.... Each one of them represented a different emotional and psychological characteristic that all humans have.... In spiritual terms, these Beings went far beyond the signs of the zodiac....
>
> Now more than ever I knew that this was a place of learning.... In the presence of these Beings of Light, I would become knowledge, and would know everything that was important to know....

> I had only to think a question to explore the essence of the answer.... Ask and you shall perceive, is the way I sum it up.
>
> ... these Being were among the greatest of their kind.... [They] came at me one at a time. As each one approached, a box the size of a videotape came from its chest and zoomed right at my face.
>
> The first time this happened I flinched, thinking I was going to be hit. But a moment before impact, the box opened to reveal what appeared to be a tiny television picture of a world event that was yet to happen. As I watched I felt myself drawn right into the picture, where I was able to live the event. This happened twelve times, and twelve times I stood in the midst of many events that would shake the world in the future.[166]

Here, we meet a kind of surreal world: a 'spiritual' dimension with mountains and buildings, and a landscape that strikes us as a *sensory* realm through which one can fly. With all the respect we should of course accord the narrator, with this we are not far from Superman illusions.

In the excarnate phase, we find that angelic beings have a consciousness that is simply alien to our time-bound mode of reflection, and that they can experience vast aeons as simultaneous. They know of the developmental powers at work in our cosmos. In the same way that a gardener knows the blossoms of developing plants, so higher beings see the outcome of our thoughts, feelings and actions. Accordingly, Brinkley was granted a view of developmental forces at work in history. These beings do not fly through space, like that world-famous caricature known as Superman, but are simply 'present' wherever their consciousness moves to. The more God-filled their nature, the closer they are to the all-embracing godhead. This is also true of human beings in life after death. If the forms of consciousness that we bear with us across the threshold are full of *one-sided materialism*, we will find little power to unfold our 'wings'. In fact, the human soul often takes a long time to free itself from the habits of its consciousness and gradually grow in knowledge and perception into worlds of spirit. For 'there', knowledge is, in fact, movement and action in the spirit. Agnosticism, or simply a rejection of all spiritual reality during earthly life, quite logically conduct us into a region of the spirit where initially only leaden darkness holds sway. As far as our modern culture is concerned, we can assert, without pathos, that action is urgently needed in developing a spiritual view of life.

The 'spiritualism'–materialism polarity should by now be quite apparent. Birth is the embodiment – incarnation – of the pre-existent spirit, the beginning of a further development that we owe to the earth's 'solidity'. But at the same time we must ensure that our existence in matter does not too greatly overshadow the presence of the spirit within us and the world. This is an urgent task also of a form of pedagogy that meets modern needs.[167]

We have a sense of our own individuality thanks to the body in its self-contained seclusion. In English we speak of a person as 'some*body*' and no one as 'no*body*'! The integrity of our whole constitution – of spirit, soul and body – is the foundation of our individuation. Here, a purely materialistic experience of the world provides an indispensable service to us. But equally indispensable for an *enlargement* of our individuality is the proper inclusion of spiritual insights. Materialism has to do with birth processes, and 'spiritualism' with death processes. To immerse ourselves in matter and to find ourselves in the spirit is an interplay that can only be fully accomplished in *realism*, as we will see. In his compressed and deeply expressive sayings, which are well worth meditating on, Novalis left us significant insights into these things. Again, the boundaries with pneumatism are of course fluid here:

> Humanity is, as it were, the higher sense of our planet, the eye that it raises to the heavens, the nerve that links this part to the higher world.
>
> Doctrine of spirit. The world of spirits is in fact already open before us – it is always apparent. If we suddenly became as elastic as necessary, we would see ourselves fully within it.[168]
>
> It is the most arbitrary prejudice to think that we are precluded from reaching beyond ourselves, from having consciousness beyond the senses. At every moment we can be a supersensible being. If this were not so, we would not be a citizen of the world but an animal.[169]
>
> When a spirit dies, he becomes human. When the human being dies, he becomes spirit.[170]

But Novalis also knew that the 'mortal' part of the human being, to which our materialistic consciousness also belongs, is not so easy, let us say, to reconfigure or rebalance. Thus, at the end of his uncompleted novel, *Heinrich von Ofterdingen*, we read words that also apply to psychist I experience, but especially to a 'spiritualist' experience of the cosmos as a part of the world that also belongs to us: 'The mortal rumbles in its underlying structures, but the immortal begins to shine more brightly, and acknowledges itself.'

The complex theme of 'reincarnation' is also connected with 'spiritualism'. The Western view of reincarnation sees humanity's evolution as an ongoing rhythm of incarnation and excarnation. The seed of the plant that penetrates the earth is comparable to the birth of the eternal core of our being in a material body, whereas its further development resembles the progressive formation of leaves and flowers. Fading and decay of the flower correspond to death. In the new seed that forms lives the outcome of all the plant's former stages and generations, and in the disembodied core of our being, likewise, there lives the outcome of this and all former earthly incarnations. In Goethe's terms, this is the 'configured, living and developing form' that 'no time or power can dismember' – of which 'spiritualism' *also* speaks. Still more apt is the image of the caterpillar's metamorphosis into the butterfly, passing through the pupa stage. A person with a 'spiritualist' outlook sees how a similar lawfulness comes to expression in plant, butterfly and human being.

Thus, we approach the close of this chapter. We began with the biblical image of Jacob's ladder and spoke of the two cornerstones of 'spiritualist' experience of the world: of absolute spirituality as a quality of being contrasted with an entirely material view of the cosmos, with its fundamental solidity and cohesion; and of the graded, hierarchically interacting ranks of the angelic orders. We then briefly examined the dangers of one-sidedness in both outlooks – flight from the earth and enchainment to it – and touched on the worldview of realism as a balance between them.

To end, we will let the great Dante Alighieri show us a glimpse of his paradise, as he depicts this in *The Divine Comedy*. Like many before and after him, he founds his ideas on the writings of Dionysius. Dante passed through the circles of hell and ascended the Mountain of Purgatory. Finally, Beatrice, his beloved who died young, leads him to the highest spheres of heaven. In the supra-spatial realm of stars, he perceives an indescribably bright point, around which moves a 'ring of fire', circling 'more swiftly than the fastest motion that pulsates around the universe'. This point is God, whose light streams from the fiery heaven through infinite distances into the crystal heaven.

> And this sphere was encircled by another,
> that by a third, and the third by a fourth,
> the fourth by a fifth, the fifth then by a sixth.
>
> The seventh followed, by now spread so wide
> that the rainbow arc of Juno's messenger
> would be too narrow to encompass it.

So too the eighth and ninth, and each of them
revolved more slowly in proportion to
the number of turns distant from the centre.

And that sphere spinning nearest the point of fire
shone with the clearest flame because, I think,
it partakes most of its essential truth.

My lady, seeing me so rapt
in deep suspense, then said, 'Upon this point
hang all the heavens and the whole of nature.

Look at that circle closest linked to it
and understand its motion is so rapid
because of burning love which spurs it on....

Materially, the spheres are wide or narrow
depending on degrees of more or less
power that flows down through their zones.

A greater power seeks to work greater good,
which lives in turn in body commensurate
to the good at work in it.

This circle, then, which sweeps along with it
the rest of all creation, corresponds
to the circle that knows most truth and loves the most.

If you then take the spiritual power,
and not the outer form as measure of the beings
that here appear to you within these rings,
you will observe an awesome interplay
of greater and lesser heavenly spheres
with its angels' greater strength or weakness.'

Just as our hemisphere of air becomes
serene and splendid when the North wind blows
breezes from his gentler cheeks,

and with these breezes clears and wafts away
the overhanging mists, so that the sky
smiles on us with the beauties of each quarter,

so I became the moment that my lady
bestowed on me her crystal-clear reply
that like a star in heaven shone with truth.

And after she had finished speaking,
the rings all round began to sparkle
like red-hot iron shooting out bright sparks.

Each sparkle stayed within its fiery ring,
so many that their number runs to more
thousands than the redoubling of the chessboard.

From choir to choir I heard Hosannah sung,
to the still point gathering them for ever
and keeping them in their eternal path.

And she who saw the hesitating thoughts
within my mind then said, 'The first two circles
have shown you Seraphim and Cherubim.

They pulse so swiftly in their inner loops
the more to liken themselves to the central point;
the more they can, the loftier their vision.

Those other loves that whirl in the next circle
are called the 'Thrones' before the great Lord's countenance,
and bring the first triad to a close.

And you must know that they all draw bliss
in measure as their sight probes to the depths
of truth in which each mind finds rest.

From this we see the state of blessedness
is founded first upon the act of *vision*
and not upon the love that follows it.

And vision is rewarded appropriately by grace
and purity of will: and so
their ranks unfold from grade to grade.

The second triad germinates and flowers
in an unending springtime that
no wintry night-time Aries may despoil:

unceasingly sings Hosannah
with triple melodies that warble from
these three jubilant choirs.

The holy beings of this hierarchy are
first, Dominions; then Virtues; and the third
found there are Powers.

In the next to last rings, Principalities
and Archangels circle around,
while in the last the hosts of angels play.

These orders all gaze upward and pour out
their power downward, so that all of them
are drawn – and draw each other – towards God.

And Dionysius with such deep desire
gave himself up to contemplate these orders
that he named them and their ranks as I do here.[171]

12

Universal Relation – Monadism

The word 'relation', or also 'relative', is a wonderful and multi-layered word. It derives from the Latin *relatio* – roughly, 'report' or 'account' (and retaining this sense in our word 'to relate' or tell a story) – and its meaning has undergone a remarkable change over the centuries. 'Relative' from the late Latin *relativus* – meaning 'relating to' or 'concerning' – acquired in the twentieth century a universal significance that would have dumbfounded the ancient Romans.

In sociology and psychology, in logic and mathematics, the paired terms 'relation/relative' now enjoy a great diversity of meaning and acquire a different hue in each discipline. As an umbrella term, a kind of conceptual archetype, we find 'relation' in the table of Aristotelian categories – one of the most fascinating products from his workshop of thinking.

Einstein's special and general theories of relativity, with their fundamental speculations on space, time, mass and gravity, constitute a highly significant paradigm of the twentieth century and brought about a real revolution in physics, but also in people's view of the world. Einstein's theory of relativity and Max Planck's quantum theory are a luminous pair of twins in the heavens of mathematist physics. But relation – *pros ti* in Greek – as Aristotle saw it, points far beyond mathematical and mathematist calculations. Thus, based on the idea of time as a fourth dimension and of 'curved space', it was possible to arrive at both forms of the theory of relativity, with their conclusions. Einstein came to think that the universe was 'finite but unlimited'. It would go beyond the scope of this book to study the detailed content of the theory of relativity.[172] What we are primarily interested in here – which is why the above examples were chosen – is the fact that Einstein's basic statements have also been relativised! In the January 2001 issue of the journal *Bild der Wissenschaft*, for instance, we can read the following: 'Measurements of background cosmic radiations lead us to suspect that the universe is infinite and "shallow", or in other words is not curved in its greater dimensions.'[173]

Whatever the truth here, we do not wish to use 'relation' or 'relative' in their narrower sense, but in their original import: the interrelationship of two or more entities; a way of seeing, in fact, that can be applied to all worldviews. All parts of the universe, not only its particles, have the most manifold interrelationships. In the human world, 'relationship' is the core of sociological dynamics: family relationships, love relationships, work relationships, stable relationships, loose relationships, small and big relationships, bad and conflict-ridden relationships and the relationships in religion between human beings and a spiritual world. The list goes on.

And what is a relationship founded upon? On the respective attributes of the beings who enter into relationship with each other: qualities that – in human terms – are connected with genetics, temperament, character, appearance, education and ideals. To put it another way, this involves the respective 'world content' living individually and differently in each instance of the human species, and changing, enlarging and perfecting itself continually from hour to hour, and year to year. Thus every being – in terms of the whole cosmos – is furnished with manifold attributes and enters into multiple relationships with the most diverse entities. If I depart initially from unifying tendencies and look at the world, let us say, from the aspect of individualism or pluralism, then I am a monadist.

Monadism is in opposition to mathematism, and is its primary complement. *Monas* means, first, 'unity', and at the same time also a delineation from other monads. The unity of mathematism is a quantitative determination, whereas the monad is a qualitative experience in relation to the other.

The term was coined by the great mathematician, philosopher, physicist and diplomat Gottfriend Wilhelm Leibniz. His monadology ranges from the simplest entity through to the *ur*-monad, God:

> Every monad, in union with its intrinsic body, forms a living substance. Accordingly, there is not only life everywhere, bound up with limbs or organs, but even infinitely many degrees amongst the monads, since some more or less rule over the others. If the monad now possesses purposefully formed organs, by virtue of which emerging and diverging distinctions come about in the impressions they receive, and consequently in the perceptions produced by them (for instance, rays of light concentrated by the eye's fluids to act with greater force) then this can

> lead to *sensation*; that is, to a perception accompanied by memory, of which a certain echo remains for a longer period, and which can be interrogated when the occasion arises. We call such a creature an *animal*, and its monad, *soul*. When this soul is now raised to *reason*, it becomes something more noble, and is counted amongst the spirits.[174]

For Leibniz, nothing in the world is truly real except the monads and their thoughts. In his *History of Philosophy*, Gerhard Kropp gives an excellent brief account of this key idea in Leibniz's thinking:

> That the monads are thinking forces signifies for Leibniz that they contain the multiplicity of the whole world within them: each monad is a microcosm, a living reflection of the universe that develops pictures of things from its own seeds. All monads embody the same universe, but from different perspectives. And this diversity becomes apparent in the degree of clarity of the idea: whereas a clear idea corresponds to full, uninhibited activity, an unclear one reveals suffering. Only God has clear and precise ideas. He is the chief monad above all, and as such is pure activity, whereas every other monad is impeded in its activity, depending on the degree to which it is prevented from developing it.
>
> Leibniz especially emphasised three classes of monads: the 'naked' monads never rise beyond unconscious thoughts, and in a sense are always slumbering. Clear, yet not precise thoughts are, secondly, possessed by souls: their thoughts are already sustained by consciousness and by sensations accompanied by memory. Clear and precise thoughts, thirdly, are the possession of the mind or spirit alone: it has consciousness of itself, and the capacity to perceive general laws.
>
> Leibniz teaches that every higher level encompasses and includes the lower ones. The endeavour to link one idea to another is called 'drive' in the unconscious, and 'will' in the conscious realm. While all monads act spontaneously out of their own imperative, only thinking monads are free: freedom consists in acting without external compulsion solely according to the law of one's own reasonable nature.
>
> How do mutually independent monads ultimately develop thoughts that are nevertheless mutually compatible? This is due to 'prestabilised harmony': God created the universe so that individual monads can only develop thoughts that, taken all together, represent or depict the whole universe. The harmony of the whole is thus predetermined.[175]

Here we can recognise the basic gesture of mathematism again, but imbued with the reality of life. The orders of individual soul-spiritual beings, with their diverse degrees of consciousness, modes of thinking and powers of impulse, are regulated by their mutual relationships: thus, my surroundings belong to me. It would be abstract to form an image of a person without including their whole circle of friends and destined relationships. Nicolai Hartmann is right to say:

> The individuality identifies itself not only with its own inner holism but also with a certain part of the world with which it feels a destined connection in the flow of occurrences, or with which it also unites actively as a goal of endeavour. Whatever plays into this sphere it feels to be something that happens to itself, and it is affected by it as by its own destiny. *This living sphere of people and their influence, this magic circle, if you like, is a fundamental trait of the personality, shaping reality, configuring the world far beyond the person's consciously active scope*: it is a tangible and palpable miracle of its being. The key to understanding this sphere of influence lies in our transcendent acts, in which, surpassing conscious interiority, we form threads of living *solidarity*, and enter into a relationship with the world by virtue of which a part of the world belongs to us as ours, just as we come to belong to it.[176]

With these formulations, Hartmann is feeling his way towards a realm that, seen from the point of view of interpersonal relationships, probably constitutes the core of monadism: the law of karma, according to which human relationships, naturally transforming in manifold ways through each respective zeitgeist, pass through recurring lives on earth. At work in each human individual who steps on to earthly ground at birth is a potential complex of relationships, inclinations and disinclinations that have their origin in a certain incarnation, or in several former incarnations. To recognise this, to configure and shape it anew, is, in the terms of monadism, one of the most urgent and at the same time most difficult tasks of today. Monadism also signifies communication.

Thus, monadism has diverse degrees of intensity: it can grant me a profound intuition of the true, individual being of the person standing before me, and the quality of laws of destiny that hold sway in any particular configuration – ranging, let us say, from intimation to vision. It therefore has a certain affinity with phenomenalism (Chapter 3).

How much richer our pedagogical practice, our upbringing of children in general, would become through a power of perception schooled in monadism! Teachers do not have to be 'seers', but they ought to have a sense of the unique nature, gifts and destiny of a child. In principle, we can say that anyone who occupies a leading or managerial position in the world of work should have a sober, objective, monadistic capacity to perceive their colleagues – instead of which, in our schools primarily, everything is usually tarred with the same brush. One-sided mathematists have the greatest difficulty here, for a wholesome, holistic mathematism will usually also contain a good dose of monadism. A narrow mathematist will say, 'One rule for all!' Or: 'One examination system for all!' Or also: 'All children should be treated the same!' While monadists know that justice must prevail, they also know that life is full of exceptional instances and that every person is, in a sense, an exception. Many human tragedies could be avoided if educators and managers were to take this more on board. The great musician Pablo Casals once expressed this very aptly. In relation to the assassination of J.F. Kennedy, whom he knew personally and whom he esteemed, he said:

> Sometimes I look around me with a feeling of complete dismay. In the confusion that afflicts the world today, I see disrespect for the very values of life. Beauty is all around us, but how many are blind to it. They look at the wonder of this earth and seem to see nothing. People move about hectically but give little thought to where they are going. They seek excitement for its own sake, as if they were lost and desperate. They take little pleasure in the natural and quiet and simple things of life. Each second we live is a new and unique moment of the universe; a moment that will never be again.
>
> And what do we teach our children? We teach them that two and two makes four, and that Paris is in France. When will we also teach them what they are? We should say to each of them: do you know what you are? You are a marvel. You are unique. In the entire world there is no other child exactly like you. In the millions of years that have passed, there has never been another child like you. And look at your body – what a wonder it is. Your legs, your arms, your cunning fingers, and the way you move. You may become a Shakespeare, a Michelangelo, a Beethoven. And when you grow up, can you then harm another who is, like you, a marvel? You must cherish one another. You must work – we must all work – to make the world worthy of its children.
>
> What extraordinary changes and advances I have witnessed in my long life! Magnificent advances in science, industry, space travel. And yet hunger, racial injustice and tyranny still plague the world as ever.

> We still behave like barbarians. Like savages we are afraid of our neighbours on this earth, arm ourselves against them, and they arm themselves against us. I regret that I have had to live at a time when killing your neighbour was the law. When will we finally get used to the fact that we are human beings?
>
> It's natural to love your homeland. But why should love stop at the border? We are a single family – each of us has duties to his brothers. We are all leaves on one tree, and this tree is humanity.[177]

Casals goes to the heart of monadism here – which is love. On the one hand, monadism is connected with the strongest individualism – and in this it has an affinity with psychism – while on the other hand, in the vulnerable place of human relationships, it practises the greatest possible openness and willingness to perceive the other. How other than through genuine, feeling interest towards people and the world should the growth of one's own monad proceed? Leonardo da Vinci said that one can only perceive what one loves. And philosophy means, of course, nothing other than 'love of wisdom'.

Trust also belongs to the 'relating' category, and to a comprehensive monadism. In line with St Paul, whose theology is clearly founded on relationship, we can say: In love lives trust; in faith – inconceivable without love – lies a primary trust in God; and in hope is expressed a fundamental trust that the future, however it turns out, has its deeper meaning.

Leibniz himself was aware of a meaningful harmony rooted in God, as we have already seen. Here he touches on the realm of rationalism, which also comes to expression in the fact that, through his theodicy, he attempted to show why God was justified in allowing evil to exist. Nor is it surprising that Leibniz sought to establish peace between the confessions. In a fragmentary dialogue in Latin which he wrote in 1673, at the age of just 27, he tells of a small band of travelling companions,[178] and, among other things, of a discussion between a Catholic and a Calvanist on questions of faith. He himself appears here as arbiter and feels himself to be 'free of either party's fervour'. He goes on to suggest that all participants are seeking a unifying formula for their religious differences. In another work that he conceived around the same time, he sought to achieve reunification of the churches.

The worldview of monadism is thus, on the one hand, a formal outlook, as is mathematism, in that it starts from a harmonious system of 'unities', whether these be realms of nature or stars. On the other hand, its content remains very open, since, for example, it does not foreground its own opinions, conclusions or solutions to a problem, but has a gesture of openness and outgoing interest. To put it metaphorically, we could compare mathematism's point-focused gesture to the tip of a lance, and the openness, respect, love and interest of pure monadism to an open vessel. Interest (from the Latin *inter esse*) means, after all, 'being between' and thus 'creating relationship'!

Relativism itself, as a philosophical stance, and in a sense as a precursor of relativity theory, is very ancient. In a book we have already referred to, Jean Gebser's *Western Transformation* – a summary, still largely valid, of modern research in diverse disciplines – the author describes the concept of relativity as 'ancient'. Zeno of Eleate, he says, 'prefigured this theory of Einstein's, albeit in a primitive form'.[179] In the relevant literature we repeatedly find the suggestion that Aristotle regarded Zenon as the inventor of dialectics. And Plato, too, esteemed his thinking very highly. In Anaxagoras, by contrast, we find a marked monadist approach: he spoke, among other things, of a wealth of physical-spiritual primal beings, as diverse and manifold degrees of the spiritual '*ur*-seeds', the germinal forces of all things and creatures.

All-penetrating cosmic reason orders these ideal primal beings into a harmonious whole or cosmos. These indivisible (individual) *ur*-beings could equally be called spirit germs or soul atoms; for the word 'atom' likewise describes the indivisible unity of a being, like the word 'individual'. For this reason, the much-cited 'atoms' of Democritus are, when we examine them more closely, by no means purely material-originating particles, but are etheric and elemental in nature, and even, indeed, ensouled.[180]

But it was the 'monad' doctrine of Leibniz that would exert an unmistakeable influence on many thinkers of subsequent centuries, Goethe included. He gladly adopted the term, which for him was already a reality he experienced. Richard Friedenthal, who wrote an interesting, albeit not exactly congenial, biography of Goethe, writes the following about a conversation between Goethe and Eckermann:

> And to Eckermann he said: 'My conviction of our enduring existence arises from the idea of activity; for if I work tirelessly until my demise, nature is obliged to assign me a different form of existence if my spirit can no longer endure the present one.' There is no prouder or more arrogant way of putting it. He regards himself as an enduring and indestructible unity of energy. For this he uses the philosophical expression 'entelechy', which originated with Aristotle but which he remoulds, for his concepts, too, are governed by the law of metamorphosis. The *telos*,

> or goal, is the thing of primary importance in this word: an infinite goal towards which a once-created form strives. From Leibniz he takes the term *monad*, understanding by it the 'obstinacy of the individual, and that a person discards what is not appropriate to him'. This obstinately self-preserving unity is immortal: I do not doubt our continued existence, for nature cannot do without the entelechy; but we are not all immortal in the same way, and in order to manifest in future as a great entelechy we must also already be one.[181]

We can *also* apply the interpretative outlook of psychism to these sentences.

Goethe's monadism is very clear in many of his comments – for instance, on the day of Wieland's funeral (25 January 1813) in a conversation with the writer and pedagogue Johann Daniel Falk, which the latter subsequently transcribed (Falk's memoirs and conversations with Goethe were published posthumously):

> It would scarcely surprise me, and indeed I would even find it in full accord with my views if I were to encounter this Wieland again after millennia as a world monad, as a star of the first order, and witnessed how, with his lovely light, he enlivens and exhilarates everything... and how in general, as soon as we consider the eternity of this world condition, we can also regard monads as nothing other than eternal participants in the joys of the gods, as blissfully co-creating powers. The growth of Creation is entrusted to them. Invoked or uninvoked, they arrive by all paths, from all mountains, all stars. Who can halt their progress? I am certain, as you see me here, that I have been here a thousand times before, and I hope to return a thousand times more.

And then we can recall the passage quoted earlier from Eckermann's conversations (see p. 3) about Goethe's outlook on tolerance:

> It is a great foolishness to demand that people should adapt to and harmonise with us. I have never done this. I have always regarded a person only as a self-contained individual whom I sought to understand and with whose particularity I endeavoured to acquaint myself, without demanding from him any further sympathy. By this means I have now become able to relate to every human being, and through this alone arises a knowledge of manifold characters as well as a necessary adroitness in life. You see, especially when one encounters obstinate natures one must get a grip upon oneself to get through to them, and by this

> means all the different aspects in us are enlivened and developed, so that one soon feels equal to every encounter.... You must venture forth into the greater world, whatever position you wish to adopt.

Before we engage more closely with the realms of art and religious tolerance, I want to cite a striking account of monadist experience, paired with the alert sensory openness of phenomenalism. This is an excerpt from Rudolf Steiner's autobiography, in which he relates his encounter with the Austrian poet Fercher von Steinwand:

> I had been wrestling with the enigma of recurring human lives on earth. I had gained certain insights in this regard when I came close to people whose mode of life and form of character easily reveal the traces of an essential content that may not be sought in what they inherited through birth or have experienced since then. In his countenance and its expressions, in every gesture of Fercher's, I witnessed a soul being that could only have developed around the time Christianity began, when Greek culture of a pagan kind still played into its development. We do not gain such insight by reflecting on a person's immediate utterances; rather, we can feel it to be kindled by intuited traits of the individual that seem to accompany such utterances but in reality infinitely deepen them. Nor do we gain such realisations by seeking them while in a particular person's company, but only in the reverberation of the strong impression their presence has made, in a kind of enlivened recall in which the aspects primarily figuring in outer life are extinguished, and what is otherwise 'inessential' starts to speak a very definite language. Anyone who 'observes' people to decipher their previous lives will quite definitely not reach their goal. Such observations must be felt as an insult to the person observed. Only by virtue of something arriving from the outer world of spirit as a boon of destiny can we hope that the long-distant past of a human being will reveal itself in their present life.
>
> At this period of my life, I gained particular insights about human beings' recurring lives on earth. Previously, though these were not something far removed from me, they had not yet emerged, either, from vague apprehensions into clear impressions.[182]

This testimony is important for our reflections for two reasons, especially since Steiner is extremely sparing in his works with accounts of his own spiritual experiences. We can see here a marked ethos of respect and regard, as well as of meditative contemplation, following a particular encounter. While we ought not to make such experiences the *goal* of our social encounters, nevertheless the respect modelled here, and the subsequent contemplation, would certainly enhance our social competency, whether in school contexts, partnerships and relationships[183] or in the world of work, quite irrespective of whether this granted us deeper insights or not. Steiner's whole anthropology, which he calls 'anthroposophy' because the wisdom that makes the 'world most inwardly cohere' gradually emerges in the act of self- and world-knowledge, has an inherent and fundamental monadist orientation. While Steiner's chief work of philosophy, *The Philosophy of Freedom*, is founded on rigorous psychist experience – as we can tell from its subtitle, 'The results of inner observation scientifically acquired' – his ethical individualism nevertheless culminates in sentences that are highly relevant to a slowly developing multicultural society. Steiner has previously stated that we are free 'in so far as we are able to follow our own dictates at every moment of our life'.[184] He then continues:

> Acting out of freedom does not in any way preclude ethical laws, but rather includes them, yet such action does turn out to be of a higher order than one merely dictated by these laws. Why should my action serve the general good any less well if I do it out of love than if I have *only* done it because I believe it is my duty to serve the common good? Mere duty is a concept that excludes freedom since it does not wish to acknowledge the individual aspect, instead subordinating this to a general norm. Freedom of action is only conceivable from the point of view of ethical individualism.

Steiner continues:

> But how is it possible for people to live in community if each person endeavours only to assert their individuality? This is an objection characteristic of a mistaken moralism, which holds that a human community is only possible if all its members are united by a commonly agreed ethical order. Such moralism fails to comprehend the consensus of the world of ideas. It does not understand that the world of ideas active within me is one and the same as that living in my fellow human beings. Yet this unity is merely an outcome of our experience of the world, and inevitably *must* be so. If it could be perceived by anything other than observation, it would be an expression not of individual experience but of general norm. Individuality is possible only when each individual

> entity knows of the other solely through individual observation. The difference between me and a fellow human being is certainly not due to the fact that we inhabit two quite different mental worlds, but that the other receives different intuitions from the world of ideas common to both of us. The other desires to express *their* intuitions just as I desire to express *mine.* If we are both truly drawing from the idea, and not hearkening to some outward (physical or mental) impulse, we can meet each other in the same endeavour, the same intentions. In ethically *free* human beings, ethical misunderstandings or collisions simply cannot arise. Only someone ethically unfree, who hearkens to natural drives or an assumed commandment or duty, repudiates their neighbour for not following the same instinct and commandment. The fundamental maxim of the *free human being* is this: to *live* in love for one's actions, and to *let live*, with understanding of another's will.

These are the foundations of a broad-minded and open-hearted tolerance in all realms of life.

When reading the following comments (also from *The Philosophy of Freedom*), it is a good idea to recall what we said previously in Chapter 6 on mathematism.

> There will be many who say that the concept of the free human being you have posited here is a chimera, something not actually realised anywhere; they will say that their concern is with actual human beings, who are only likely to be ethical if they obey ethical commandments, regarding their ethical mission as a duty, as opposed to hearkening freely to their inclinations and their love. I have no doubt whatsoever that this is true. It would be blindness not to. But then let us dispense with all the hypocrisy of ethical conduct if this is to be the *last* word on the matter. Let us then say that human nature has to be *compelled* to its actions as long as it is not *free*. Whether such unfreedom is enforced by physical constraints or ethical laws – whether a person is unfree because they obey boundless sexual desires or because they are enchained by the bonds of conventional morality – is quite irrelevant from a certain point of view. But let us not assert, then, that such a person can rightly call an action their *own*, since they are driven to it by an external power. Yet amid this enforced order emerge *free spirits* – those who find themselves within the mass of ethics, legal constraint, religious practice and so on. They are *free* in so much as they hearken only to themselves, *unfree* in so far as they subject themselves to compulsions. Who of us can say that

> we are truly free in all our actions? Yet in each of us lives a deeper nature in which the free person comes to expression.

Only in this context does Steiner's fundamentally pluralist outlook in questions of aesthetics become comprehensible. We cite here again the relevant passage (see p. 91):

> Just as every true artwork is the individual, personal expression of an individual person, so any critique can only be a very individual reflection of the feelings and thoughts that rise in the soul of the reflecting critic as they attend to the artwork in question. I can never say whether a poem is objectively good or bad, since there is no norm for good or bad here.

Or to put it another way: each actual individual – rather than any norm or fashion – becomes the source of aesthetic judgement.

The two poles of all art are: creator and spectator. Expressed in the categories of our worldviews, this gives rise to the following picture, which can now serve as a continuation of our comments on art.

So far we have seen that practically every worldview relates more or less significantly to the triad of science, art and religion.[185] We cited various examples of this, though of course every argument developed in this volume can only be a stimulus for readers to pursue their own studies. If we consider the many kinds of art, those that take spatial form as well as the arts of speech and music, we naturally find the source of all these manifestations in ourselves as human beings. Thus, every art is of anthropological concern. We could also say that speech embodies the primary nature of all artistic endeavour. Just as thoughts, feelings and impulses rise up from invisible and inaudible depths of our human nature by means of words, assuming sound and shape, so the artist transforms inward experience into visible or audible manifestation. Whereas speech and song, along with dance and eurythmy, manifest through the human organism, pictorial artists use a particular material, available to them in the world, to 'inform' it with the configurations that seek manifestation through the creative act. If an artwork is successful, we can discover that the merely subjective sphere of the artist is, as it were, transformed and appears at a higher, or enhanced, level: a piece of 'substance' – whether this be voice, body or material – has been transformed. A third, new thing arises: essence manifests.

So is every work a work of art? I will follow Steiner here and say: let everyone decide for themselves! This places dialogue at the heart of things, entirely in line with monadism. We can and may certainly reject a work, since in art, as everywhere else, light and shadow are in close proximity. But our judgement about this ought not to have any normative power. In terms of monadism, this means forming your own aesthetic verdict through mathematist thinking, by observation and analysis. If you reject a work, never forget to accept the person who made it. And if you enter into dialogue with them – even into dispute – it is possible you may have to end up revising your judgement, since a conversation can open eyes and ears.

Basically, this applies also to tolerance in matters of religion, where the chasm between a necessary certainty of mathematist perception and a necessary monadist openness can be a very big one. Radical fundamentalism and sanctimonious indifference are the two great shadows of these two bright suns of knowledge. Pluralist theology has become a positive, active current in these questions, especially over the last ten years, and this is intrinsic to the monadist stream. In some of its representatives it establishes a very specific stance towards Christianity, which we will examine in more detail in the last chapter of this book. In its television series, *Stations*, the Bavarian Radio network broadcast a programme on 14 February 2001 entitled 'How Dangerous Is Pluralist Theology?' I will end this chapter with a quotation from the transcript of the programme which was sent to me.

During the programme, various theologians were interviewed and asked for their opinions. Francis X. D'Sa from Puna, India, is a Jesuit priest and was questioned while on a visit to Munich. Asked whether understanding was possible between the Christians' idea of God and that of the Hindu world, he replied:

> I don't believe that we can use the symbolic language of one religion to understand the symbolic language of another. We can only understand one another through dialogue. Only when I know how others understand me, can I speak in a way that avoids them misunderstanding me.

The interviewer then said, 'For Francis X. D'Sa, therefore, one great unified religion is not the ultimate end of all world religions; but rather, he can conceive of unity within diversity.'[186]

13

'I Am Dynamite' – Dynamism

Let us imagine a pair of spectacles with an infrared-type detector something like the Kirlian technology we mentioned earlier – the only difference being that it perceives all energy or force fields. As we walked about, we would see nothing but energy everywhere.

From the simplest glow-worm through all kingdoms of nature to the human realm, and beyond it to the divine, we would perceive a graded domain of forces and potencies: mechanical energy, nuclear energy, heat, chemical and electrical energy, hydro-energy, radiation energy, biomasses, muscular power and much, much more. And then also vital energy, soul strength and spiritual energy.

This is the empirical field of dynamism, which has come to reign victorious in recent centuries, especially since the invention of the mechanical loom, which inaugurated the first Industrial Revolution. Even without wearing such a pair of spectacles, countless people today – not only economists – think in terms of categories of energy: vigour, power, resonance, force fields, capacity, terrestrial radiation, kilojoules, potency, vitality – to name but a few. To these can be added products such as power foods, energy diets and even 'turbo muesli'! Even what is called the 'obsession with youth' belongs here. We don't have to be well versed in philosophy to be a confirmed dynamist! Everyone knows that when a stone falls to earth, gravity is at work, while magnetic force is at work in a magnet. And it has become almost self-evident that the sunlight of Zarathustra and Ekhnaton can be used as solar energy. Any contradiction here? Not at all: just two ways of seeing *one* all-embracing phenomenon.

Study of the twelve worldviews – this dodecahedron of wisdom and life – everywhere reveals the justification and, in principle, the equal value of every worldview *as part of the whole.* While such study uses long-established analytic and syllogistic tools, these are integrated into the whole fabric of the twelve outlooks, and are not founded on any kind of reductionist or agnostic premise. The approach characterises and determines the place of each worldview within the overall context, so that each separate aspect seeks its position within a living whole. This is no shallow pluralism but a keen activity of discrimination, one that also looks for the purity and transparency of each colour within the context of the whole colour-circle. I would like to call the ethos of such discriminating insight, and its cognitive technique, a kind of *ars magna,* expressed in the quest for meaning and truth both today and in future.

The dynamist certainly perceives correctly. His experiential field encompasses not only knowledge of the world but also special depths of self-experience. His introspection is less focused on conscious or feeling aspects of complex I experience than on the energy potential lurking in the depths of the will. The proximity to psychism becomes especially apparent. Yet here the concern is not, let us say, with a compact experience of one's own core being but with the discovery of a vital energy capable of anything. One's own I is transcended here in so far as we descend into depths – chthonic depths of the soul – which in a sense withdraw from the I's dominion. Chthonic divinities, thus gods of the earth's depths, were feared by both the Greeks and the Romans. We can gain an inkling of these powers at work in us in a poem by Nietzsche:

> *Ecce Homo*
> Yes! I know where I come from!
> Unsatisfied always, like the flame
> I burn and glow, myself consume.
> All I touch on turns to light,
> Blackened all I leave behind:
> Flame I am without a doubt!

Let us stay for a moment with this interior aspect of dynamism, which assumes a great many philosophical forms. José Ortega y Gasset once described the nature of a strong personality in very dynamistic terms: 'A strong personality, of whatever kind – moral, scientific, artistic, erotic – is completely impossible without a fulsome supply of vital energy accumulating in the under-depths of our inner being.'[187]

If we savour this pregnant sentence, with its somewhat explosive dynamism, we can have a very clear sense of its opposition to its complementary pole – that is, to rationalism. Where the first is irrational, the latter is rational and reasonable. Where the one is in principle chaotic and unordered, the other is formed and ordered. Whereas the rationalist is on the look-out for calm, clear, starry harmonies, the dynamist sees volcanoes on the earth and exploding star bursts in the universe: we have here the collision of Apollo with Dionysus. Nietzsche erected a true memorial to these divinities and the modes of experience they embody in his *The Birth of Tragedy*. He himself swung back and forth between these two extremes. Ivo Frenzel writes, 'Nietzsche's life was in general a restless passage, a path between extreme moods: he was torn hither and thither between two poles, between delirious joy and another state characterised by… rational detachment… towards persons and things.'[188]

The brilliant poet-philosopher was increasingly sucked into a one-sided, destructive dynamism at odds with both men and gods. He once wrote, 'I am dynamite.' The tragedy of his life can be seen especially in the fact that the contrary dispositions that wrestle for peaceful co-existence in each of us could not come to equilibrium within him. Inevitably we recall here the words of Faust as he strives 'in the night' for knowledge of the world and self-knowledge:

> Two souls live – alas! – within my breast,
> The one seeks severance from the other:
> one looks to the world with an urgent lust
> and clings to it with all its grosser organs;
> the other raises itself powerfully from the dust
> back to ancient progenitors' lofty realms.

Goethe was by no means an easy or straightforward person, but he succeeded in riding both 'horses' – as we might (following Plato) call the divergent and mutually resisting soul forces – and harnessing them to lifelong creative accomplishments. Nietzsche, by contrast, ended his life in complete benightedness and derangement. The abysses that exist in *each and every one* of us broke him asunder. Human destructiveness is a daily recurring theme, one made palpable to us in wars, battles and conflicts. Faust's words resound strongly with an erotic capacity that binds us to the world – an ambivalent aspect of dynamist reality that is by no means always free of violence. Goethe was also aware that there was no crime of which he would not have been potentially capable. To put it differently, in line with what we already stated in relation to Plato in Chapter 7 on rationalism, both the idea of good and the idea of evil are active cosmic forces. A huge power indwells both, and mastering them in the context of an ethical individualism is perhaps the most difficult task for a civilisation in which sexuality and criminality have become more widespread and more commonly portrayed than ever before. Countless people now hungrily devour stories and images of sex and crime. These are some of the darkest aspects of dynamism: intoxication and violence are very close neighbours, but they too belong in the realm of 'vital energy accumulating in the under-depths of our inner being'.

Let us now listen to what Nietzsche says in his *The Birth of Tragedy*, before turning to further aspects of this especially topical worldview. As mentioned several times already, in the course of history, worldviews undergo periods of greater public prominence and then times of relative quiet. But in the quest for truth and meaning, it is worth accentuating yet again that all twelve belong to our full humanity and its expression: they are the Herculean tasks of a humanity awakening to its full self- and world-awareness. Like a hero of classical tragedy, Nietzsche, a mind full of acuity and sensitivity, went under in the battle against Cerberus, the guardian of the gates of hell. Here, in brief outline, is his view of Apollo and Dionysus:

> This joyous necessity of dream experience was likewise given expression by the Greeks in their Apollo: Apollo as the god of all sculptural powers is at the same time the truth-saying god. He, who at root is the 'shining one', the divinity of light, also rules over the beautiful luminosity of the inner world of imagination. The higher truth, the perfection of these states by contrast to a daily reality only partially comprehensible, and then a deep consciousness of the healing and helping power of nature in sleep and dream, is at the same time the symbolic analogy of the capacity to speak truth, and altogether of the arts that make life possible and worthwhile. But in the picture of Apollo, too, we must not lack that delicate line across which the dream picture should not venture if it is not to act pathologically so that appearance might deceive us into thinking it coarse reality: the measured limit, that freedom from wild arousals, that wise tranquillity of the shaping god. His eye must be 'sunlike' in accordance with his origin. Even if it gazes with ire and annoyance, the sanctity of lovely appearance still lies upon it.

Then Nietzsche speaks of an irrational moment, a losing of faith in forms of knowledge governed by appearance, which is described as dread:

> If we add to this sense of dread the voluptuous ecstasy that rises, with this same fragmenting of the *principia individuationis*, from the inmost

> ground of the human being, indeed from nature itself, then we find ourselves gazing into the essence of the Dionysian. We come closest to it through an analogy with intoxication. Either by the influence of the narcotic potion hymned by all primal people and races, or through the mighty approach of spring as it penetrates all nature with its joy, the Dionysian stirrings awaken, and, as they intensify, the subjective element vanishes into complete self-oblivion.[189]

Nietzsche then uses the oppositional pairing of Apollonian–Dionysian as a lens through which to view and characterise forms of art that first blossomed in ancient Greece. In my view these powers are universal in nature. In the language of C.G. Jung, we would refer to them in psychist terms as archetypes, while 'spiritualism' sees in them pictures of spirit beings.

Rationalism and dynamism have accompanied our cultures from way back, through into modern times. Today the 'vital pole' is idolised. Fitness-fever, performance addiction, anabolic steroids, energy drinks and Viagra are ingredients of vitality rituals and eternal youth – which people also try to access by dyeing their hair, face-lifts, liposuction and medically dubious implant surgery. I am not casting moral aspersions here – these things can simply be observed as part and parcel of the dynamist impulse.

On the other hand, what Ortega y Gasset describes as 'vital energy accumulating in the under-depths of our inner being' is a power that can express itself in many culturally beneficial forms: full-blown human *eros* just as much as artistic, moral, religious and scientific creativity, and everything fertile and productive in our nature.

But there is also a different kind of energy, which we rediscover in the cosmos. Putting it somewhat simply,[190] a direct line leads from the divine fire logos of Heraclitus and St John the Evangelist[191] to the morphic resonance fields of Rupert Sheldrake, a modern biologist. Sheldrake is concerned with form-creating powers throughout nature. In his book, *A New Science of Life: The Hypothesis of Formative Causation*,[192] first published in 1981, Sheldrake expresses ideas that cohere very well with the context of this volume, although they are not necessarily identical with the 'etheric formative forces' referred to on p. 119:

> At present, the orthodox approach to biology is given by the mechanistic theory of life: living organisms are regarded as physico-chemical machines, and all the phenomena of life are considered to be explicable in principle in terms of physics and chemistry. This mechanistic paradigm is by no means new; it has in fact been predominant for over a

century. The main reason why most biologists continue to adhere to it is that it works: it provides a framework of thought within which questions about the physico-chemical mechanisms of life-processes can be asked and answered.

The fact that this approach has resulted in spectacular successes such as the 'cracking of the genetic code' is a strong argument in its favour. Nevertheless, critics have put forward what seem to be good reasons for doubting that all the phenomena of life, including human behaviour, can ever be explained entirely mechanistically. But even if the mechanistic approach were admitted to be severely limited not only in practice but in principle, it could not simply be abandoned; at present it is the only approach available to experimental biology, and will continue to be followed until there is some positive alternative.[193]

Sheldrake then writes of possible ways to revise mechanistic theories:

> The organismic or holistic philosophy provides a context for what could be a yet more radical revision of the mechanistic theory. This philosophy denies that everything in the universe can be explained from the bottom up, as it were, in terms of the properties of atoms, or indeed of any hypothetical ultimate particles of matter. Rather, it recognizes the existence of hierarchically organized systems which, at each level of complexity, possess properties that cannot be fully understood in terms of the properties exhibited by their parts in isolation from each other; at each level the whole is greater than the sum of its parts. These wholes can be thought of as *organisms*, using this term in a deliberately wide sense to include not only animals and plants, organs, issues and cells, but also crystals, molecules, atoms and sub-atomic particles. In effect this philosophy proposes a change from the paradigm of the machine to the paradigm of the organism in the biological *and* the physical sciences. In A.N. Whitehead's well-known phrase: 'Biology is the study of the larger organisms, whereas physics is the study of the smaller organisms.'[194]

In a later passage of this remarkable book, he summarises a few of his research findings:

> In addition to the types of energetic causation known to physics, and in addition to the causation due to the structures of known physical fields, a further type of causation is responsible for the forms of all material morphic units (sub-atomic particles, atoms, molecules,

> crystals, quasi-crystalline aggregates, organelles, cells, tissues, organs, organisms). Form, in the sense used here, includes not only the shape of the outer surface of the morphic unit but also its internal structure. This causation, called *formative causation*, imposes a spatial order on changes brought about by energetic causation. It is not itself energetic, not is it reducible to the causation brought about by known physical rfields.[195]

To understand a 'formative causation' that is not itself energetic in nature, we need to consider the miracle of speech. This most human of all forms of communication, which we considered a little in the previous chapter, will now be studied in somewhat more detail from a different perspective, and *in connection with* the worldviews that have already been explored in this book.

Let us briefly trace how situational speech arises, and do so very simply, in a phenomenological-psychist manner.

A content that we wish to utter, a certain intuition, surfaces in our awareness. Initially it is an inwardly intuited form of consciousness coloured by our own I – as it were, a *form potential.* This immaterial *ur*-concept is pervaded by a certain intensity of feeling and will, and becomes an audible, physically measurable, technically ascertainable and recordable reality by means of our speech organisation. Thus, a word or a sequence of words is born: a *supersensible* element becomes *sensory.* A mental or spiritual awareness potential becomes 'flesh' and dwells among us. It was, first, impulse – that is, *life* – then life became the *light* of consciousness, and for a moment this light may, perhaps, illumine a dark interpersonal situation where there seems to be no way forward.

However clear and self-evident this process may appear, the thoughts we can draw from it are profound. This 'becoming flesh' of a content grasped purely in the mind is a daily repetition in miniature of what, according to the Gospel of John, occurred at the primordial beginnings of the world. Accordingly, everything arose from the resounding, creative, cosmic Word, and nothing arose except through its cosmic power: through the Logos which is at the same time thought. Every word, sustained and pervaded by a higher will, became living being. From the spirit, sensory substance consolidated.

Human beings themselves, as beings endowed with spirit, soul and body, were formed according to this archetypal process. At every birth we meet, basically, the ensoulment and embodiment of a very particular 'content', one that immerses itself in the proffered genetic stream at conception and configures it in order to be able to come to ever-more apt *expression*. In this sense the growth of a child is a continuous self-disclosure.

Word, world and human being have this same signature. In perceiving the archetypal plant, which contains the as-yet unborn energy form of every plant, Goethe began to penetrate and gain insight into this creative realm. Like the uttered word, nature initially shows us only what has developed: a lawfully configured, sense-perceptible world.

From this perspective, the human being also appears a product of outward evolutionary conditions. But if, by developing our 'unacknowledged and unknown' spiritual organs of perception in a way suitable for modern conditions – and entirely in accord with pneumatism – we learn to decipher the 'song' that 'sleeps in all things', as Eichendorff says, then frozen form starts to come into movement again: creative forces appear through a nature that has now grown transparent, and the world 'begins to sing'. A poetic metaphor? No: an experience available at any time! Human word and cosmic Word – seen as a creative power – belong to dynamism.

As a *forming or configuring* force, they are also to be found in idealism, rationalism and mathematism; and as something ready-formed, in materialism, sensualism and phenomenalism. In the profoundest depth of psychism we experience the divine creator (see p. 109), in some instances as the 'I in the I AM' or also as the epitome of the world soul, which we increasingly *intimate* in pneumatism. In 'spiritualism' and monadism, this experience intensifies into a personal one: that is, rather than being universal and pantheistic, it acquires the character of the person. In one of his 'Tame Invectives', Goethe, who decidedly asserted this position, mocked the idea that 'the professor' should be regarded as a person, but God should not:

> What is all your mockery to me
> Of the universal and the one?
> The professor is a person but
> God is none.

If we focus particularly here on the aspect of energy or power, we cannot avoid pointing once again to the inexhaustible dimension of the divine Trinity. The many triads that we find in some religions – from Osiris, Isis and Horus in Egypt through Brahma, Shiva and Vishnu in India to the Celtic triads, to name but three examples – all seek to do justice to the great 'world enigma' in triadic form, even though they cannot be hermeneutically equated with the Christian Trinity. The threefold human being of body, soul and spirit, of whom Paul speaks (for instance, in 1 Thessalonians 5, 23), was felt to belong to this enigma as an image of the godhead.

A particular aspect of the Trinity can help us further when we approach the question of the nature of primal cosmic energy, which is itself in a sense threefold. The primordial power present at the beginning is initially concealed, undisclosed – like all that is unexpressed in us human beings. Everything is still pure potential. That is the 'Father'. The Logos-Christ then, in a sense, breaks God's silence and becomes his Word: creation begins. The realms of nature are, as it were, finished sentences: the letters, syllables and words of God. The cosmos reveals itself to humanity as phenomenon, as sensory experience and as 'matter': in the consciousness of ensouled beings, through to the human being, the 'spirit' comes to expression. Thus, we have: being, becoming and consciousness.

In Chapter 6 on mathematism (see p. 56), I wrote of the unity of God being divided into the active Trinity of Father, Son and Holy Spirit, this 'three-in-one' acting in both historical and time-transcendent fashion. We called the Father the foundation of existence; the Logos-Son, the power of God, which stimulates creation and inwardly penetrates the world through into the profoundest depths of the human heart; and the Holy Spirit, the consciousness of both earthly and divine nature in the human being and the cosmos. Thus, we have the power of existence in the Father, the power of development in the Son and the power of consciousness in the Spirit. In the realm of becoming, a further trinity emerges: in concepts of classical physics, these can be called potential development in the Father, kinetic development through the Logos, and actualised development through the Spirit. And finally there is consciousness in the Father, consciousness in the Son and – forgive the tautology – consciousness in the Spirit.

But being, becoming and consciousness are in turn a unity in God, reflected in evolutionary terms in the human being as God's image. The 'Farewell Discourse' in the Gospel of John is a unique meditation on these very briefly outlined contexts. It is important to dwell on this for a moment, especially since much in this chapter has already touched on the shores of *realism*, to which we will return later in more detail.

> Thomas said to him, Lord we do not know where you are going. How should we know the way? Jesus replied, I am the way and the truth and the life. None finds the way to the Father except through me. If you had known me, you would have known my Father also. Henceforth know him, for you have seen him.

Then Philip spoke to him: Lord, show us the Father – that is all we require. Jesus answered: Have I been so long among you, and you have not known me, Philip? They who have seen me have seen the Father also. How can you therefore say, Show us the Father. Do you not believe that I am in the Father and the Father is in me? The words I speak to you I do not speak from myself. The Father who lives in me accomplishes his works through me. Believe me that my I lives in the Father, and the Father lives in my I. If you cannot trust in me, then trust at least in these works. Yes, I say to you, They who take up my I into them will also be able to do the works that I do, and will do greater deeds, for I am going to the Father....

If you truly love me, take up my cosmic goals into your will. And I will ask the Father, and he will give you another support, one who dispenses spiritual courage, and he will be with you for this whole cosmic era, the spirit of truth and knowledge. Not all people can take him up into themselves. They do not see him or acknowledge him. But you perceive him, for he holds sway as your higher being over you, and will enter into you. I will not leave you orphaned. I come to you. A little while still and the world will see me no longer; but you will see me. I live, and you are to have a part in this life. On that day you will know that I am in the Father, and you in me, and I in you. They who know my cosmic goals and take them up into their will are they who truly love me. And they who love me will be loved by my Father, and I will love them and reveal myself to them....

But now I go to him who sent me, and none of you asks, Where are you going? Now that I have said these things to you, sadness enters your hearts. But I tell you the truth: it is for your salvation that I go. For if I did not go, the helper, the one who dispenses spiritual courage, would not come to you. When I now depart, I will send him to you.

... The hour comes when I will no longer speak to you in parables. Then I will speak openly and directly to you from the Father. Upon that day you will pray in my name. I do not say that I will pray to the Father for you, for the Father himself loves you, because you have loved me and because you have believed that I come from the Father. I came forth from the Father and came into the earthly world. And now I depart from the world of the senses again and go to the Father....

When he had spoken these words, Jesus raised his eyes to have vision of the spirit and said: Father Ground of the world, the hour is come; reveal your Son's being so that your Son may reveal your being. You have made him a creative power in all earthly human bodies so that

> he may lend true life to all who have come to him through you. But this is the true life: that they know you truly as the one ground of the world, and Jesus Christ as the one whom you have sent to them. I have manifested your being on earth, and completed the work that you laid upon me. And now, Father Ground of the world, let my being become apparent in the light that shone round me with you before the world yet existed.
>
> I have brought your name to light for the people who came from the world to me through you. They were yours, and you gave them to me, and they have preserved your word within them. And so they have acknowledged that everything that you have given me comes from you; for all the power of the Word that you have given me I brought to them. They have filled themselves with it, and have really known that I come from you; and have come to believe that I was sent from you. (John 14, 5–17, 8).

The scope of these words spans from psychism through pneumatism, 'spiritualism' and monadism, all the way to dynamism. And so we can sense that the twelve worldviews are an expression of the creating Logos.

A particular aspect of dynamism becomes apparent here: death. Christ's path to the Father is at the same time into death. And he knows that new life will come from death. For sensory eyes, death signifies decay and an end to existence. But from a cosmic perspective it signifies nothing less than a return of 'kinetic' energy into the state of potentiality. The dynamic cycle of creation is thus in a sense between source and return. Between these, in union with the spirit, the Logos ever and anew creates a fire that always 'kindles in measure and extinguishes in measure', as Heraclitus says. Only from this perspective can we understand what Goethe says in his essay about nature:

> Life is her loveliest invention, and death is her stroke of genius for having much life.… She is whole and yet always incomplete. The way in which she governs things is one that can continue perpetually. To each she appears in a unique form. She conceals herself in a thousand names and terms, yet always remains the same. She brought me into life and she will lead me forth from it again. I entrust myself to her.

In relation to language we would have to say that every word arises and fades, must always be reborn anew from silence and is wedded to death. In this rhythm of becoming and vanishing, we discover a further fundamental principle of creation, and also a significant aspect of dynamism. These realities are ones that important modern scientists have also noted. Hans-Peter Dürr, for many years director of the Werner Heisenberg Institute at the Max Planck Institute for Physics and Astrophysics in Munich and winner of the Alternative Nobel Prize, and among other things involved in the environmental movement, has made some remarkable scientific discoveries. He regards the traditional materialistic worldview as no longer contemporary. In the following account we see motifs that have also repeatedly surfaced in our reflections here and aptly complement the account given on p. 43 of this book.

> [In the traditional view] nature is material, is substance. We can dismember it without it losing its material properties. We speak of the smallest particles, atoms, that cannot be further disassembled, and which are in a sense infinitely hard. They ought to have the property of always remaining identical with themselves over time. Through matter's temporal continuity, a continuity of the world is assured. Observable changes in the world occur through a reordering of these smallest particles. Thus, we can see things like this: substance, matter, is primary, and remains the same; the form, by contrast, is secondary, and arises through the structural context of substance, through the reciprocal action of matter, and this changes continually as time elapses.
>
> The modern view is quite different from this. It comes to recognise that at the most microscopic level the world is not simply a smaller reflection of the world we know, that it does not have the structure of a Russian doll that, as we take it apart, largely keeps reiterating itself. An atom is, if you like, not a small apple, or a grain of sand, or a small planetary system. No, nothing of the kind: if we increasingly take matter apart, in the end nothing remains that reminds us of matter. Ultimately there is no matter any more, but only form, shape, symmetry, relationship. Matter is not composed of matter!

Dürr continues:

> What does this mean? We have a reversal here: the primary thing is context, relationship, while substance itself is secondary. Matter is a phenomenon that only appears to a certain, coarser level of observation. Substance is coagulated form. Perhaps we can also say that at bottom we are left only with something that more resembles spirit – holistic, open, living: a potentiality. Matter is the waste product of this spiritual element

> – reducible, sealed off, determined: reality. In potentiality there are no clear cause–effect relationships. The future is basically open. Only probabilities can be cited for what is 'shed' or 'vitrified' and assumes reality. No indestructible particles exist that remain self-identical, but rather we have a 'fiery simmering', a continual arising and fading away. The world is newly created at every moment, but in mutual correspondence with the world that is, by vanishing, opening up a 'field of expectancy'. The old potentiality in its totality gives birth to the new, and forms new realisations without, however, absolutely delineating them. In this ongoing process of creation, something new and never-yet-existent is continually created. Everything participates in this. The interplay obeys rules – physically described as an over-layering of complex waves that can reinforce and weaken each other. It is a plus-sum activity where collaboration leads to strengthening, and which can, interestingly, imitate a teleological orientation (the Hamilton principle of smallest effect). The temporal process is not simply development and unfolding, an 'unwrapping' of what already exists by a permanent matter that gives itself one form alone. It is true creation, rather: the transformation of potentiality into reality.

And finally:

> This may be bad news for those who manipulate nature and ultimately seek to get a 'handle' on it. You see, we simply cannot precisely know what will happen in future under predetermined circumstances. And this – we should note – is not because of a lack of knowledge but as a consequence of the 'both one thing/*and* another' structure of potentiality, which resembles the loose associational structure of independent thoughts.
>
> But this is good news for all those who regard and experience the human being as a part of the same, single, great reality, without this participation in the overall unity meaning that we must reduce ourselves and all living creatures to lifeless parts of a machine. No one can absolutely reliably manipulate the world around us, but each person, and everything, can to a certain degree creatively collaborate in shaping the future.[196]

'Transformation of potentiality into reality'! Thus, aspects of the cosmic side of dynamism explored in this chapter cohere into a sustainable picture.

Previously, with reference to Plato, we referred to ideas of good and evil in connection with human destructiveness, which we termed an aspect of dynamism. We can actually only speak of evil in relation to human beings. Emergence and disappearance, formation and change, death and new life are naturally sustaining powers in the greater balance of the cosmos. Autumn, or the month of November with its chills, is certainly not 'evil'. The power of the Father is in fact what Plato calls the primordial good! Even Christ repudiates the appellation of 'good master':

> As he went on his way, one hurried to catch up with him, then kneeled before him and asked: Good Master, what must I do to attain life beyond time? Jesus said to him, Why do you call me good? None is good except for the one God. (Mark, 10, 17)

Thus, the problem of evil arises when we one-sidedly wreak destruction – violence always attracts violence – or when we one-sidedly seek only 'life', that is, joy, progress and eternal harmony, or an eternally enduring 'Dionysian' intoxication of whatever kind, or at least a never-ending 'high'. It is well known by now that even 'bliss' and 'ecstasy' as a basic, hedonistic penchant – whether achieved by sexuality, drugs or alcohol – eventually leave us with an existential 'hangover'. Healthy human nature is dependent on a state of balance between all its forces and processes, and losing this leads to illness. Depletion and renewal are simply a law of life!

How, therefore, can we overcome, or even tame, the Cerberus within ourselves? Greek mythology offers us a wonderful answer here: Orpheus conquered Cerberus through the soul-transforming *power* of art. That this power promotes creativity in children and adults is well known, as are its therapeutic effects. When we witness art, and still more when we create it, we activate deep forces within us that lend a creative character to everything we undertake, or what we refrain from doing. This also means acting, rather than being acted upon, in social contexts; thinking and feeling on our own initiative instead of being stuck in yesteryear. A progressive momentum then increasingly pervades our daily life. The aim of all education ought really to be the creative human being, for inner creativity is the best way to find meaning in an environment riddled with the most diverse contradictions. Then an outlook that is basically passive and resigned can make way for a true art of living.

The philosopher Ludwig Wittgenstein once said that the meaning of the world must lie beyond it. If we want to apply this principle to life, then we will have to stop the world and get off. An artistically active person fundamentally contradicts this outlook. Just as we can give form to an unworked block of stone, say, or colour and content to an empty page – and in other words give these a *purpose* – so we likewise inform whatever we create with *meaning*. The true artist of life can give meaning even to the refractory material of life – their destiny – just as artists give to their material. In this sense, art is also an expression of the creative Logos.

Something similar is achieved through a vibrant religiosity, perhaps intensified through acts of worship or ritual. Here gateways open for us to a life of whose existence we previously had only a faint idea. The eternal nature in us receives nourishment that does not fade. Irrespective of whether I am more a thinker, or a feeling person, or a person of action, this living dynamic is inherent in all forms of religion that are 'pure' in the sense of our colour-circle. Of course there are also destructive cults, such as the 'black mass' and so on.

In the Gospel of John, once again we find a lovely instance of this palpable spiritual nourishment in relation to powers of knowledge, feeling and action, these three being seen here in *only* a single accentuation. In this life force, the whole person resonates. First, here are passages, quoted earlier, from the 'high-priestly prayer' that Christ addresses to the father:

> But this is the true life: that they know you truly as the one ground of the world, and Jesus Christ as the one whom you have sent to them. (John, 17, 2f.)
>
> And they continued to ask: From what sign that you make can we see your true being, and have trust in you? Of what nature is your working? Our fathers ate manna in the desert, as it is said in the holy script: 'Bread from heaven he gave them to eat.' Jesus replied to them: Yes, I say to you, it was not Moses that gave you bread from heaven, but it is my Father who gives you the spiritually real bread from heaven. That is the bread of God, that descends from heaven and gives true life to the world. And then they said: Lord, give us this bread always.
>
> Jesus replied: I am the bread of life. For whoever comes to me will hunger no more, and whoever places trust in me will no longer thirst. (John 6, 30–36)

Those who perceive and trust, who realise the will of God, can expect a strengthening of their whole nature, for this 'life' to which reference is repeatedly made in the Gospels is the element of a real, inspired power of cosmic youth, which each one of us, however late in the day, can achieve here and now:

> His disciples urged him: Master, eat! But he replied to them: I have a food of which I eat, which you do not know. Then the disciples spoke amongst themselves, asking, Did anyone bring him something to eat? Jesus answered: My food it is to work out of the will of he who sent me, and to perfect his works. (John 4, 31–34)

> Then Jesus said to her [Martha]: I am the resurrection and the life. They who, believing, fill themselves with my strength will live, even when they die; and they who take me up into them as their life are liberated from the power of death in the whole cycle of earthly times. (John, 11, 25f.)

This, too, belongs to dynamism in its cosmic-human dynamic.

Thus, the overarching concept of dynamism comprises all existing forces in the world: nuclear physics and nutrition, morphic resonance fields and etheric forces, eros and thanatos, art and religion…

14

The World Scales – Realism

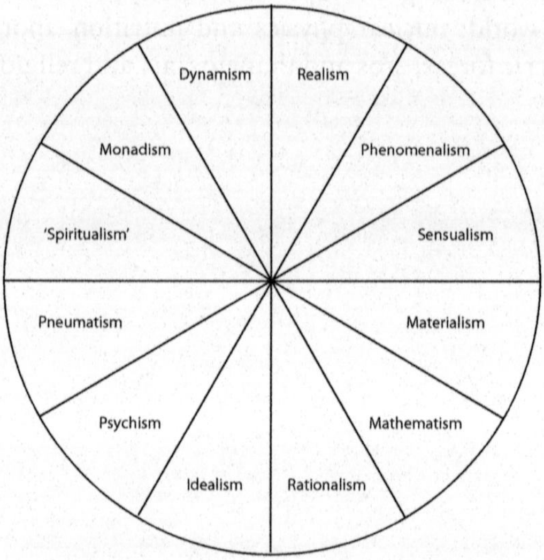

If we compare this diagram to a clock, we have now reached twelve o'clock, and thus are slowly coming to the end of our reflections on what we said, at the very outset, would be twelve different gateways for understanding human beings and the world. We also referred to these as a means to gradually penetrate the mysteries of humankind and cosmos and, as it were, read their script. These 'mysteries', it becomes clear, are creative and constituting principles at work in the world and in us. They are not just justified outlooks, but – in the pure colour-circle of 'diverse unity' – also absolutely equal in value. We also spoke of them somewhat later on as the manifestation of truth about the world and the human being. To avoid the suspicion of hubris, of whatever kind, we compared the full truth to an ocean in which we swim while staying close to the shore. Our mind is not capable of fully encompassing its breadth and depth, but we are in the water, at least, and our further learning will help us in swimming out further.

It was also important to note that we can hazard the great venture from shores other than our own. As mentioned in various places, the great problem does not primarily consist in the seeming irreconcilability of these worldviews, but in the one-sidedness in which they can appear. The intense activities of enquiry necessary in studying the twelve worldviews involve, first, grasping their archetypes or overarching ideas, so as to advance towards their multi-layered mutual connections and interdependencies. In doing so we explore the purity and transparency of a 'worldview colour', and also, as we saw earlier (pp. 154–155), draw on the usual, long-proven analytic or syllogistic tools – not founded, however, on reductionist or agnostic preconceptions. Starting from the whole, this mode of enquiry characterises and specifies the position of each strand within the living whole. Rather than a shallow pluralism, therefore, this study – in its fundamental ethical structure, in its acceptance and invariable affirmation of other views – is an *art* that can breathe only in the utmost freedom. We also spoke of it as a dodecahedron of wisdom and life.

When we survey our whole journey in this book, we can realise that some worldviews look more to the external aspect of world and humanity, while others are concerned more with their interiority. *Phenomenalism* (Chapter 3) is the objective manifestation or revelation of 'inmost living being' in the form of 'an alien truth and reality' as Herman Lotze puts it. *Sensualism* (Chapter 4) departs from this more objective plane initially and is subsumed primarily in sense experience, seeking its orientation in sense impressions. Thus, it occupies a middle position between phenomenalism on the one hand and *materialism* (Chapter 5) on the other, the latter founded on the principle of attributing all natural processes to material processes.

The worldviews that primarily employ thinking reflection are mathematism, rationalism and idealism (Chapters 6–8, respectively). The mathematist investigates the mathematical and geometrical structure of world and human being, but also possesses the tool of crystal-clear cognition. Mathematism seeks to reduce everything to a common denominator: one God or an archetypal force or an equation to explain everything. Its magic formula is 'unity in diversity'. In this way, mathematism connects with monadism (Chapter 12) as true pluralism. And while pneumatism (Chapter 10) finds fulfilment in an intimating vision of the universal world soul, there is only a very fine line dividing it from its complementary counter-pole in sensualism. Here we touch on two worldviews that are more concerned with the interiority of world and humanity. '*Spiritualism*' (Chapter 11) also approaches us from this direction, and, with its assertion that everything is spirit, stands in crass opposition to materialism. Our twelvefold study here tells us that matter and spirit are *two* aspects of the *one* reality. And this is the core statement of *realism* (Chapter 14).

But now let us go further: *psychism* (Chapter 9) as pure introspection reaches the eternal and primordial ground of our own individuality. The deeper this experience, the more the contrary phenomenality of existence becomes the manifestation of a 'living essence' intimately related to our I-hood. To progress further here, we need the eyes and ears of a pneumatic and 'spiritualist' outlook, as well as the further means provided only by monadism. These carry us through into dynamism (Chapter 13).

The dynamist, in the Dionysian–Appollonian interplay of human interiority, descends into the unfathomable depths of the 'Father'. Here, we have one side of the cosmic Trinity: the essentially silent and unmanifest. In contrast to this – in phenomenalism – we have complete manifestation, revelation, the *spoken word* of creation. 'Spirit' has entered phenomenality, becomes sense-perceptible and coagulates into 'matter'. Let us recall here the previously cited words of the great Oetinger: 'Corporeality is the end of the ways of God.' And in Paul we read, 'Do you not know that your body is a temple of the holy spirit indwelling you?' (1 Corinthians 6, 19). Solomon even calls the spirit the 'master-workman' of God (Proverbs 8, 30).[197]

Here, we see a mysterious contradiction, one that could scarcely be any greater: energy becomes form, inner becomes outer, essence becomes manifest phenomenon. And in the middle, as it were at the heart of all creation and evolution, the Logos holds sway, the creative grammar of a cosmic speech whose script constitutes visible nature – precisely as Novalis puts it at the beginning of *The Novices of Sais*:

> Many are the ways pursued by men. Whoever traces and compares them will see wondrous forms emerging; forms that belong to that great script of ciphers that we see everywhere: on wings, eggshells, in clouds, snow, in crystals and rock formations, on ice-clad waters, in the interior and exterior of mountains, plants, animals, human beings, in the lights of heaven, on lumps of pitch and panes of glass, in filings gathering round

> a magnet and in strange conjunctures of chance. In these we intimate a key to this wondrous script, its very grammar.

This is the Logos that endowed us with the capacity for speech as a continuous creation in miniature, as we briefly described earlier. *This* is the highest spirit of realism, of a worldview that starts where, in our encounter with the world, we take it as it is – the world of both outer and inner phenomena. We can therefore say that all worldviews rest like a bud within this realism that adheres to what is; and thus it is *the* fundamental human outlook par excellence. We are all endowed with it at birth as a tool that helps us to find our way in the world, in our apprehensions, emotions and daily work.

Realism is not intrinsically more valuable than other outlooks. Just as every worldview can grow beyond its own confines, this is also true of the potentiality of this last worldview. It has a deep affinity with the apprehensions of the child, where, of course, it still wears the garb of naivety, which in the course of life must be exchanged for the more critical stance of the adult. And yet it is never lost entirely, for without it we could never freely and openly embark on a new challenge or embrace a new outlook. This openness is the child still alive in a man or woman! Openness and lack of preconception or prejudice are blossoms on the strong stem of a new childhood that we need to attain if we really wish to become equal to life's fullness. With the Gospel, we can say, 'Strive for the sagacity of the snake and the innocence of the dove' (Matthew, 10, 16). This also means that we should *become* like children once again. Christ once said this when he summoned a child into the circle of disciples. Then he added a phrase worthy of the deepest contemplation: 'They who, with trust in me, engage with the being of such a child, will find me in that child' (Matthew 18, 5).

In philosophy, people speak of realism as opposed to idealism, and often, at the same time, point to the two great pillars of Western culture: to Aristotle and Plato. We broached these matters in Chapters 7 and 8 on rationalism and idealism, but now let us study this fundamentally harmonious contrast in more detail.

The epithet 'realist' for Aristotle and 'idealist' for Plato relates to their stance towards the creative world of ideas. In Plato's outlook we recognised, basically, the metaphysical distance of the world of ideas. He saw this realm as the true nature of being in contrast to the mutability of things, and thus also their inessential quality. Aristotle, who belonged to Plato's academy for nigh-on 20 years, here adopts a position in striking contrast to that of his teacher, Plato. Throughout his *Metaphysics*, we can discover something like a polemical undertone in regard to Plato's views. For Aristotle, while ideas are active powers, they are *immanent* in things rather than transcendent. They bring about form in material substance. This substance, which Aristotle calls 'hyle', relates to creating form as reality does to potential. Only in the unity of the forming element and this mysteriously immaterial yet primordially substantial 'stuff' of hyle does reality emerge as essential, tangible phenomenality. This view is termed 'hylomorphism'. It can be illustrated in terms of the sculptor who, in the artistic process, informs the soft, undifferentiated clay with idea and thus creates a third element, the immanence of artistic reality – the artwork as unity of form and substance.

Here, the aesthetic approach of realism is at home: beauty is not the reflection of the idea in the artwork, but the artwork itself is formed and *transfigured* matter, which has assumed an ideal character. Nature differs from this only in being complete and concluded, whereas, thanks to the Logos power indwelling us, we human beings as artists can extend the natural process further and continue it. Goethe, whose artistic and scientific approach largely accords with realism, speaks clearly of this continuation of nature's works: 'They to whom nature begins to unveil her open secret will feel an irresistible yearning for her worthiest interpreter, art.'[198] As we saw earlier in Chapter 3 on phenomenalism, we are concerned here with *Impressionism* as an artistic stance. *Expressionism*, by contrast, likewise understood in its broadest sense, basically reveals interior worlds. In Goethe's terms, both are connected with the 'secret laws of nature' active within us, which, without the manifestation of beauty, 'would have remained eternally hidden from us' (see p. 24). A spiritualism that is indivisible from a higher realism belongs here, too, in the sense of the artwork as transfigured reality. At the age of 27, Rudolf Steiner gave a talk at the Goethe Association in Vienna on 'Goethe as the Father of a New Aesthetics', and there stated:

> Beauty is not the divine in the garb of sensory reality; no, it is sense reality in a divine garment. The artist does not bring the divine to earth by allowing it to flow into the world, but rather by raising the world into the sphere of the divine. Beauty is 'seemly', is appearance, because it conjures before our senses a reality that inherently depicts an ideal world. 'Consider *what*, but still more consider *how*' [Translator's note: the latter is a quotation from Goethe, referring also to the dichotomy of content and form]; for this, the *manner* of what is shown is the important thing.

Just before this, he had quoted from Johann Heinrich Merck, the literary critic, who, very much in terms of the artistic realism we have been discussing here, once characterised Goethe's work in the following words: 'Your endeavour, your unswerving intent, is to give reality a poetic form, whereas others seek to realise the "poetic", the imaginative.' With regard to the artist as someone who continues and extends natural processes, Steiner said at the end of his lecture:

> In this sense, the artist appears to us as someone who continues and carries further the spirit of the world. Where this spirit relinquishes its labours, the artist continues creation. Thus, the artist appears to us to have an inner fraternity with the world spirit, and art can be seen as the free perpetuation of the processes of nature. As such, artists rise above ordinary life and raise us with them too when we contemplate their works. They do not create their works for the finite world, but they grow beyond it. Goethe expresses this view in his poem 'Artist's Apotheosis', placing into the mouth of the Muse these words to the artist:
>
> Thus mightily the noble man works on
> For centuries upon his kind:
> For what a good person can achieve
> Is not attained in life's constricted scope.
> He lives on too beyond his death
> Still influential as in life:
> Good deeds and lovely words still strive
> Immortally as he once, mortal, strove.
> And so you too [the artist] live on through measureless time,
> Enjoying immortality.[199]

After these thoughts on art, let us return again to our starting point.

Aristotle coined the term 'entelechy' to describe a shaping, form- and purpose-giving power. He also gives the name 'entelechy' to the human soul, which 'contains its goal within itself'. We see here a principle at work similar to Goethe's 'living form configured and self-developing', which 'neither time nor any power can break' (see p. 105). This, therefore, is the indivisible essence within us, the 'in-dividual'. In this book we regard it as identical with what has been called the human 'I'. It is clear here that this term – this reality – can, like truth, be compared in its depths and breadths to a more or less unfathomed ocean. (This Aristotelian definition of the nature of entelechy is also an extremely fertile perspective for gaining a deeper understanding of psychism and monadism.)

In the works of Thomas Aquinas, the concept of entelechy became *the* key reference point in his endeavour to demonstrate the immortality of the human individual. Here, he was primarily confronting the monopsychism of the Arabic philosopher Averroes, according to which the separate souls of human beings are not in themselves, and originally, diverse, not individually immortal, but instead materially and bodily determined modifications of a single soul substance. The Averroists likewise regarded the active power of human thinking connected with this soul substance as non-individual. Martin Grabmann, a scholar profoundly knowledgeable about medieval philosophy, summarises Aquinas's outlook very aptly and succinctly:

> Thomas now superimposes Aristotelian hylomorphism, as he developed it, upon the realm of psychology, by expressing the relationship of soul and body in the following fundamental thesis: 'The principle of thinking activity, the rational soul, is the essential and intrinsic form of the human body.'... He specifies and illumines this thesis through many further clauses of his argument. Contrasted with the monopsychism of Averroes, he demonstrates that there are as many intellectual principles, as many substantial forms, as there are human bodies.... Since the soul is the essential, intrinsic form of the body, it exists as a whole in the whole body, and as a whole also in each separate part of the body.... In this way, Thomas Aquinas applied the idea of substantial form in a consistent way to the relationship of soul and body in the human being, thereby sharply characterising the essential unity of the human being.[200]

Earlier we spoke of the continuing influence of Platonism and Aristotelianism through into our own times. In Christianity, until roughly the death of Alanus ab Insulis in 1203, philosophy and science – as well as theology – largely accorded with Platonic thought. As Aristotle's scientific reputation consolidated, he then came to be regarded as an authority who legitimised an ever-increasing desire for empiricism, for mundane reality. Around the seventeenth century, unfortunately, Aristotelian-influenced thought became ever-more dogmatic in nature, and as such was a hindrance to modern enquiry and research. It is known that Galileo, for instance, devoted himself energetically to refuting Aristotelian–Scholastic physics. And yet both these figures, Aristotle and Plato, remained influential into the modern era – and no wonder! Aristotelian realism and Platonic idealism are, after all, two worldviews rooted in human experience of the world. Over the course of history, much ingenuity was expended in efforts to connect or harmonise these two outlooks.

In his book *The Brilliance of Copenhagen* (not available in English), the popular science author Jos Verhulst offers an incisive and comprehensible account of the different approaches to research of the two great physicists Werner Heisenberg and Niels Bohr. The following passage from this important work aims to consolidate what was stated above:

> Werner Heisenberg, who read Plato's *Timaeus* at the age of 18 (on the roof of a priest seminary in revolutionary Munich in the summer of 1919), always regarded himself as more of a Platonist, invoking Platonic ideas to the end of his life in order to refute atomistic views of reality: 'It seems to me that modern physics has clearly decided in favour of Plato (as opposed to Democritus). The smallest units of matter are in reality not physical objects in the ordinary sense, but rather forms, ideas, that can only be unequivocally expressed in the language of mathematics.'...
>
> There is no doubt of a certain tension between the 'Platonist' Heisenberg and the 'Aristotelian' Bohr. The essence of this is that Heisenberg has a tendency to regard the mathematical 'idea' as such as a reality, whereas Bohr is not satisfied with a merely mathematical account, and instead seeks further: for a physical reality to which mathematical formalism relates.

Then he continues by describing the sometimes fierce disputes that arose between Bohr and Heisenberg in 1927:

> [Heisenberg] was happy with a mathematic formalism that satisfactorily described reality, whereas Bohr wished to break through to a formulation of *physical concepts* capable of encompassing newly discovered aspects of nature. The so-called 'Copenhagen Interpretation' of quantum mechanics – which is still accepted today – arose from the dispute between the 'Platonist' and the 'Aristotelian'. That it was possible in 1927 to achieve a synthesis between these two outlooks was of great significance for the history of physics.
>
> Later in his life, Heisenberg expressly cited Aristotle when interpreting the true meaning of mathematical structure (of the wave function in quantum mechanics). This wave function, which we can establish with the aid of the physical system theory, in general describes which

fields of possible phenomena can be demonstrated in the observed physical system. At the same time it stipulates the degree of probability with which every possible phenomenon can be realised:

> '... The idea that the occurrence itself is not inevitably pre-determined, but that the potential or the "tendency" for an occurrence itself possesses a type of reality – a certain intermediate level of reality, midway between the mass-type reality of matter and the mental reality of the idea of the picture – plays a decisive role in the philosophy of Aristotle.'[201]

If we also add here what Franz Herwig Schopper said about Plato (see p. 93), we can gain a vivid sense of the topicality of these matters. Not only do these two worldviews not conflict with each other, but like the other ten they, too, are in an interacting and reciprocal relationship. This comes very clearly to expression in Steiner's spiritual-scientific work, in anthroposophy, which itself represents a contemporary continuation and connection between the substance of Platonist and Aristotelian culture: on the one hand, extending into 'spiritualism' and, on the other, also encompassing materialism. Somewhat simplifying, we can say of the 'wheel' of the twelve worldviews that from the point of departure of idealism, passing to the left and rising further, we find a 'Platonic' element at work whereas, looking to the right half of the wheel, we find realms that more strongly invoke Aristotelianism in us.

Both Goethe and Steiner can further bear witness to the degree to which the relationship between Aristotle and Plato preoccupies human thinking. In his *History of the Theory of Colours*, Goethe writes:

> Plato relates to the world as a blessed spirit that deigns to dwell a little while upon it. He is less concerned to acquaint himself with it, since he already accepts it as a given, than to amicably impart what he brings with him, which is so necessary for it. He penetrates the depths more to fill the world with his own being than to enquire into it. He moves towards the heights with the longing to own again his own origin. Everything that he expresses relates to what is eternally whole, good, true and beautiful, enhancement of which he seeks to stir in every breast. The diverse aspects of the earthly knowledge he acquires merge, or even, one might say, evaporate in his method, in his form of address.
>
> By contrast Aristotle relates humanly to the world, as a master builder. Here he is, and aims to work and create. He enquires into the

> soil but only to the point where he finds ground and foundation beneath him. From here downwards to the centre of the earth is a matter of indifference to him. He draws an enormous ground plan for his edifice, procures materials from everywhere, orders them, layers them upon each other, and thus rises in regularity of form up into the heights like a pyramid, compared with Plato, who seeks heaven like an obelisk, or even a pointed flame....
>
> Yes, like the nations, the centuries divide in their reverence for Plato and Aristotle: sometimes peacefully, sometimes in fierce dispute; and it is to be seen as a great advantage of our own age that honour is given to both in equal measure, as Raphael already conceived of both men in his *School of Athens*, and placed them opposite each other.[202]

And Steiner:

> The worldview of Aristotle... is not at odds with that of Plato. The difference between them lies more in the manner in which both these men were captivated by the different aspects of reality (the world of ideas, and the world of the senses). For Plato, the sense world is merely a preliminary to reaching the world of ideas; it only has significance in so far as it enables us to attain this. For Aristotle the opposite is the case: he wanted to explain the sense world, and sought to do so through ideas. We can say that, to a sober appraisal, both philosophers are of the same view, but that their interest focuses on opposite things.[203]

As stated earlier (see p. 104), Steiner elaborates the aspect of human entelechy into a science of reincarnation and karma, on the one hand; and, on the other, he establishes a path of knowledge of the unified reality of the world and the human being which depends on the immanent, spiritual power of thinking enacted by this entelechy of ours. Let us enlarge on the three passages from his autobiography cited at the beginning of the book with excerpts that relate to his book *The Philosophy of Freedom*:

> In my book I sought to show that an unknown reality does *not lie behind* the sense world, but that the world of spirit is immanent within it. And in relation to the human world of ideas I sought to demonstrate that this world is rooted in, and consists of, the world of spirit. In other words, the essence of the sense world is only hidden from human awareness *for as long as* the soul *only* perceives through the senses. If we experience ideas

> along with sense perceptions, then consciousness experiences the sense world in its objective essence and being. Cognition is not the depiction of intrinsic being but rather the soul living its way into this intrinsic being. *Within* our consciousness we advance from the as-yet inessential sense world to its reality. And thus the sense world only remains appearance (phenomenon) while consciousness has not yet completed its work upon it.

This process then undergoes an intensification or enhancement that, in connection with the totality of the twelve worldviews, we can certainly see as the living expression of the whole human being:

> In order to achieve the right relationship with the world through meditation, I repeatedly summoned this thought: the world is full of enigma. Knowledge may approach it, but will mostly come up with a thought content as the solution to the enigma. But these enigmas, I said to myself, *cannot be resolved through thoughts*. They lead the soul towards solutions, but they themselves do not contain them. An enigma arises in the real world and exists there as phenomenon; and its solution similarly *arises in reality*. One thing, a being or process, arises, and will be the solution to the other.
>
> And so I also told myself that the whole world, apart from the human being, is an enigma, the world-enigma as such; and *the human being is its solution*.
>
> And this led me to think that at any moment we can say something about the world-enigma, but that what we say can offer only as much of the solution as we have discovered about ourselves as a human being.
>
> Thus cognition becomes a process occurring in reality. Questions manifest in the world as realities; knowledge within us is our participation in what the beings and processes in the spiritual and physical world have to tell us.

And finally, Steiner's fundamental position:

> In my whole soul lived enthusiasm for what I later called 'knowledge that accords with reality'. And it was clear to me, especially, that with such knowledge a person could not encapsulate themself in some remote corner of the world while existence and development occurred outside them. For me, knowledge became something that does not belong only to a person but to the being and growth of the world. Just as the root and

> trunk of a tree are not complete if they do not grow on into blossom, so the world's being and development cannot truly endure if they do not live on to become the content of knowledge. With this insight I continually repeated to myself, whenever appropriate, that humans are not beings who *create* a content of knowledge *for themselves,* but rather their soul is the *arena upon which the world first experiences her existence and development.* If knowledge did not exist, the world would remain incomplete.[204]

The world of sense phenomena and that of spiritual thinking activity in a sense merge and, in this realist, almost alchemical process, intensify into a dimension of reality for which appropriate terms really are lacking. This is an intensification of the sense realm, on the one hand – like a dissolution – and a substantiation of the corresponding concepts, on the other: a process resembling the artistic 'transfiguration processes' described earlier. In the sense of a higher realism we would have to name this 'element' the true *foundational substance* of the world.

In 1907 Steiner wrote a sentence from which it is clear that he defines *reality* neither in 'spiritualist' terms alone nor in narrowly material ones: 'For the whole reality of a thing consists of spirit and substance.'[205] In this statement we find realism – and an encounter of the two halves of the circle of worldviews. Confirmation of the existence of this dual-poled but unified underlying substance is to be found in the *evidence of immediate experience* – an experience that proceeds from ordinary consciousness, doing so thanks to the Aristotelian–Thomist principle of thinking activity as creative spiritual power latent in our depths. But this is nothing other that the power of the Logos!

So we have three stages of realism, each embedded in a very particular historical and cultural context. Aristotle took the first of these steps. The principle of entelechy in the human being and nature, as he formulated it philosophically, then becomes – and this is the second step – the foundation of certainty in the soul of Aquinas that each person is immortal through the power of their thinking soul as entelechy. Here is a key passage from his argument against the adherents of Averroes:

> Amongst all errors, the most crass is that relating to intelligence, by virtue of which we are after all capable of avoiding errors and acknowledging truth. Long enough already, this erroneous view of intelligence has insinuated itself into many, taking its origin from certain statements by Averroes, in which the endeavour is to claim that 'Intelligence

> is an entity completely separate from the human soul, and is one and the same in all people'. In regard to this view we must especially be surprised that it originates with those who desire to be of the school of peripatetics, yet prefer to follow Averroes on misguided paths than to know the truth with other peripatetics – indeed, with Aristotle himself. From the words of this same Aristotle it is clear, apparent and beyond objection that *this* was his view of the intelligence of the human soul, through which it [intelligence] grasps ideas and forms insights: namely, that, first, it is a part of the soul; secondly, that it is not a part of the body nor possesses any bodily organ like the other soul faculties; thirdly, that one rightly regards it as being separate from the body, coming to it from without, since it does not proceed from matter, of which it is fully independent, but originates from a nobler source, like other entities also that excel matter; fourthly, that nothing prevents intelligence from outlasting matter, given that its intrinsic efficacy is fully independent of the body etc....
>
> But also the other assertion, that 'Intelligence is numerically only *one* in all human beings', appears impossible for many diverse reasons. For from this it would follow, first, that *this* individual person would be in no way other than *that* individual person, and that *all* people would only be *one* person, indwelled by only a single soul. Furthermore, it would necessarily follow that there would be only *one* understanding for all people, such that, when *I* encompass a stone with my understanding, *you* would inevitably also grasp it at the same time and in the same way. Yet this does not accord with experience.[206]

The third stage or step is that taken by Steiner. He undertook it in an era neither of intellectual upheaval, as was true for Aristotle, nor of scholastic contemplation, as for Aquinas, but in the midst of a century of classical materialism, and he founded it on the conceptual world of Fichte, Haeckel, Hegel and Stirner.

As we saw earlier, in Steiner's realism – enhanced or intensified in the Goethean sense – he went beyond mere knowledge of a power of entelechy in the world, and also beyond a Thomist substantiation of individual immortality. He connects thinking to the world in a way that enables the ideas engendered *in us* in the sense world to manifest their *real* essence and inner being. Steiner's entelechial realism is concerned, on the one hand, with intensifying human powers of cognition from ordinary waking consciousness into a thinking clairvoyance that overcomes the limits of space and time. In scope, this knowledge ranges from mathematism to monadism. On the other hand, he establishes a view of 'reality-attuned knowledge' capable of shedding a higher light on our experience of phenomenalism, sensualism and materialism; that is, as enhanced, heightened hylomorphism, at a level where the opposition between spirit and matter completely disappears and both are perceived, as it were, as a new earth substance: concentrated thought light and liquefied life substance in one. That is the 'foundational substance' to which we referred above.

Human consciousness is an essential part of this process. Here, we are compelled to use religious terms, since the ontological plane of this process is nothing other than the sphere of the omnipresent resurrected Christ Logos, both within us human beings and in the natural world. The words with which the resurrected Christ sends his disciples into the world must certainly be understood as words of the 'Logos':

> All creative power has been given me now in heaven and on earth. Therefore depart and be the teachers of all nations, and baptise them in the name and with the power of the Father, the Son and the Holy Spirit. And teach them to hold to the spiritual goals that I have given you. And behold, I am in your midst always, to the very end of the earth. (Matthew, 28, 18ff.)

The Logos, the creative might of cosmic reason, became human being in Jesus of Nazareth at the Jordan baptism. In the hyle of Jesus, its formative power, its essential form of being – or, we can also say, its entelechy – developed the germ of a new corporeality that was to unfold – through the 'Father' – only after death. Just as, at the world's creation, the Logos 'expressed' what became manifest from the silent and hidden ground of the cosmos, through the Holy Spirit as 'master workman' (see p. 173), so now, after the silence of the grave on Easter Saturday, a new creation is initiated: the new 'body' as foundation of 'God's Citadel', as Novalis puts it in one of his 'Spiritual Songs'. Here, we encounter an octave, or higher level, of hylomorphism in its original conception. We can also put it like this: the Logos becomes a human being, and the human being – the resurrected one – appears, as new Logos, as the creator of a new humanity and a new earth, described by the author of the Apocalypse in the picture of the heavenly Jerusalem.

Thus, we have three manifestation of the cosmic Word: the first, original creation, then the creative Word principle within us, and finally the resurrected Logos-Christ in the human being, simultaneously as the 'creative might' in heaven *and* on earth. Heaven and earth within him, in his earth-encompassing resurrection aura: that is cosmic realism. Thus, it is the entelechial power of Christ that is capable of so humanising the human element in us that the Logos power resting in the I, ordinarily largely unconscious, penetrates daily consciousness, *raising* and transubstantiating it. And this 'eternal duration of a heightened human condition, sealed by the day of Easter', symbolised by the Rose Cross, is what Goethe is speaking of in his poem 'The Mysteries':

> The cross stands there, with roses woven thickly.
> Who was it who with roses adorned the cross?
> The coronal wreath on all sides unfurls richly,
> Softening the stark wood's loss.

The resurrected Logos-Christ, the divine principle that, as Paul says, indwells the temple of the human body, is the loftiest spirit of realism, and the assurance of a perpetual transformation of human nature: it is *he* who adorned the cross with roses.

In the midst of war and the thundering of cannon, a mystic and scientist – a palaeontologist – wrote an essay on 'Cosmic Life' and prefaced it with this motto:

> There is a communion with God
> And there is a communion with the earth
> And there is a communion with God through the earth.[207]

This was the Jesuit Pierre Teilhard de Chardin, one of those who participated in this mystery. Each and every person has their own most highly individual doorway that is gradually opened. To put it another way, in the language of Christ's farewell addresses and, in our view, in the sense of a genuine pluralism, 'In my Father's house are many dwellings' (John 14, 1). The 'house' is Christ himself. It seems to me that Sadat, in 'Cell 54' (see p. 116) began to open *his* doorway, as did Gandhi, Albert Schweitzer and many others from all parts of the globe and all religions who may not ever have told anyone else about it. This is a universal process that can manifest at many different levels, not least through the genuine Christian sacrament of the Eucharist in which bread and wine become Christ's 'body' and 'blood' by the mediation of an ordained priest. That, too, is realism.

And Steiner? He too found his doorway. Through the 'path of knowledge' he established, 'that seeks to lead the spirit in the human being to the spirit in the universe' (see p. 14), he was able to open up contemporary ways by means of which anyone who wishes can come closer to their own 'dwelling'. At the same time it should not be forgotten that it is the prerogative of 'Another' to open the door. I will return to this later.

Steiner's path led him from a Platonist-type idealism – if we recall his 'Credo' – to a cognitive and existential realism, latent in him from the outset and rooted in a direct experience of Christ. Towards the end of the nineteenth century, his ethical and epistemological individualism turned him fiercely against all one-sided, otherworldly Christianity. In *Nietzsche, the Fighter against His Age* (the title of one of Steiner's early books),[208] he felt he had found a like-minded companion. It is probable that these words from Nietzsche's *Thus Spoke Zarathustra* met with complete endorsement from Steiner:

> Stay true to the earth, my brothers, with the might of your virtue! May your bestowing love and your knowledge serve the earth's purpose! Thus I beg and beseech you... May your spirit and your virtue serve the purpose and meaning of the earth, my brothers, and may the worth of all things be renewed by you! This is why you should be fighters! This is why you should be creators![209]

For Steiner, who sought to 'know reality through thinking', engagement with the materialistic forms of thinking of his day was what the thunder of cannon and the rattling of machine guns were for Teilhard de Chardin. Following extreme experiences of loneliness, it is my conviction that this was reinforced by the abyss of extreme individualism that had opened up before him in his spiritual assimilation of the thoughts of Max Stirner and in his friendship with Stirner's publisher, John Henry Mackay. Here are two significant statements about that period, before he was able to pass through *his* doorway:

> In the thinking that can emerge from science – but was not yet emerging then – I saw the foundation upon which human beings can gain insight into the world of spirit. I therefore strongly accentuated knowledge of natural foundations that must lead to spirit knowledge. For those who, unlike myself, do not have direct experience of the world of spirit, such immersion in a school of thought signifies mere activation of thinking. But for those who experience the world of spirit, it signifies something very different. They are brought into the proximity of beings in the spirit world who desire to make such a school of thought the sole, prevailing

> and dominant one. Here, one-sidedness of knowledge and perception is not merely the cause of abstract confusion, but what is simply error in the human world there becomes living, spiritual intercourse with beings. Later on, when I sought to point in this direction, I spoke of 'ahrimanic' beings. For them it is an absolute reality that the world must be a machine. They live in a world that directly adjoins the sense world.
>
> With my own ideas I did not for a moment succumb to this world, not even unconsciously. I carefully ensured that all my cognition occurred in calm, reflective awareness. All the more conscious, therefore, was my inner battle with demonic powers that were seeking to conjure a mechanistic-materialistic mode of thinking rather than to lead natural science towards spirit vision.
>
> In seeking spiritual perception and knowledge, one has to *experience* these worlds; merely thinking about them theoretically is not sufficient. At the time I had to save my spirit vision in inner tempests. These tempests stood behind my outward experience.[210]

And the other trial:

> Destiny shaped my experience of J.H. Mackay and Stirner in a way that meant I was compelled to immerse myself in a world of thought that became, for me, a *spiritual probation.* I sensed my ethical individualism to be a purely inward human experience. As I elaborated it, I had no inclination to make it into the basis for a political view. But then, around 1898, my soul's purely ethical individualism was to be dragged down into a kind of abyss. From purely inward human experience it was to be made into something outward. The esoteric was to be diverted into the exoteric.
>
> But at the beginning of the new century, having come through this probation, when I was able to convey my spiritual experience in texts such as *Eleven European Mystics* and *Christianity as Mystical Fact*, 'ethical individualism' once more stood in its rightful place.[211]

Looking back to that time of trial, Steiner then wrote that he was only able to get further by conjuring the development of Christianity before his spiritual gaze:

> I found the Christianity that I was compelled to seek in none of the available confessions. After facing arduous inner battles in my period of inner trial, I had to immerse myself instead in a contemplation of Christianity in the world in which the spirit speaks of it....

> At the period when I made comments on Christianity in words whose content so greatly contradicted what I later said, its true content started to unfold in me germinally as an inner manifestation of insight. Around the turn of the century, this germ increasingly developed. The soul's probation I described occurred before the new century dawned. It was central to my inner development that I had stood spiritually before the Mystery of Golgotha in an inmost, and most profoundly earnest, festival of knowledge.[212]

The 'eternal duration of a heightened human condition, sealed by the day of Easter' became for Steiner, the Goethe scholar and philosopher of freedom, an *immanent* reality. Henceforth, he no longer sought, as Nietzsche had, to battle *against* his age, but rather *for* a new age. During those years he also gained a comprehensive insight into the truth

> that beings and occurrences in the world are not truly explained by using thinking to 'explain' them; but instead, one can use thinking to perceive occurrences in the context in which one thing explains the other, in which one thing becomes the solution to the other's enigma, and human beings themselves become the word for the outer world they perceive.
>
> And thus it was possible for me to experience the truth that the *Logos, wisdom, the Word,* holds sway in the world and its workings.[213]

Let us now briefly summarise what has been said in this chapter, in the awareness that we have already reached the religious dimension of realism: as a worldview of transfiguration and, if you like, inner resurrection founded on existential experience. Here, I have to emphasise that I have only elaborated things in this book that have arisen through my own quest and research. Others may have come to different conclusions. It is ultimately up to readers to decide what is plausible for them or not. As already mentioned, I see this study only as stimulus for each person's own further search.

Thus, we started from the fundamentally realist outlook of taking the world altogether as it is, but in an expectant intimation that outer and inner worlds conceal more within them than either sensory observation or introspection initially reveals. The gaze of the true realist – not to be confused with a narrow pragmatist or positivist – resembles that of an innocent child who, in their own way, seeks to decipher the 'enigma' of the world. However essential it is to have a critical capacity when seeking knowledge about the human being and the world, a childlike eye, without preconceptions, can lead us a long way in our search for comprehensive truth. We could enlarge on the saying of Christ that we should *become* – not remain – like little children – by adding the thought that we should do so with the full freight of our own entelechy.

Next, we considered Plato and Aristotle as representatives of idealism and realism, respectively, and traced these two currents of thought all the way down to Heisenberg and Bohr. We also touched on the world of art and aesthetics from a realist perspective, and likewise the hylomorphism of the great Thomas of Aquinas.

In the work of Steiner we saw a third development of Aristotelianism beyond Aristotle himself and Aquinas. As we see from his autobiography, Steiner, like Paul and many later figures through into our own time, bore witness to the reality of the 'Mystery of Golgotha', which became *his* doorway. In the Christological aspects of his work he tells us what he perceived of this. He also emphasises that an 'ordinary healthy' sense of things is enough to enable us to experience the workings of the Father in the world. But to find the Christ, he says, is 'in a sense a matter of destiny'.[214] It is grace. It cannot be compelled, although one can embark on the journey towards it. Both Christ and the human being are in this respect completely free, for the highest genius of realism to which we have referred is at the same time the presiding spirit of freedom.

We also spoke of anthroposophy as a path of knowledge. Due to this developmental character, it is not a 'worldview' in the same way as those described in this book, but can open our eyes to this whole colour-circle of outlooks. The twelve worldviews, as an expression of the Logos creatively active in the world and the human being, are centred in the resurrected Christ as in a focal point. He, after all, is 'the way, the truth and the life'. Novalis knew this. In one fragment he writes, 'Should there not also be a heaven in philosophy, that is, an *infinite* epitome of system potencies? Continually predicated upon an infinite central body – which is none other than heaven – in which we live, move and have our being?'[215]

These last words are a quotation from Paul, when speaking to the Athenians (Acts, 17, 27), and in turn originated from the Stoic Cleanthes; for Paul was speaking to an audience well versed in philosophy. Thus, a broad span reaches from the origins of conceptual thought through to our own day, and continues on into the future, for transformation of our now outmoded thinking through the power of the Logos is one of the great missions for today and the future.

We are now approaching the end of this complex chapter, and I will conclude with same verse by Steiner in which he offers further testimony of his realism. Precisely when we discern his ethos of life here, we can understand why Steiner's life's work turned out to be eminently practical: from it emerged schools, hospitals, farms, medicine, cosmetics, artistic impulses, socially committed banking institutions, and much more. These are all the outcome of a realism that encompasses science, art and religion in equal measure. Below is a credo that reckons with the 'meaning and purpose of the earth':

> Seek truly practical material life,
> But do so in a way that does not allow it to dull you
> to the spirit at work within it.
> Seek the spirit,
> But do not seek it by revelling in supersensible delight,
> out of supersensible egoism,
> But seek it rather
> Because you wish to use it selflessly
> in practical life in the material world.
>
> Apply the old principle:
> 'Spirit is never without matter, matter never
> without spirit', in such a way that you say:
> We wish always to act materially in the light of the spirit,
> And we wish to seek the light of the spirit so
> That it kindles warmth for us in our practical deeds.
> The spirit that we conduct into matter,
> The matter that we work upon until it manifests
> By expelling the spirit from it;
> The matter that receives from us spirit manifested,
> The spirit that is driven by us towards matter:
> These form the living existence
> That can bring true progress to humanity –
> A progress that the best of modern souls
> Can only long for, in their profoundest depths.[216]

15

Humanus: The New Human Being in the Third Millennium

The end of the twentieth century threw up questions whose answer will determine how we shape the future. Strange and unsettling contrasts became apparent: fundamentalism on the one hand, calls for tolerance on the other. Neo-nationalisms are clashing with a globally increasing sensitivity to the rights of minorities. Materialistic lifestyles come up against a broad and diverse search for spiritual values. Ecology and exploitation of the natural world collide.

The situation today is very different from the beginning of the twentieth century, before the raging of world wars, before such events as Hiroshima; and different also from the period of reconstruction in the shadow of the Cold War. In so far as events in the world are an expression of human thought, their potential dynamic acts within each one of us. Questions of *meaning* newly posed today are thus also about human integrity in an environment torn apart by diverse conflicts. These are not new questions, of course. But old, traditional answers cannot maintain their validity. Millions of new cases of depression, and the hosts of people debilitated by drugs and intoxicants, are surely a global cry for meaning.

Many even ask whether we might need a new kind of human being altogether. Some answers to this question reveal trends that may remind us of the horrors of the Fascist and Communist regimes of past decades. To illustrate this we will quote some passages from Jens Heisterkamp's lucid study, *Biotech Man: Genetic Utopias and How 'Bioethics' Justifies Them*:

> Never before have we been more liberated from creaturely conditions than in our century. We have made eating independent of natural

rhythms; machines relieve us of a great part of our daily work; we master the elements to procure inconceivable amounts of energy; we overcome the boundaries of space and have plunged deep into the cosmos; electronic data processing enables us to achieve things far superior to our own intelligence. And ultimately human beings, following endlessly long evolutionary periods, have lifted themselves free of evolution and are taking their own development, and that of nature, into their own hands. It seems that the eighth day of Creation has dawned, and that the world is beginning anew for humankind....

The eighth day: the end of the old and a transition into a new creation lorded over by the human being; the end of our creaturehood and the beginning of self-creating responsibility. The idea of the 'Superman' has been around since the nineteenth century, initially as pure promise or expectancy, as yet unsullied by the disfigurements that would later appear. But what inner content do we give to this new trend in creation and humanity?...

In this context, the totalitarianism that manifested in many forms during the twentieth century can appear as a perversion and materialisation of spiritual evolutionary perspectives that had dawned on humankind with the new century, but assumed a warped form in the delusion of the perfect human being, the 'Superman'. Leninist and Stalinist socialism seeks to compel human perfection by establishing a classless society. By brutally eradicating real distinctions between people – we may think here of measures enforced by Stalin or Pol Pot – it destroys the very nature of humanity. The delusion of biological perfection in a racially homogeneous, thus supposedly superior, society holds sway in nationalistic Fascism. This demands the complete subordination of the individual to principles of biology and functionalism, leading to a denial of human rights, and the suppression and ultimate destruction of all who are not seen as conforming to this biological functionalism.

Heisterkamp continues:

In relation to this deluded idea of genetic perfectionism, Klaus Dörner has taken a surprising new look at the strategies of Nazism. He thinks that the key aim of the Nazis was 'to demonstrate to the world, in the single example of Germany, that a society that rids itself of absolutely all social ballast would be economically, militarily and scientifically unbeatable'. From this perspective, racist and eugenic totalitarianism would no longer be seen as moral deviancy but as the inevitable consequence of a logic of industrial and scientific progress. This aim in fact was formulated as far back as the eve of the First World War (and thus long before the Nazi era) by the physician and social reformer Forel:

> We certainly do not intend to create a new human race, an *ubermensch*, but only to gradually eradicate... defective lower types through voluntary sterilisation of the carriers of poor seed, at the same time encouraging better, more social, healthier and happier people to multiply in ever-greater numbers.

Heisterkamp now points out that the 'horrors of Nazi eugenics, especially the murder of people with learning difficulties or handicaps, and the repugnant racial purity policies of the Third Reich... have – at least in Germany – rendered completely taboo any idea of artificial, state-enforced or planned interventions in human reproduction'. In the further course of his book he refers to questions arising from the decoding of the whole human genome, and comes to this conclusion:

> Eugenics has become socially acceptable again. Benefitting from enormous medical progress in previous decades, modern eugenics, it is true, no longer advocates an openly racist programme as it did in the thirties. Nevertheless, this neo-eugenic thinking has unmistakeable connections with the 'bio-politics' of the new right. A fixation on the purity and health of the genotype along with increasing nationalism are descendants of the same ill wind.[217]

Such ideas, involving the total manipulation and disenfranchisement of the individual, are issues that threaten to erupt beneath us. From the perspective of our overall humanity, we can only agree with Heisterkamp when he writes, towards the end of his book:

> If we are to owe biotechnology any debt of gratitude, then it is this: that it alerts us to the question of the real nature of the human being. Without renewal and redoubling of endeavours to answer this question, biotechnology will take possession of the human body and thus the very foundations of our evolution. In still more extreme forms than environmental dangers, climate change or food quality, our 'most intrinsic arena of life' (Herbert Witzenmann) is at stake here. All further trends towards 'human qualities' produced by biotechnology (including a 'happy' personality as outcome of genetic manipulation) signify a

> limiting of individual human existence. This is the most radical attack on our evolution towards freedom.[218]

The whole thing is still more explosive in nature if we consider – and such thoughts are already being loudly voiced – that the many who 'do not wish to worship at the altar of the new (old) idol of an "improved humanity"... may soon have to reckon with compulsory measures (such as partial withdrawal of health insurance protection if a patient refuses certain procedures)'.[219]

The author closes his remarkable book with an appeal to 'work to become more conscious and to engage in practical actions'. Basically, the question of meaning and purpose is here placed in a context that will not allow much delay.

A book by Andreas Steffens published in 1999, as a philosophical summary of the state of play at the end of the century, concerns itself with the question of human nature, and what kind of people we *wish* to be in future.

> A history of the ruin of our human self-conception extends from the battlefields of the world wars through to the research laboratories of molecular biology today; and at the end of the twentieth century one of its central legacies is the uncertain nature of human existence.[220]

Steffens pleads for a rejection of monist positions on consciousness, which he describes as absolutism:

> The few 'results' apparent at the end of the century include a growing tendency to relinquish such absolutism, as it flourished under the spell of metaphysical traditions, and to refashion the loss of truth that seemingly results from this into the advantage of an unlimited 'pluralism' in thinking.[221]

In relation to the twelve worldviews, this is a perspective that offers much food for thought! A key chapter in his relentlessly clear analysis of the recent past deals with the theme of 'anthropolitics', which, among other things, concerns racial discrimination and so on. He then also speaks of the 'longing for a new human being' apparent in the past century:

> The century began with a longing that has not lapsed as it ends, but reaches far beyond it: the longing to be different. In its testimonies a tendency is at work that we cannot conceive of sufficiently strongly,

> and whose distant vanishing point is the desire to be a different kind of human being.[222]

Then he quotes words by Hermann Bahr on the eve of the First World War:

> It's about this: that human beings wish to find themselves again. Can it be human destiny that we neglect ourselves through adherence to some goal? That was Schiller's question. The inhuman endeavour of our era is to urge this upon us against our nature, making us into a mere tool, an instrument of our own works, with no meaning any more.... We no longer live but are only lived. We have no freedom any more, we are no longer allowed to decide, we have gone absent, the human being has been deprived of soul, and nature has been dehumanised. Only a moment ago we lauded ourselves as lords and masters, but now her gorge has swallowed us. We need nothing short of a miracle! This is what it's about: whether, through a miracle, the desouled, sunk, buried human being will come back to life again.[223]

This outcry came with, as yet, no knowledge of the Second World War or Nazi anthropolitics, let alone modern bio-ethics. Steffens then focuses his attention on the darker years of the past century and, interestingly, accentuates the anthropological momentum of that era:

> The totalitarian dynamic of an exclusively controlled and directed community life followed various marked principles that together constitute an anthropology. Nazism was not only declared by a few dominant ideologues as the basis for a new human type, but was organised from the first moment the Nazis came to power to such a degree that they could take practical and political steps to enforce this shaping of human nature. This was a conscious policy of *human reformation*.[224]

Steffens concludes his overview with a quotation from Michael Landmann about anthropology as self-knowledge, and assigns philosophy a mission that we have also discovered in the context of the twelve worldviews, not least in relation to the question of meaning:

> *'Anthropology is humankind's knowledge of itself.'*
> This statement no longer holds true now that human self-confidence founded on self-determined action has imploded during a history of ever-more excessive forms of destruction of human nature. At least,

> anthropology has not yet come to be this (again). The extreme potential contained in human nature, as we have experienced it, has expanded our knowledge so profoundly that the validity and sustainability of everything that went before have been cancelled out. Even where it has not become completely devalued, its value has nevertheless changed.
>
> It has become surface knowledge only, and as yet there is scarcely any acknowledgement of the deep strata from which those all-relativising experiences emerged.
>
> As we look back on this century, it is certainly philosophy's most essential mission to establish this deep knowledge of human nature, and to form it into an awareness capable of acting upon human self-understanding; and of doing so in ways that will allow it to become once again a factor in the genesis of a culture that consists in creating and assuring human potentiality.
>
> By culture I mean the self-creation of human modes of being. This cannot be naturalistically founded. While there are conditions that must be respected when culture is created which set limits to it, or advance it, these do not determine it. There is no natural limit to the way in which human beings wish to be and exist; such confines pertain only to forms of organic life. Even here, given the potential of biotechnical interventions, the limit may no longer be absolute.
>
> Naturally this mission is a hypothetical one, since no philosophy, no science, can seriously undertake to *attain* such a goal. But what is possible, and an obligation on us, is to pursue what we seek as if it were attainable.
>
> One has to forget *the* human being so that *human beings* do not become unendurable to us, and so that we can continue to cope with the idea of being one....
>
> Could anyone have dared wish to create the human being who gazes back on the human deeds of this past century?
>
> In retrospect, we can therefore know fairly precisely what kind of people we would prefer *not* to be; but do we know who we would like to become?[225]

From the stance of this book, we find a plausible perspective here: it is rooted in human potential, in the inner sovereignty of our self – as we have discussed this in various ways – to become *the* human being that we seek to be. This perspective can be seen in ongoing practice of the anthropology of the twelve worldviews, and, as we said almost programmatically at the beginning, as a gateway to an all-embracing understanding of the human being and the world. In our view, this task, or in Steffens's word, 'mission', can only be gradually realised, but is not, nevertheless, a 'hypothetical' one. It becomes actual and real to the degree that *I set about practising it*, here and now. Naturally I am under no illusions that this practice could happen all of a sudden, or that the diet proposed in this book can be digested immediately by everyone. But thoughts also have a scope and a destiny that can only be determined by actual life; and no mere assumption, whether optimistic or pessimistic, can set itself up as the arbiter of destiny.

Each and every person can awaken the 'Humanus' in themselves by finding the gateway through which this figure approaches us. This book is only an *image* of a large-scale housing complex, with its infrastructure and its facilities. Every reader can use it as orientation in order, where possible, to gain an idea of what the dwelling assigned them in the 'house of the Father' may look like. In my experience, since the resurrection of the Logos-become-man, entering this house has become an immanent event, and therefore a picture of this kind can already show us our 'front yard'. Paul says, 'For the spirit searches all things, also the deep things of God' (1 Corinthians 2, 10). This quest and enquiry is a path that all of us can pursue.

The basic stance of this book is largely a monadistic pluralism, above all in its social or socio-cultural concerns. But how, now, does our view of the central significance of the Easter events in their historical context – right up to the present day – relate to the equality of the twelve worldviews, or to the theoretical parity of religious outlooks? Have we perhaps, in some undercover way, created a whole new hegemony after all? Let us look back again to the movement for pluralist theology which we touched on briefly at the end of Chapter 12 on monadism. I'll quote again from the radio script I was sent:

> *Announcer:* What is known as pluralist theology relinquishes Christianity's traditional claim to superiority over other religions. It considers, instead, that there are other pathways to God. Rome regards this as a danger, the greatest challenge since the theology of liberation.

The interviewer asks the English philosopher of religion John Hick, the most prominent representative of pluralist theology, what significance Jesus Christ has in his outlook. It seems to me that a great many contemporaries would give the same answer that he does:

> Jesus was a historical figure. That's certain, there's no doubt about it. But if you identify him with God, I'd prefer to use other terms. I see him as a human being, albeit one of manifold significance – as someone who was open to, and in touch with, God in an extraordinary way. In this sense God incarnated in his life. Wherever a human being acts towards other people in selfless love and compassion, so that God's will is fulfilled on earth, then you can say that God or the will of God has incarnated in human life. We should reflect on this, and see the divine incarnation in the life of Jesus as a picture of Jesus incarnating the ideal of a human response to God. But he is not the only person with this openness to God in the history of humanity.

There is nothing at all to object to, of course, in the wonderful contemporary ethics conveyed in these words, nor – in the terms of pluralism – anything to be said against Hick's view of Christ's identity. But I would like to offer another – albeit rather unorthodox – view, as a possible answer to this really very unusual question: Is Christianity actually a religion at all in the usual sense?

Novalis once said this: 'There is no religion that would not be Christianity.'[226] To understand this sentence – which I agree with – the first thing to shed from it is the character of religion as identical with a particular confession based on a creed that encompasses *all* believers. There are a great many Christian confessions, and likewise differing groups within all other religions in the world, in a sense related to the great diversity within humanity, ever since the Tower of Babel and the 'confusion of tongues'. If we regard the first half of humanity's evolution – wherever each person may be located in it – as a mighty process of individuation from racial, tribal and clan connections, we can see this emancipation culminating at last in the absolute individual, lonely in their faith or lack of it, wedded to their own hard-won outlook and willing only to lead an intrinsically personal religious life. When Novalis, in his essay 'Christianity or Europe', states that true anarchy is the element that engenders religion, I believe he means it in this sense. Here, all idea of a church community *in the usual sense* ceases, along with all claims that one is better than another, and any striving for hegemony by a unified religion founded on an obligatory confession with a hierarchical structure. From the individual perspective, the only unity there can be is the one we referred to as 'unity in diversity'.

Above all, any claim to power must cease here; for all these things are shadows cast by the great light of mathematism.

If we seek to understand the nature of Christ and *his* Christianity from this aspect, we must become absolute monadists. It is a matter not of me convincing or even converting others, but rather of entering into dialogue with them; for each person is in a sense someone unique in creation, from whom I can learn new perspectives on the world, whether in the fields of science, art or religion. Basically what is said here tends towards the 'I–Thou' relationship formulated by Martin Buber. We can only affirm what Buber says in his fundamental work:

> Relationship is mutuality.... The relationship to the Thou is direct.... Everything real in life is encounter.... Love is the responsibility of an I for a Thou... Creation reveals its configurability in encounter.... In the beginning is relationship.... Through the Thou a person becomes an I.[227]

This is monadism!

In monadism we are in fact concerned with the category 'relation'. Only this can be the real foundation of a developing multicultural society in which listening acquires at least as much value as utterance. But this applies to every relationship: in the family, in friendships, in partnerships, in the world of work – everywhere. When the claim to power over others, and the wish to convince them ceases, then the original social renewal occurs as Christ established it: 'For where two or three are gathered in my name, I myself am in their midst' (Matthew 18, 20).

What does it mean to be gathered 'in his name'? It can only mean: as he intends, or in accord with his being and nature. A key aspect of this is that the Logos-Christ is simply the epitome of 'relation'. And what does 'relation' mean? Relation or relationship means 'being between'. In Buber's terms we could say, 'When we say Thou, we are not speaking of some quantity.... When we say Thou, we do not possess something or other. We have nothing. But we do stand in relationship.'[228] Or to put it another way: if A stands here, and next to them B, and then C alongside, the 'empty space' between them is the *relational space*.

Christ is the relational space of the cosmos. Or we could also say he is the mediator or cosmic grammarian who gives the letters of creation their *order*; or the cosmic artist who gives the Father's substance of being – as Logos, as the logic of cosmic laws – to the 'master workman' of the spirit so that it can be configured and made manifest.

We can try to apply this manner of reading to the Gospels and release the nature of this 'power in the world' from the claims of any earthly church. Only indications can be offered, for readers to enlarge on and diversify. The first example is the beginning of the Gospel of St John:

> In the beginning was the Word,
> And the Word was with God,
> And the Word was a divine being.
> The same was in the beginning with God.
> Through this did all things become,
> And nothing that arose became other than through the Word.
> In it was life,
> And the life was the light of humankind.
> And the light shines in the darkness;
> But the darkness has not taken up the light.

The Logos was *with* God. In the original Greek, we can recognise here the Aristotelian category of *pros ti*, the 'relationship to something'. Then the text continues: *through* this did all things become. The Word was like the creating gateway through which silent being articulated itself in – rationally ordered – speech. We spoke of creation earlier as Word coagulated into matter. Then life becomes light. The realm of the living is, surely, a manifold network of infinite, harmonious relationships. And light is the element that allows us to enter into relationship with something. Light makes visible, not urging itself upon us but illumining everything. Light is selflessness: we do not see it as such, but it encompasses everything. From this perspective we might also say that light is love.

Below are three further testimonies from the Logos Gospel of John:

> And Jesus began anew to speak to them: I am the light of the world. Whoever follows me will not wander in darkness but will have the light in which is life. (John, 8, 12)

> I am the door. (John 10, 1)

And then the passage we have already quoted, where Christ's mediating role becomes especially apparent:

> Then Thomas said to him: Lord we do not know where you are going. How should we know the way? Jesus replied, I am the way and the truth and the life. None finds the way to the Father except through me. (John, 14, 5)

We could cite many more instances. If we think of the 'relation' category in the sense discussed above, we discover the true nature of religion: creating a *relationship* with God. The moment we find in the Christ Logos the primal element of connection between the human being and God – both before and after Christ – it becomes the impulse underlying all religion, as the human search or quest for God. And we can understand in these terms what Novalis means by saying there is no religion that 'would not be Christianity'. Earthly churches cannot be 'Christianity' but only the world-encompassing love of the Logos become man is 'Christianity', and as such this lives in *every single human being*, initially irrespective of any ecclesiastical affiliation. A Church community, an *ecclesia*, a 'gathering' as Paul called it, can only be called Christian if the mystery of meeting and encounter unfolds within it, which in turn signifies that the encounter becomes love. In the Christian sense, God is simply love: 'God is love, and whoever remains in love, remains in God, and God remains in him' (John 4, 16).

In this sense, too, it is of no interest whatever to Christ which Church anyone belongs to: he looks upon the individual whom he can lead to the Father. He is the true door to our dwelling in the house of the Father. His temple is the world in which we all live, his parish the whole of humanity, his family all kingdoms of nature. *He* is, in fact, the truly pluralistic religion. In so far as earthly churches, or those organised on earth – whether in Judaism, Islam, Christianity or other religions – have not yet discovered or do not yet practise universal love (for, at this level, truth and love are identical), they are not yet pervaded by the breath of freedom and truth: 'You will perceive the truth, and the truth will lead you to freedom' (John 8, 32). That is the Christianity of Christ that can live in every religion: truth, freedom and love. And in this spirit he seeks to lead each and every individual, into whom he has entered since the resurrection, out of the 'anarchy' into which the process of individuation inevitably led us and towards a new relationship with other people, nature and the all-encompassing godhead.

In this sense, there are three stages in religious development: ecclesiastical organisations that are 'pre-anarchic' or pre-emancipation, and whose task was to guide and govern people; then a great emancipation movement of the individual, extending as far as inner anarchy (which should in no way be understood in political terms); and, finally, the realisation of the threefold Gospel in truth, freedom and love by ever-increasing numbers of people from all religious camps and worldviews. This ideal shines as a future beacon for humanity in the images of the first Whitsun, as recorded at the beginning of the Acts of the Apostles: the Babel of many tongues is redeemed by each disciple speaking his own language, yet understanding and being understood by all. This is a Logos mystery of the future that can only be gradually realised: a true *ecclesia.*

This is the relational aspect of Christianity, connected with Christ's omnipresence, as described also at the end of the Gospel of Matthew: 'He is *with* us until the end of the world.' If we exclude the Easter events – which is the danger of pluralist theology as embodied by John Hick – then we also omit the future of the earth. Does this mean Christianity is a better religion than others? The question is misplaced. Christ is not a 'religion', but the impulse driving everything religious, all search for God and for cosmopolitan-spiritual community-building. However, there is not only good in the world. The power of evil also has its own kind of light: yet this is either a compelling, seductive, *blinding* light, or a *slanted* light of lies and deception. It is up to each of us to examine carefully what light we live in and perhaps also the church we may belong to.

If we wish to school ourselves in the quality of the Logos light, there is scarcely a better manual for this than the Gospel of John. In the complete acceptance that love can engender – but this has nothing to do with an absence of critical faculty – there is simply no longer a question as to which religion is the 'best'. Instead, as a twenty-first-century person, we can recognise that 'to live in love for one's actions, and to *let live*, with understanding of another's will, is the fundamental aim of the free human being'.[229] In other words, not only tolerating others but acknowledging them!

Goethe once took a basically similar stance when he said that tolerance should really only be a 'passing outlook', and that acknowledgement should come to replace it (see p. 3). Here is the passage from Rudolf Meyer's book, which was quoted at the very beginning of this book:

> But tolerance can also culminate in an unfruitful neutrality of view, one that makes no effort to engage with the specific and particular nature of a different stance. For this reason Goethe says: 'Tolerance should actually only be a temporary position: it must lead to recognition and acknowledgement. Sufferance signifies insult.' It is clear that this high ideal at the same time points to a developmental goal embracing all human society and the community of nations. The figure of Humanus who, in the sign of the Rose Cross, gathers around himself representatives of all religious and cultural currents and can unite them in true fraternity, seeks to embody this outlook of a future interdenominational Christianity.

On another occasion, Goethe wrote that 'there is no salvation except love in the face of another's great qualities'.[230]

What has been said here about the category 'relation' can shed light on the mysterious departure of Humanus from the company of the twelve 'after long living together'. Goethe himself said this was because 'his spirit is embodied in all of them, belongs to them all, and no longer needs an earthly raiment'.[231] Humanus had become pure 'relation', was omnipresent as the Christ-filled relational power of love. This is the only way to understand Goethe's remark that Humanus's departure is connected with the events of Easter and with the process initiated then of earth's permeation by the death-vanquishing power of Christ's love:

> If this whole enactment takes place in the week of Easter, and the chief symbol of this community is a cross inwoven with roses, it is easy to envisage that the eternal preservation of higher human conditions will have also been revealed here, in consoling fashion, at the point when Humanus departs.

The Easter events – that lead on to Ascension, Whitsun and through to the moment when Paul witnessed the resurrected Christ as light and word near Damascus – can, as we saw earlier, be understood at least tentatively with the aid of two Aristotelian categories, as long as we grasp them dynamically and on diverse planes of existence. In the enhanced hylomorphism of the actual resurrection we can draw on the category of 'substance' – *ousia*. This is neither spirit alone – that is, form – nor exclusively matter (see p. 181). This Christ-permeated new founding substance is comparable to a cloud that, on the one hand, can condense into *points* of precipitation and, on the other, can evaporate into the *universal* atmosphere. That is the context described in the Ascension scene as Christ's disappearance into a cloud. The risen one becomes, as it were, atmospherically omnipresent: he has become relational space.

Relation and space provide open-minded thinking with a first, important aid in grappling with one of the most complex questions in humanity's cultural history. In connection with our twelve outlooks, too, we have spoken at various places of the categories. Sigismund von Gleich repeatedly refers to them.[232] Basically, the twelve worldviews are a further evolution of the core statements, established in antiquity in mathematist manner by the genius of Aristotle, about the various mode of being.[233] Just as the categories are an expression of the thinking human being, the twelve worldviews in principle embody the *thinking*, *feeling* and *will-enacting* human being as an answer to the world's enigma: they are an expression of our fully awoken I. In reality, they appear in the most varied forms and connections, and their path to the truth is at the same time a path to the core of our humanity: to the Logos-become-human in all of us, the Humanus.

Rudolf Steiner, who, to my knowledge, was the first to point to this twelvefold unity of worldviews, knew that progressively engaging with these matters would offer not only a path to the cosmos, but also a distinctive path of self-knowledge, a means for discovering our all-encompassing self. In a lecture in which he started from the level of the imaginative faculty – one of the higher stages of human knowledge – he once said this:

> The moment we enter into the imaginative world through this schooling path, and see our I as an image, we must be clear that we can see twelve different pictures of this I. There are twelve different pictures of every individual I, and only when we have regarded our I from without from twelve different perspectives have we understood it in its completeness. This view of the I from without has precisely the same relation as that reflected in the relationship between the twelve pictures of the zodiac and the sun. Just as the sun passes through the twelve zodiac signs and possesses a different power in each and, as it were, shines upon our earth from twelve different positions, so the human I also illumines itself from twelve different perspectives as it looks back from the higher world. For this reason we have to say that when ascending into higher worlds we must not be satisfied with a single perspective. One has to school oneself in this to avoid confusion, and we can only do so if we accustom ourselves in the physical world already to seeing that observing anything from one angle is not the be-all and end-all. Some people are materialists, others 'spiritualists'... etc. The 'spiritualists' assert that everything is spirit and accord meaning only to the spirit; the monists assert that everything must be explained in terms of a unity. All these different people dispute with one another, and may even fall to squabbling. But if you want to prepare the ground for real insight, you must consider this: materialism is to some degree valid; we have to acquire the ability to think according to material laws, but apply this thinking only to the material world, not to the mental or spiritual world. We have to grasp these laws, for otherwise we do not get to proper grips with this world.

He then goes on to say:

> But by adopting different perspectives we can accustom ourselves to discovering wherever each is valid. And in doing so we educate ourselves to see things from the most diverse points of view... this ability to depart from our own position and to describe objectively through another's eyes is something we must necessarily acquire.[234]

In this whole context, Steiner relates each of the twelve worldviews to the zodiac forces, as these have been known since antiquity:

Phenomenalism – Virgo
Sensualism – Leo
Materialism – Cancer
Mathematism – Gemini
Rationalism – Taurus
Idealism – Aries
Psychism – Pisces
Pneumatism – Aquarius
'Spiritualism' – Capricorn
Monadism – Sagittarius
Dynamism – Scorpio
Realism – Libra

Looking back at our whole journey through this book, we could say that Goethe's work continues, or to some degree fulfils, the intention characterised but not realised in his poem 'The Mysteries': that of describing the twelvefold unity of 'the most diverse modes of thinking and feeling'. We have tried to illustrate how Rudolf Steiner picks up on this work that Goethe began. To locate and isolate him, therefore, in a particular fixed and locked outlook, as many over-eager critics of his work have done, is either an error based on lack of knowledge, or perhaps intentionally misleading. He is neither a gnostic nor a theosophist, neither a syncretist nor an eclectic. Ultimately, what he did was to gain access – in a manner available to everyone – to these twelve worldviews and thereby seek to enliven many fields of practice. To a certain degree he gained initiation in the mysteries of truth, freedom and love.

The work Steiner left – anthroposophy – is in his words a 'path of knowledge'. Building on this path, we have tried to develop these twelve qualities, as stimulus for an emerging multicultural society, in a way that continually shows illustrative links with science, art and religion. In this sense, the book is conceived as a workbook or practice book and needs complementing with other aspects or from other perspectives. Doubtless there are other ways to reach the goals described here, especially since this kind of study is not everyone's cup of tea. But I have repeatedly found that these fields of study have indeed proved fruitful in a social context – in the actual world of work, in negotiations and in biographical counselling; and not least as a help on the path towards finding deeper meaning in everyday life.

Besides Goethe we have often spoken of another figure, and quoted from his works: Friedrich von Hardenberg, who took the pen name of Novalis – or 'clearer of new ground'.[235] When he died at the age of 28, he left poetry and philosophical works that we can regard as nothing less than a seed for future centuries. He himself once said in one of his profound aphorisms, 'Everything is seed.'[236] A contemporary of Goethe and connected with the most important artists and scholars of his day, he continually learned and absorbed new things, and was able to compress his brilliant insights and the fruits of his meditations into a wealth of masterful and seminal aphorisms. He had a view of the world and the future rooted in a youthfully impelled Christianity. Christ himself became, for him, the presiding genius in the quest for an eternal spiritual youth – one who, as John tells us in the Apocalypse, sets about making everything *new*. In Novalis's view of the new human being and a new earth, we see the same foundation that underlies the growth of this book; and in the poet himself we recognise the very spirit and embodiment of this same rejuvenating power that each and every person – whether young or old – can attain. What our contemporary world needs in the third millennium is not the dynamistic worship of everlasting biological youth in an otherwise spiritually decrepit civilisation, but a youthful heart, full of interest in and love for nature and humanity, and a readiness to act where it is needed; and this too is completely in accord with Novalis, who wrote, 'Our mission is this: to form and develop the earth.'[237]

Or to put it another way: this is about developing truth, freedom and love in all theoretical and practical concerns of daily life. Too lofty an ideal? Each person will have to decide for themself.

Epilogue

From *Sacred Songs* by Novalis:

I tell each person that he lives
And has arisen; that he
Hovers in our midst and is
With us eternally.

I tell each person, each one tells
It to their friends again:
That soon and everywhere will dawn
The new kingdom of heaven.

To new eyes only now the world
Appears a Fatherland;
A new life, enraptured, we receive
Out of his offering hand.

Down into the ocean's depths
Baleful death has sunk,
And every person, light, sublime
Can to his future look.

The path of darkness that he trod
Ends in the heavens above,
And we come to the Father's house also
If we hearken to his word.

Nor is there any weeping now
When someone's eyes by death are sealed:
Knowing we'll meet again, soon or late,
This pain is sweetened, healed.

For every good deed, each one now
Can glow with fresher joy,
For glorious this seed will flower
In meadows lovelier.

He lives and will be with us now
When we're bereft of all!
And so this day shall be for us
A world-rejuvenating festival.

Notes and References

1 J.W. Goethe, *Die Geheimnisse – ein Fragment* ('The Mysteries – a Fragment') with Goethe's essay in Cotta's *Morgenblatt*, 1816. Quotations from the poem are taken from the Hamburg edition, vol. III, pp. 271–284. All poems in German in this volume have been translated by this book's translator, Matthew Barton.

2 Quoted in Fredrich Hiebel, *Goethe, die Erhöhung des Menschen*, Frankfurt a.M., 1982, p. 141.

3 See, for instance, F. Lienhard, 'Montserrat, der Gralsberg', in *Das Buch vom Gral*, ed. B. Kircher, Munich, 1989, pp. 299–308.

4 J.P. Eckermann, *Gespräche mit Goethe*, ed. F. Bergmann, Frankfurt a.M., 1994, p. 104.

5 Rudolf Meyer, *Goethe: Der Heide und der Christ*, Stuttgart, 1999, p. 227.

6 Ibid., p. 104f.

7 G.W.F. Hegel, *Vorlesungen über die Philosophie der Geschichte*, Frankfurt a.M., 1973, p. 76.

8 Ibid., p. 86.

9 Thomas S. Kuhn, *Die Struktur wissenschaftlicher Revolutionen*, Frankfurt a.M., 1996, p. 115f.

10 Neil Postman, *The End of Education: Redefining the Value of School*, Vintage Books, 1996.

11 Hartmut Böhme, 'Wer sagt, was Leben ist?', *Die Zeit*, 30 November 2000, p. 41.

12 Max Scheler, 'Der Formalismus in der Ethik und die material Wertethik', quoted in G. Schischkoff, *Philosophisches Wörterbuch*, Stuttgart, 1991, p. 773.

13 Rudolf Steiner, lecture on 21 January 1914, in GA 151, *Human and Cosmic Thought*, Rudolf Steiner Press, 1991. All quotations from the works of Rudolf Steiner cite the volume number in the complete catalogue of his works (GA) as published by Rudolf Steiner Verlag, Dornach, Switzerland.

14 *Brockhaus Enzyklopädie*, vol. 24, p. 20 in the 19th edition, Mannheim, 1994.

15 Cf. Johannes Hemleben, *Diesseits – vom Lesen im Buche der Natur*, Hamburg, 1982.

16 Rudolf Steiner, GA 28, *Mein Lebensgang* (published in English as *Autobiography*), p. 245.

17 Ibid., pp. 319–320.

18 Ibid., p. 235f.

19 Ibid., p. 237.

20 Ibid., p. 279f.

21 Rudolf Steiner, GA 26, *Anthroposophische Leitsätze* (published in English as *Anthroposophic Leading Thoughts*), p. 14.

22 See note 13.

23 Sigismund von Gleich, *Die Wahrheit als Gesamtumfang aller Weltansichten*. Disseminated in 1947 as a cyclostyled manuscript, this first appeared in book form in 1957 from J.Ch. Mellinger Verlag, Stuttgart (2nd edition, 1989).
24 Quoted in S. von Gleich, op. cit., p. 23.
25 Ibid., p. 43.
26 J.W. Goethe, *Sprüche in Prosa*, edited with a commentary by Rudolf Steiner, no. 165 (re-issued Stuttgart, 1999).
27 Ibid., no. 178.
28 Ibid., no. 188.
29 Ibid., no. 811.
30 Novalis, *Werke und Briefe*, Munich, 1962; from the fragments on 'Cosmology and Religion', no. 537.
31 P. Antes (ed.), *Grosse Religionsstifter: Zarathustra, Moses, Jesus, Mani, Muhammad, Nanak, Buddha, Konfuzius, Lao Zi*, Munich, 1992; see H.P. Hasenfratz on Zarathustra, p. 11.
32 Ibid., p. 14.
33 Quoted in Hans Baumann, *Die Welt der Pharaonen*, Ravensburg, 1967, p. 106.
34 See, for instance, V. Poulsen, *Ägyptische Kunst*, Königstein im Taunus, 1968, Part II, p. 13.
35 Genesis, 9.
36 See for instance Peter Heusser (ed.), *Goethes Beitrag zur Erneuerung der Naturwissenschaften*, Bern, 2000. In addition, see the Goethean studies by, amongst others, Jochen Bockemühl, Thomas Göbel, Ernst-Michael Kranich, Wolfgang Schad and Andreas Suchantke.
37 Quoted by Michael Ende in *Fantasie, Kultur, Politik*, Stuttgart, 1982, p. 33.
38 See, for instance, Konrad Lorenz, *Er redete mit dem Vieh, den Vögeln und den Fischen*, Munich, 1964; and *So kam der Mensch auf den Hund*, Munich, 1985.
39 Lorenz., *Er redete mit dem Vieh, den Vögeln und den Fischen*, p. 12.
40 Rudolf Steiner, GA 10, *Wie erlangt man Erkenntnisse der höheren Welten?* (published in English as *Knowledge of the Higher Worlds*), 1972, p. 48ff.
41 Quoted in S. von Gleich, op. cit., p. 78f.
42 In R.F. Schmidt (ed.), *Grundriss der Sinnesphysiologie*, Berlin, 1985, p. 8f.
43 Ibid., p. 1.
44 Franz Mechsner, 'Das Problem mit der Seele', *GEO*, 25 May 1987, p. 146ff.
45 Alfred Gierer's reply to the question about the 'limits to knowledge' in *GEO* (see note 44), p. 166f.
46 See, for instance, Jean Ayres, *Sensory Integration and the Child*, Western Psychological Services, 1970.
47 See, for instance, W. Aeppli, *Sinnesorganismus, Sinnesverlust, Sinnespflege: Die Sinneslehre Rudolf Steiners in ihrer Bedeutung für die Erziehung*, revised edition, Stuttgart, 1996.
48 Rudolf Steiner, GA 1, introductions to Goethe's scientific writings, published in English as *Goethean Science*, Mercury Press, 1988, in the chapter 'The Ur-Phenomenon'.
49 Qur'an, 4, 14, translated into German by L. Ullmann, Munich, 1959.
50 Ibid., 47, 16.
51 Ibid., 56, 12–25.
52 Bacon IV [1901], 50: *Novum Organum*, I, Aphorism XIX.
53 German source: *Geschichte de Philosophie in Text und Darstellung*, vol. 4, Stuttgart 1980, p. 29f.

54 Rudolf Steiner, GA 293, *The Foundations of Human Experience*, Anthroposophic Press, 1996; especially lecture 8 on 29 August 1919. In general these lectures concern the whole human configuration of body, soul and spirit.
55 R.F. Schmidt, op. cit., p. 2ff.
56 Hugo Kükelhaus, *Organ und Bewusstsein*, Cologne, 1987, p. 12f.
57 Ibid., p. 35.
58 Ibid., p. 47.
59 J.W. Goethe, *Pandora*, verses 164–193.
60 Barbara C. Sproul, *Schöpfungsmythen der westlichen Welt*, Munich 1994.
61 *Die Vorsokratiker*, selected and translated into German by E. Bergs, Aschendorff, 1971, p. 75.
62 Klaus Strobach, *Vom Urknall zur Erde: Werden und Wandlung unseres Planeten im Kosmos*, Melsungen, 1983, p. 194ff.
63 G. Gamov is a pioneer of the big bang theory.
64 See the outstanding study by Alfred Schütze, *Die Kategorien des Aristoteles und der Logos*, Stuttgart, 1972. The ten categories are: substance, time, space, quantity, quality, action, suffering, state or habitus, position and relation.
65 Quoted in Werner Heisenberg, *Der Teil und das Ganze: Gespräche im Umkreis der Atomphysik*, Munich, 1975, p. 52.
66 See Emil Bock, *Boten des Geistes: Schwäbische Geistesgeschichte und christliche Zukunft*, Stuttgart, 1955. In relation to the origins of matter, see also Hermann Beckh, *Alchymie: Vom Geheimnis der Stoffeswelt*, Dornach, Switzerland, 1987.
67 James Jeans, *The Mysterious Universe*, Cambridge, 1930, quoted in Jean Gebser, *Abendländische Wandlung*, Berlin, 1968, p. 57.
68 Walter Schubart, *Geistige Wandlung*, 1940, quoted in Jean Gebser, op. cit., p. 57f.
69 Quoted in von Gleich, op. cit., p. 37.
70 In relation to this whole issue, see also Jens Heisterkamp, *Der biotechnische Mensch: Genetische Utopien und ihre Rechtfertigung durch 'Bioethik'*, Frankfurt a.M., 1994.
71 From *Süddeutsche Zeitung*, quoted in *Info3*, p. 8, no. 10, 2000, Frankfurt a.M.
72 Quoted in Johannes Hemleben, *Das haben wir nicht gewollt: Sinn und Tragik der Naturwissenschaft*, Frankfurt a.M., 1981, p. 125f.
73 Von Gleich, op. cit., p. 37.
74 See Emil Bock, *Rudolf Steiner: Studien zu seinem Lebensgang und Lebenswerk*, ed. Erich Gabert and Gundhild Kačer-Bock, 3rd edition, 1990: the chapter 'Von der okkulten Bewegung in Deutschland am Ende des 19. Jahrhunderts'.
75 Sheila Ostrander and Lynn Schroeder, *Psychic Discoveries behind the Iron Curtain*, Englewood Cliffs, NJ, 1971, p. 203.
76 Ibid.
77 See, for instance, Rudolf Steiner, GA 13, *Occult Science – an Outline*, the chapter 'World Evolution and the Human Being'.
78 Hemleben, op. cit., p. 166.
79 Quoted in Hemleben, op. cit., p. 52.
80 Novalis, op. cit., from the fragments on 'Mathematics and Science', no. 354.
81 Ibid.
82 Ibid., no. 353.
83 Ibid., no. 354.
84 Aristotle on the categories, rendered here from the German version by Schütze, op. cit., p. 9.
85 See also Ekkehard Meffert, *Nikolaus von Kues: Sein Lebensgang, seine Lehre vom Geist*, Stuttgart, 2001.
86 Hemleben, op. cit., p. 26.

87 *Der Anticlaudian*, translated from Latin and introduced by Wilhelm Rath, 1983, p. 199f.
88 Qur'an, 2, 256.
89 Ibid., 3, 20; 3, 200; and, for instance, 5, 5.
90 Hamburg edition, vol. I (1960), p. 367.
91 Quoted in Alfred Schütze, *Das Rätsel des Bösen*, Stuttgart, 1969, p. 107f.
92 The passages are taken from *Der Spiegel*, no. 42, 1988.
93 Quoted in G. Kroppp, *Philosophie: Ein Gang durch ihre Geschichte*, Munich, undated, p. 176.
94 Quoted in Hemleben, op. cit., p. 38f.
95 V. Vontin (ed.), *Das Weltbild*, Braunschweig, 1952, pp. 188f., 191.
96 Quoted in von Gleich, op. cit., p. 174f.
97 J.W. Goethe, 'Der Verfasser teilt die Geschichte seiner botanischen Studien mit', Hamburg edition, vol. XIII, 1960, p. 163f.
98 Albert Steffen, *Pilgerfahrt zum Lebensbaum*, Dornach, Switzerland, 1982, p. 58f.
99 Albert Einstein, *Mein Weltbild*, Frankfurt a.M., 1984, p. 18.
100 Plato, *The Republic*, Books VI and VII.
101 Plato, *Timaeus*, 2.2.
102 Marcus Aurelius, *Meditations*, II, 9; IV, 10, 51; and VI, 1.
103 Epictetus, 'What Does the Good Consist of, and What Should One Most Practise?', III, 3, here from *Geschichte der Philosophie in Text und Darstellung*, vol. 1, Stuttgart, 1978, p. 310.
104 Antes, op. cit., the essay by H.-J. Klimkeit, p. 155.
105 Translations of passages from the Bible in this book are based on the German by Emil Bock, Stuttgart, 1980.
106 G. Mensching (ed.) *Die Söhne Gottes: Aus den heiligen Schriften der Menschheit*, Wiesbaden, undated, p. 50.
107 Niccolo Machiavelli, *The Prince*, here from *Geschichte der Philosophie in Text und Darstellung*, vol. 1, Stuttgart. 1978, p. 365.
108 Giovanni Pico della Mirandola, *Die Würde des Menschen*, Fribourg, undated, p. 52f.
109 Wilhelm von Humboldt, *Ideen zu einem Versuch, die Grenzen der Wirksamkeit des Staates zu bestimmen*, Stuttgart, 1962, p. 21.
110 G.F. Kennan, address given in German on the occasion of the award of the German Book Trade Peace Prize, Frankfurt a.M., 1982; see also 'George Kennan Calls on the West to End Sanctions against Soviet [Union]', *New York Times*, 11 October 1982, accessed at goo.gl/jqmDj8 (18 March 2019).
111 Quoted in von Gleich, op. cit., p. 208.
112 E.W. Bödefeld, 'Kein Weltethos ohne Religion: Über das Projekt Weltethos', *Novalis*, 1/2, 2001.
113 Rudolf Steiner, GA 40, *Wahrspruchworte*, 'Credo – der Einzelne und das All'.
114 See note 26, proverbs 136, 183, 151, 185.
115 Rudolf Steiner, GA 6, *Goethe's Conception of the World*, Anthroposophical Publishing Company, 1928, the chapter 'Plato's World View'.
116 Rudolf Steiner, GA 30, *Methodische Grundlagen der Anthroposophie*, p. 541.
117 Franz Herwig Schopper, 'Die Grenzen unseres Weltbilds', *Bild der Wissenschaft* no. 5, Stuttgart, 1991. On this theme, see also J. Guitton, G. and I. Bogdanov, *Gott und Wissenschaft*, Munich, 1993, p. 99ff.
118 Bergs, op. cit, p. 65.
119 From A. Borbély, *Das Geheimnis des Schlafs: Neue Wege und Erkentnisse der Forschung*, Zurich, 1987, p. 70.
120 Marcus Aurelius, op. cit., X, 24; XII, 33.
121 Hildegard von Bingen, *Worte lebendigen Lichts*, Freiburg, 1996, p. 39f.

122 *Geschichte der Philosophie in Text und Darstellung*, vol. 6, Stuttgart, 1978, p. 126.
123 Quoted in von Gleich, op. cit., p. 55.
124 Quoted in Kropp, op. cit., p. 169.
125 Ibid., p. 171.
126 *Geschichte der Philosophie in Text und Darstellung*, vol. 7, Stuttgart, 1981, pp. 207, 225.
127 Goethe, *Proverbs in Prose*, no. 1
128 Ibid., no. 53.
129 Ibid., no. 793.
130 *Geschichte der Philosophie in Text und Darstellung*, vol. 8, Stuttgart, 1981, p. 175.
131 Carl Gustav Jung, *Erinnerungen, Träume, Gedanken* (published in English as *Memories, Dreams, Reflections*), ed. Aniela Jaffé, Zurich, 1967, p. 415.
132 Ibid., p. 416.
133 Ibid., p. 410.
134 Ibid., p. 182f.
135 Ibid., p. 408.
136 For instance in books such as *The Philosophy of Freedom*, GA 4, and *Theosophy*, GA 9. Steiner also described therein exercises for acquiring competency in spiritual-scientific enquiry.
137 Gerhard Wehr, *C.G. Jung und Rudolf Steiner: Konfrontation und Synopse*, Stuttgart, 1982, p. 186.
138 Jung, op. cit., p. 418.
139 Novalis, op. cit, from the collection *Blütenstaub* (*Pollen*), nos 16 and 28.
140 Goethe, *Proverbs in Prose*, no. 482.
141 V.I. Khan, *Sufismus - der Weg zum Selbst. - Stufen einer mystischen Meditation*, Bern, 1975, p. 68f.
142 Walter Nigg, *Das mystische Dreigestirn: Meister Eckhart, Heinrich Seuse, Johannes Tauler*, Zurich, 1990, p. 73f.
143 See note 136, especially *The Philosophy of Freedom*.
144 Sigismund von Gleich, *Der Seele Aufstieg zu den Sternen: Ein Mitgehen im sinnenden Gedenken*, 1954, p. 30.
145 J.W. Goethe, *Naturwissenschaftliche Schriften*, Hamburg edition, vol. XIII, 1960, p. 315.
146 In the essay 'Nature', James Munroe & Co., 1836.
147 Friedrich Hölderlin, 'Hyperion oder Der Eremit in Griechenland', vol. 2, Book 2, in *Sämtliche Werke*, ed. Friedrich Beissner, Munich, 1961, p. 630f.
148 J. Pesch, Bonn, 2001.
149 Mensching, op. cit., p. 264f.
150 Anwar Sadat, *In Search of Identity: An Autobiography*, London, 1978.
151 Jacques Lusseyran, *And There Was Light*, Edinburgh, 2014, p. 17ff.
152 Ibid., p. 72.
153 In many of his works, Steiner made fundamental comments on the etheric forces. See also the study and research based on this by Ernst Marti, *Das Aetherische*, Basel, 1989, and *Erscheinungsformen des Ätherischen*, ed. J. Bockemühl, Stuttgart, 1985.
154 *Faust* I, Night.
155 Steiner offers decisive insights and exercises in *Knowledge of the Higher Worlds*, GA 10, and *The Threshold of the Spiritual World*, GA 17. See also Mario Betti, *Das Sophia-Mysterium der Gegenwart: Die Geburt der Imagination*, Dornach, Switzerland, 1992.
156 Manfred Kyber, *Genius Astri*, Munich, 1960.
157 *Die Bhagavad Gita*, translated by F. Hartmann, Leipzig, 1904, pp. 12–14.
158 See, for instance, W. Müller, *Dionysios Areopagites*, Basel, 1990.

159 See Rudolf Steiner, GA 110, *The Spiritual Hierarchies and the Physical World: Zodiac, Planets & Cosmos*, SteinerBooks 2008; also Mario Betti, *Engel:– Ihr Wesen und Wirken in der Gegenwart*, Unterlengenhardt, 2001.
160 W. Müller, op. cit., p. 18.
161 *Geschichte der Philosophie in Text und Darstellung*, vol. 2, Stuttgart, 1982, pp. 151–152, .
162 See Mario Betti, 'Okkulte Fragen der Gegenwart', *Der Europäer*, 2/3 December/ January 1997/1998.
163 Betty J. Eadie, *Embraced by the Light: What Happens when You Die?*, London, 1992, pp. 90–91.
164 George G. Ritchie and Elizabeth Sherrill, *Return from Tomorrow*, Revell, 1988.
165 Dannion Brinkley, *Saved by the Light*, Piatkus, 1994, pp. 25–26.
166 Ibid., pp. 29–31.
167 See lectures by Rudolf Steiner on education, especially *The Foundations of Human Experience*, GA 293.
168 Novalis, op. cit., from the fragments on 'Cosmology and Religion'.
169 Ibid., from the collection *Blütenstaub* (*Pollen*), no. 22.
170 Ibid., from the fragments 'On the Secret World', no. 246.
171 Dante Alighieri, *The Divine Comedy*, *Paradiso*, Canto 28. This version is based on a translation at http://www.italianstudies.org/comedy/Paradiso28.htm, but modified in many places by the translator of this volume in line with the German, which was translated from Italian by Karl Vossler, Zurich, undated.
172 See Jean Gebser, op. cit.; Gebser gives a clear, succinct account of these matters.
173 *Bild der Wissenschaft*, no. 1, 2001, Stuttgart, p. 21.
174 *Geschichte der Philosophie in Text und Darstellung*, vol. 5, Stuttgart, 1979, p. 241.
175 Kropp, op. cit., p. 72f.
176 Quoted in von Gleich, op. cit. (note 23), p. 186.
177 Pablo Casals, *Joys and Sorrows: Reflections*, Simon & Schuster, 1970.
178 See the comprehensive study by E.C. Hirsch, *Der Berühmte Herr Leibniz: Eine Biographie*, Munich, 2000, p. 58ff.
179 Gebser, op. cit., p. 28.
180 Quoted in von Gleich, op. cit., p. 180.
181 Richard Friedenthal, *Goethe: Sein Leben und seine Zeit*, Munich, 1996, p. 581f.
182 Rudolf Steiner, *Mein Lebensgang* (*Autobiography*), p. 135f.
183 In this connection see, for instance, U. and M. Betti and W. Kersten, *'Es ist nicht gut, dass der Mensch allein sei…' Frau und Mann im Zeitalter der Individualität*, Stuttgart, 1998.
184 Rudolf Steiner, GA 4, *Die Philosophie der Freiheit* (*The Philosophy of Freedom*), p. 164ff.
185 In relation to science, art and religion, see also the important work by S. von Gleich, *Geisteswissenschaft, Kunstoffenbarung und religiöse Lebensanschauung in ihrer Dreieinheit philosophisch-anthroposophisch entwickelt aus dem Menschenwesen und Ideenkosmos*, Stuttgart, 1971.
186 Bavarian Radio programme *Stationen* on 14 February 2001 at 10.30am, 'Wie gefährlich ist die pluralistische Theologie?', production number 439827, presenter B. Himmelstoss.
187 Quoted in Kropp, op. cit., p. 165.
188 Ivo Frenzel, *Friedrich Nietzsche*, Reinbek bei Hamburg, 2000, p. 40.
189 Ibid., p. 50f.
190 Since this book endeavours to get to the *core* of each worldview through chosen instances, a detailed account of some forms of energy such as electricity, magnetism and nuclear power would exceed its scope, particularly since the nature of these

forces is different from those active in the organic-etheric or soul-spiritual realms. I would therefore like to refer the reader to the work by physicist Georg Unger, *Kernenergie und Geisteswissenschaft*, Dornach, Switzerland, 1979.

191 See, for instance, Wilhelm Kelber, *Die Logoslehre: Von Heraklit bis Origenes*, Frankfurt a.M., 1986, which clearly describes the different aspects of the Logos doctrine in antiquity.

192 Rupert Sheldrake, *A New Science of Life: The Hypothesis of Formative Causation*, London, 1983 (later edition, 2009).

193 Ibid., p. 16.

194 Ibid., p. 17, original emphases.

195 Ibid., pp. 118–119.

196 Hans-Peter Dürr, 'Naturwissenschaftliche Erkenntnis und Wirklichkeitserfahrung', in *Wenn Gott verloren geht*, Freiburg, 1998.

197 On this theme see also Betti *Das Sophia-Mysterium der Gegenwart*.

198 Goethe, *Proverbs in Prose*, no. 810.

199 Rudolf Steiner, 'Goethe as the Father of a New Aesthetics', lecture on 9 November 1888, in GA 271, *Kunst und Kunsterkenntnis: Grundlagen einer neuen Ästhetik*. In another lecture, given in Munich on 15 February 1918, published in the same GA, Steiner speaks of Impressionism and Expressionism and delves deeper into the matters raised here.

200 Martin Grabmann, *Thomas von Aquin: Persönlichkeit und Gedankenwelt*, Munich, 1949, p. 132ff.

201 Verhulst, *Der Glanz von Kopenhagen*, p. 17ff.

202 Goethe, *Geschichte der Farbenlehre*, p. 53ff.

203 Goethe, *Naturwissenschaftliche Schriften*, p. 28.

204 Steiner, *Mein Lebensgang (Autobiography)*.

205 Rudolf Steiner, GA 34, *The Education of the Child in the Light of Spiritual Science*, first published in *Lucifer-Gnosis*. The essay is also available as single-lecture edition.

206 Quoted in Wilhelm Rath, *Rudolf Steiner und Thomas von Aquino*, Basel, 1991, p. 79ff.

207 Quoted in J. Hemleben, *Teilhard de Chardin*, Reinbek bei Hamburg, 1966, p. 49.

208 Rudolf Steiner, GA 5, *Friedrich Nietzsche, Fighter for Freedom*, Rudolf Steiner Publications, 1960.

209 Friedrich Nietzsche, *Also sprach Zarathustra* (*Thus Spoke Zarathustra*), in the chapter 'On the Virtuous'.

210 Steiner, *Mein Lebensgang (Autobiography)*, p. 363f.

211 Ibid., p. 372.

212 Ibid., p. 366.

213 Ibid., p. 334.

214 Rudolf Steiner, GA 182, lecture on 16 October 1918 in *Death as Metamorphosis of Life*, SteinerBooks, 2008.

215 *Novalis: Das philosophisch-theoretische Werk*, ed. H.-J. Mähl, Darmstadt, 1999, p. 221.

216 Rudolf Steiner, GA 40, *Wahrspruchworte*, p. 116 in the 1961 edition. With this verse Steiner concluded his public lecture on 24 September 1919 in Stuttgart, published in GA 297, *Idee und Praxis der Waldorfschule*.

217 Heisterkamp, op. cit., p. 21ff.

218 Ibid., p. 92.

219 Ibid.

220 Andreas Steffens, *Philosophie des 20. Jahrhunderts: Oder die Wiederkehr des Menschen*, Leipzig, 1999; from the foreword.

221 Ibid., p. 27.

222 Ibid., p. 87.
223 Bahr, op. cit., p. 87f.
224 Ibid., p. 121.
225 Ibid., p. 307f.
226 Novalis, *Werke und Briefe*, fragments on 'Cosmology and Religion', no. 557.
227 Martin Buber, *Ich und Du* (*I and Thou*), quoted in Gerhard Wehr, *Martin Buber*, Reinbek bei Hamburg, 1992, p. 82.
228 Ibid.
229 Steiner, *The Philosophy of Freedom*.
230 Meyer, op. cit., p. 226.
231 Goethe, *Die Geheimnisse*.
232 See the works of Sigismund von Gleich cited in notes 23 and 185.
233 See Schütze, op. cit., p. 88ff. on a possible enlargement to twelve categories.
234 Rudolf Steiner, GA 119, *Macrocosm and Microcosm*, Rudolf Steiner Press, 1968, lecture on 29 March 1910.
235 Friedrich Hiebel, *Novalis: Deutscher Dichter, Europäischer Denker, Christlicher Seher*, Bern, 1972, p. 9.
236 Novalis, *Werke und Briefe*, from the fragments 'On the Secret World', no. 228.
237 Ibid., from the collection *Blütenstaub* (*Pollen*).

Study/Discussion Guide, Worldview by Worldview

Mario Betti and Kathelijne Drenth

General Template Structure for Each Session

I. *Individual work*: the reader summarises what he has actually read (it is important in order to hold back from his own interpretation), and asks himself the following questions:
   (a) Why is it of key importance to engage with/enter into other worldviews?
   (b) What is genuine dialogue based upon…
      (i) when both dialogue partners hold the same opinion?
      (ii) when both are in dispute?
      (iii) when genuine agreement arises following dispute?
   (c) Why are there so many different views of the world?

   Having done this, he writes down points that stood out for him.

   Thirdly, he writes down what has touched or moved him. He does not as yet share these experiences with the other readers in the study group.

II. The readers meet in a study group. This way of working is repeated for each succeeding chapter.

   One of the members of the study group shares what he has prepared. The other members listen and note it down in writing.

   The listeners feed back to the speaker what stood out for them.

   The speaker then writes down all the points, and chooses one they find touching, and *shares this with the others*. Each member should be given the chance to be both speaker and listener. In this way, each person has the opportunity to share their findings, and the same amount of time is allowed for each study-group member.

   One of the listeners takes responsibility for time-keeping.

III. At the end, each person characterises the whole for themselves. These accounts are shared, and there is space for dialogue.

Study Questions for Each Worldview

Substitute the following questions into part I of the above template structure for each of the worldviews, as follows:

1 **PHENOMENALISM**

(a) Give an example from your own experience.

(b) Are we deceived by the way things appear, or does this reveal a truth – and if so, why?

(c) Summarise this worldview in one sentence.

2 **SENSUALISM**

(a) What connection does the 'I-experience' have with the senses?

(b) What is a sensual person?

(c) Briefly summarise this worldview, too.

3 **MATERIALISM**

(a) Is today's world materialistic? And if so, why?

(b) How do I know that I am not just a piece of matter?

(c) Say something about the three worldviews to date, and distinguish them from each other.

4 **MATHEMATISM**

(a) What does the truth of this worldview consist of?

(b) Where can mathematism and phenomenalism find accord with each other?

(c) How many forms can mathematism have?

5 **RATIONALISM**

(a) Was the French-European Enlightenment rationalism? And if so, in what way?

(b) Name a politician of today who is a rationalist. How does a true rationalist act?

(c) Say something about the ideal of rationalism in thinking and action.

6 **IDEALISM**

(a) Say something about the history of idealism.

(b) Why is idealism important for us as human beings? When does it become disastrous?

(c) How do mathematism, rationalism and idealism relate to each other?

7 PSYCHISM

(a) Is psychism always psychology? Or when does it become philosophy or religion?
(b) Does modern culture need psychism in its pure form?
(c) Are self-knowledge and psychism one and the same?

8 PNEUMATISM

(a) Is this connected with the New Age movement? if so, why?
(b) What is the difference between pneumatic experience and being high on drugs?
(c) Do we need pneumatism today?

9 'SPIRITUALISM'

(a) What is this really, and what does it have to do with materialism?
(b) What relationship does it have with idealism? And religion?
(c) How do psychism, pneumatism and 'spiritualism' relate to each other?

10 MONADISM

(a) How does the monadist see the individual person, as compared with the mathematist?
(b) How do monadism, mathematism and materialism regard the cosmos?
(c) Can monadism help us resolve social problems? And if so, how?

11 DYNAMISM

(a) What is dynamism in its pure form? How many forms does it appear in?
(b) Can dynamists and rationalists become friends?
(c) What are the shadow aspects of this very modern worldview?

12 REALISM

(a) What is the relationship between realism and idealism?
(b) What is the reality in all twelve worldviews for science, art and religion?
(c) Twelve Ways and the individual self: how do they belong together?

A final question: What is it that ultimately holds the world together?

18 September 2018

Index